Engaging Social Media
in China

US–CHINA RELATIONS IN THE AGE OF GLOBALIZATION

This series publishes the best, cutting-edge work tackling the opportunities and dilemmas of relations between the United States and China in the age of globalization. Books published in the series encompass both historical studies and contemporary analyses, and include both single-authored monographs and edited collections. Our books are comparative, offering in-depth communication-based analyses of how United States and Chinese officials, scholars, artists, and activists configure each other, portray the relations between the two nations, and depict their shared and competing interests. They are interdisciplinary, featuring scholarship that works in and across communication studies, rhetoric, literary criticism, film studies, cultural studies, international studies, and more. And they are international, situating their analyses at the crossroads of international communication and the nuances, complications, and opportunities of globalization as it has unfolded since World War II.

Engaging Social Media in China

PLATFORMS, PUBLICS, AND PRODUCTION

Edited by Guobin Yang and Wei Wang

MICHIGAN STATE UNIVERSITY PRESS | *East Lansing*

♾ The paper used in this publication meets the minimum requirements of
ANSI/NISO Z39.48-1992 (R 1997) (Permanence of Paper).

Michigan State University Press
East Lansing, Michigan 48823-5245

LIBRARY OF CONGRESS CATALOGING-IN-PUBLICATION DATA
Names: Yang, Guobin, editor. Wang, Wei, editor.
Title: Engaging social media in China : platforms, publics, and production
/ edited by Guobin Yang and Wei Wang.
Description: East Lansing : Michigan State University Press, [2021] |
Series: US-China relations in the age of globalization | Includes bibliographical references and index.
Identifiers: LCCN 2020026662 | ISBN 978-1-61186-391-8 (paperback ; alk. paper)
| ISBN 978-1-60917-665-5 (PDF) | ISBN 978-1-62895-424-1 (ePub) | ISBN 978-1-62896-425-7 (Kindle)
Subjects: LCSH: Information technology—Social aspects—China. | Social media—China.
| Social media—Government policy—China.
Classification: LCC HN740.Z9 I5665 2021 | DDC 302.23/1—dc23
LC record available at https://lccn.loc.gov/2020026662

Book design by Charlie Sharp, Sharp Designs, East Lansing, Michigan
Cover design by Erin Kirk
Cover image: Woman with Victoria Harbour in background, by YiuCheung, Adobe Stock

Michigan State University Press is a member of the Green Press Initiative and is
committed to developing and encouraging ecologically responsible publishing
practices. For more information about the Green Press Initiative and the use of
recycled paper in book publishing, please visit www.greenpressinitiative.org.

_____

Visit Michigan State University Press at *www.msupress.org*

ON THE INTERSECTION OF EDGE BALL AND COURTESY:
NOTES ON SCHOLARSHIP IN THE AGE OF GLOBALIZATION

Like America or France or Brazil, China is a nation-state riven with fault-lines along region and race, ethnicity and education, linguistics and libido, gender and more general divisions. The US media tends to portray Chinese society as monolithic—billions of citizens censored into silence, its activists and dissidents fearful of retribution. The "reeducation" camps in Xinjiang, the "black prisons" that dot the landscape, and the Great Firewall prove this belief partially true. At the same time, there are more dissidents on the Chinese web than there are living Americans, and rallies, marches, strikes, and protests unfold in China each week. The nation is seething with action, much of it politically radical. What makes this political action so complicated and so difficult to comprehend is that no one knows how the state will respond on any given day. In his magnificent *Age of Ambition*, Evan Osnos notes that "Divining how far any individual [can] go in Chinese creative life [is] akin to carving a line in the sand at low tide in the dark." His tide metaphor is telling, for throughout Chinese history waves of what Deng Xiaoping called "openness and reform" have given way to repression, which can then swing back to what Chairman Mao once called "letting a hundred flowers bloom"—China thus offers a perpetually changing landscape, in which nothing is certain. For this reason, our Chinese colleagues and collaborators are taking great risks by participating in this book series. Authors in the "west" fear their books and articles will fail to find an audience; authors in China live in fear of a midnight knock at the door.

   This series therefore strives to practice what Qingwen Dong calls "edge ball": Getting as close as possible to the boundary of what is sayable without crossing the line into being offensive. The image is borrowed from table tennis and depicts a shot that barely touches the line before ricocheting off the table; it counts as a point and is within the rules, yet the trajectory of the ball makes it almost impossible to hit a return shot. In the realm of scholarship and politics, playing "edge ball" means speaking truth to power while not provoking arrest—this is a murky game full of gray zones, allusions, puns, and sly references. What this means for our series is clear: Our authors do not censor themselves, but they do speak respectfully and cordially, showcasing research-based perspectives from their standpoints and their worldviews, thereby putting multiple vantage points into conversation. As our authors practice "edge ball," we hope our readers will savor these books with a similar sense of sophisticated and international generosity.

—Stephen J. Hartnett

Contents

PART III. Engagement and Disengagement

Acknowledgments

We are deeply grateful to series editor Stephen J. Hartnett and editor-in-chief of MSU Press Catherine Cocks for their thoughtful and thorough editorial work and their good-humored encouragement and support. For their assistance in copyediting some of the chapters, we thank Emily Hund, Roopa Vasudevan, and Andrew Wirzburger at the University of Pennsylvania. We also thank MSU project editor Amanda Frost for her careful and professional copyediting of the manuscript. Most of the chapters are based on presentations at the Second Biennial Conference on Communication, Media, and Governance in the Age of Globalization held in Beijing in 2018 by the Communication University of China and the National Communication Association. We thank the organizing committee of the conference and the faculty and staff at the Communication University of China for their support and hospitality.

—*Guobin Yang and Wei Wang*

Social Media and State-Sponsored Platformization in China

Guobin Yang

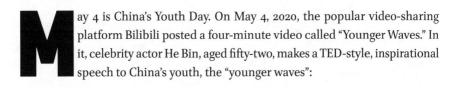ay 4 is China's Youth Day. On May 4, 2020, the popular video-sharing platform Bilibili posted a four-minute video called "Younger Waves." In it, celebrity actor He Bin, aged fifty-two, makes a TED-style, inspirational speech to China's youth, the "younger waves":

> You can freely learn a language and a craft, watch movies, and travel to distant places. Since childhood you have explored your interests freely.... You have the right which we once dreamt of having—the right to choose.... I salute your confidence. Only weak people are used to mocking and negating. People with strong hearts never hold back their praise and encouragement.[1]

The video prompted a tsunami of satirical responses on social media. It is a eulogy to freedom, but on WeChat, another major social media platform, many critics noted that it is only about the freedom to consume, not other types of freedom. Others commented that only the children of wealthy families could freely travel; poor youth could not afford it. Still others challenged the proposition that "only weak people are used to mocking and negating." Why is it a sign of weakness to be negative and critical? Why isn't it a sign of strength?

The video is a piece of political propaganda disguised as inspirational oration by a celebrity actor. During the lockdown of the city of Wuhan and the war against the COVID-19 disease in China, Chinese social media exploded with criticisms of the delayed responses and ineptitude of local bureaucracies and Party leaders. These criticisms were dismissed as "negative energy" in the official media. The video is using a celebrity's star power to tell people that it is not cool to be critical. Be positive!

At first glance, the fact that a popular social media platform like Bilibili produced and promoted this video may be puzzling. After all, Bilibili is a commercial platform known for its playful, rolling bullet comments on the screen, while "Younger Waves" is a didactic lesson. Yet the video and the public responses it generated encapsulated the complex dynamics and recent trends of Chinese social media, which are the focus of this book.

Commercial social media platforms are increasingly being co-opted into platforms for political propaganda as well as commercial advertisements, and propaganda is increasingly presented in fashionable styles and high-tech media formats to appeal to the younger generation. Like consumer culture, mainstream political ideologies call on citizens to take positive attitudes and feel positive feelings about anything and everything. Positive energy has become a new ideology, while critical thinking is suppressed and dismissed as negative energy.[2] Bilibili's video on "Younger Waves" evidently plays into this mainstream ideology of positive energy.

On the technological front, one notable trend is the popularity of livestreaming and short video applications on platforms like Bilibili. According to the forty-second internet survey report released in July 2018 by the China Internet Network Information Center (CNNIC), there were 425 million livestreaming users in China as of June 2018.[3] This report has no information about short video users, but half a year later, its forty-third report shows that China had 648 million short video users as of December 2018, meaning that 78.2 percent of all the 829 million Chinese internet users were also short video users. Not surprisingly, the popularity of livestreaming and short videos is accompanied by the growth of mobile phone usage: close to 99 percent of all internet users access the internet on their mobile phones, while only 35.9 percent of them access the internet on their laptop computers.[4]

Another technological development is the growing dominance of WeChat as a digital platform. Developed by Tencent and launched in 2011 as a mobile instant messaging application, WeChat quickly grew into a platform serving multiple purposes such as WeChat Pay, group chats, and public accounts. American readers will be familiar with debates about the ways Facebook is shaping political discourse, with critics worrying that Facebook has become an unaccountable monopoly warping democracy to the needs of advertising and misinformation.[5] In some ways, the reach of WeChat is even more extensive and more powerful than Facebook, making this communication platform a crucial site of investigation.

These developments are not purely technological, of course, for the changing online population is as much a sociological and cultural phenomenon as technological. In considering the social dimensions of these recent technological trends, what is most striking is how deeply the dual logics of politics and profit-driven market, in all their complex and entangled forms, have penetrated China's digital spheres. We see a perfect example of this blending of politics and commercialism in the above example, as well as some of the consequences of this blending. The commercial platform Bilibili gave the propagandistic video instant online attention, but instant attention also brought instant criticisms to the video.

To make things more complicated, these trends in social media are happening in the middle of fraught US–China relations and technological contestations. Within US–China relations, no issue is more complicated and potentially dangerous than the question of social media and new technologies. On the US side, we have seen elections hacked via Twitter and Facebook and Chinese technology firms such as Huawei restricted in the United States and TikTok first put under national security review[6] and then banned together with WeChat.[7] On the Chinese side, major American social media platforms such as Facebook and Twitter continue to be blocked while Chinese social media platforms are being censored and used for mass propaganda. It is fair to say that if we hold out hope for a future based on ethical communication, and ideally ethical communication within and about US–China relations, then that future hinges on the health of our social media. There are of course already many studies of these issues. To take stock of the existing scholarship and highlight the distinct features of this volume, let me begin with a survey of the field of Chinese internet studies.

The Field of Chinese Internet Studies

Chinese internet studies is an umbrella term that covers studies of all digital technological forms, including the internet, social media, smart phones, and more. As the field expands, it may be more accurate to call it digital media studies.

Notwithstanding the use of different terms, scholars from around the world have produced a large body of academic work, which is too rich and complex to capture here. Nonetheless, I will build on reviews of the field already published while highlighting some of the most recent and important publications. David Herold's review in his introduction to the 2012 book *Online Society in China* highlights four areas in academic studies of the Chinese internet. One area focuses on government control of the internet and citizens' use of it for resistance. A second area is the emergence of new forms of civic associations. The third area concerns the impact of the internet on economic development and social inequality. The fourth area is the rise of new forms of entertainment associated with digital media, including internet addiction. In Herold's review, therefore, we see the penetration of the internet into the four areas of politics, society, economy, and culture. A weakness of the field, according to Herold, is the neglect of the internet as a space of its own. By focusing on "online society," the book helps to fill a gap.[8]

Based on a review of twenty-two monographs, Weiyu Zhang and Taberez Neyazi find that what they call "the field of ICT research on China" has two broad themes—state and society. Under the category of the state, they subsume studies of both political control and political economies of telecommunications industries. The category of society includes studies of online activism, online civil society, online fandom, everyday life, and digital inequality. What they find missing in the field are studies of internet service/content providers, which "belong to neither the state nor the society."[9] This is a gap that I hope our volume will help to fill with our focus on social media platforms.

Since the review by Zhang and Neyazi does not cover edited volumes or journal articles, and their bibliography does not contain monographs published in or after 2019, let me introduce some of these publications to highlight a few additional areas of research. Among edited volumes, *Chinese Social Media: Social, Cultural, and Political Implications*, edited by three Australian scholars, features chapters on several platforms, such as Weibo and WeChat, with an particularly interesting section on social media in greater China and overseas.[10] *The Internet, Social Media, and a Changing China* examines the impact of the internet as it pertains to civil society, legal change, and international relations.[11] Two of these themes, law and international relations, contribute to relatively uncharted territories. Although civil society is a well-traveled terrain, Min Jiang's chapter raises the new question of how the internet has also helped to breed an uncivil society.[12] Jiang pursues this question further in a 2018 special journal issue on uncivil society in digital China.[13] These are particularly fascinating studies, as they map the ways online discourse in China, like recent trends in America, may be leading toward polarization, conspiracy theories, vulgar language, and increased levels of anger and resentment among users.

Another notable special journal issue is about the platformization of Chinese society.[14] By platformization, the editors of the special issue mean "the penetration of economic, governmental, and infrastructural extensions of digital platforms into the web and app ecosystems."[15] They point out, however, that the process of platformization in China has different problems and challenges than platformization in the West, the key difference being "the intrusive role of the state."[16] They highlight three vectors of platformization, namely, infrastructure, governance, and practice. The study of platform politics is an important recent trend in the field of media and communication studies, but remains largely untapped in the field of Chinese internet studies. Their special issue represents an important step forward.

Among the new books published in 2019 or forthcoming in 2020, five merit special emphasis because they each break new ground in their own ways. Two books are about online activism. Jing Wang's *The Other Digital China: Nonconfrontational Activism on the Social Web* is based on years of her personal experience of operating an NGO in China.[17] Other scholars have studied the nonconfrontational forms of online activism, but Wang takes the concept as far as it can go. She argues that nonconfrontational activism is a deliberate choice by citizens, NGOs, and members of the corporate sector and the state, and that it can be an effective way of achieving incremental change. Sally Xiaojin Chen's forthcoming book, *Resistance in Digital China: The Southern Weekly Incident*, is a study of online activism through the case of the *Southern Weekly* protest. Unlike existing work on Chinese online activism, it provides an in-depth analysis of one single case. Conceptualizing online action as a form of embodied action, which is no less authentic or "real" than bodily action in the streets, Chen offers new insights into the dynamics of online and offline protest.[18]

Luzhou Li's *Zoning China: Online Video, Popular Culture, and the State* argues that although the television industry is heavily regulated and controlled, the video-streaming industry developed under a lax regulatory regime. This differential approach configured the cultural realm into multiple zones delineated by technological forms in order to accommodate consumer needs while simultaneously retaining socialist legacies through state media. Particularly relevant to current debates about social media platforms and infrastructures, Li argues that the development of the online video industry in China was largely based on piracy.

Li treats piracy as a cultural infrastructure that provides individuals with both social and technical knowledge, which in time become crucial foundations for entrepreneurial endeavors under legitimate market conditions.[19]

Marcella Szablewicz's *Mapping Digital Game Culture in China: From Internet Addicts to Esports Athletes*, based on many years of research, will be the first systematic study of digital game culture in China, another under-studied area.[20] Silvia Lindtner's *Prototype Nation* is an ethnographic study of China's maker culture, the only one of its kind I am aware of. Lindtner argues that maker culture fulfills several different functions for different social actors (state, startup businesses, entrepreneurs, citizens), but is united by the idea of the mutual benefits of self-improvement and national progress through tech-based self-making. She shows that China's maker culture is entangled with the state project of upgrading the nation by upgrading its citizens, but also finds that the discourses and practices of maker culture in China do provide yearnings for alternative futures for both citizens and the nation.[21]

Last but not least, a large amount of exciting research on digital media is going on in China and has been published in Chinese, but has not attracted the attention it deserves. Research teams at the School of Communication of Soochow University led by Professors Zhonghong Ma and Lin Chen have published important work on youth subcultures in China, ranging from digital gaming to cosplay and youth identities.[22] The *Chinese Journal of Journalism and Communication*, edited at the School of Journalism and Communication at Renmin University of China, has consistently published high-impact work on Chinese internet studies. One of its recent special issues features studies of memes, visual culture, and fandom communities in contemporary cyber-nationalism, and was recently published as a book in English translation.[23]

As this review of recent published work indicates, the field of Chinese internet studies, or what we might call digital media studies in China, has blossomed in exciting ways, offering analyses that focus on production, distribution, user preferences and habits, technological affordances, market logics, and state imperatives. Across this work, we see one key trend: social media are increasingly structured by "platforms," especially those user-friendly apps that we all use to organize our friend groups, or our weather and sports updates, or our news feeds. As the critical literature surveyed here suggests, while these apps make our lives as consumers easier, they also leave us in self-aggregating filter bubbles, wherein we select what we want to know, whom we want to engage with, and what versions of the news we wish to consume. In the United States, these apps are built and managed by for-profit corporations, or sometimes by nonprofit NGOs and civic groups, but in China they tend to be linked, either directly or indirectly, to the Party, meaning the new platforms that structure social media in China are deeply entwined with state politics. And so I turn below to a discussion of the complicated interweaving of the market, the state, and platforms in China.

State-Sponsored Platformization in China

To this dynamic and fast-growing field of scholarship, this volume aims to make three distinct contributions. First, I introduce the concept of state-sponsored platformization, thereby adding specificity and nuance to the process of platformization with Chinese characteristics. Second, chapters in the volume show that state-sponsored platformization has multiple layers. While the state extends its influences into social media platforms, it also aspires to turn its own media agencies into platforms. Third, several chapters suggest that state-sponsored platformization does not necessarily produce the Party's desired outcomes. On the one hand, social media platforms are still used for public engagement (both supporting and opposing the state), but on the other hand, there is a growing trend of crafted resistance to hyper–social media connectivity as people begin to manage their online settings to reduce or refuse connection with certain individuals or social groups, including the state. Even state-sponsored platformization, then, may not serve the political goals of the state.

The process of state-sponsored platformization is the continuation in the social media age of an earlier history of Chinese internet politics. In this earlier history, the global internet, which had originated in the United States, gradually took on Chinese characteristics in the course of its evolution in China, such that it may have become "a monopoly board separate from the international Internet,"[24] or at least an internet heavily imprinted with Chinese characteristics, what Susan Leong has argued might more accurately be called "the PRC internet."[25] In short, state-sponsored platformization is not entirely new, but is part of a longer history of the political and cultural shaping of the internet in China.

State-sponsored platformization has three dimensions. First, like the market-dominated platformization in the West, state-sponsored platformization has a technological logic with technological affordances and constraints. These affordances directly shape user behavior on the platforms. For example, while a Weibo user can accumulate thousands and even millions of followers, WeChat users can only have a small number of WeChat friends (qua followers), because WeChat's Moments and chat features are designed mainly for personal use. To read my Moments, you will need to have already become my WeChat friend.[26] WeChat users can build "circles" of friends, but the maximum number of friends in any circle is five hundred. Thus, Weibo is a more public platform where one can easily communicate and interact with large numbers of strangers, whereas WeChat is a more private platform better suited for small-group interactions. The comparative study of American and Chinese scientists' use of social media in "Lure of Connectivity" provides some insights on Chinese scientists' different approaches to Weibo and WeChat.

Second, also like the market-dominated platformization in the West, state-sponsored platformatization in China has its commercial logic. All the major internet platforms in China—WeChat, Weibo, Baidu, Alibaba, Douban, and so forth—are first and foremost private business firms. They started as business entities relatively independent from the state, and have remained so, as long as they abide by laws and government regulations. Like their American counterparts, they hype the values of connectivity, sharing, and community to incite users to stay active by participating in social media interaction.[27] But the commercial logic of Chinese social media platforms also has its own culturally specific elements. For example, one way of promoting user participation and business is to adapt social media to age-old traditions, or rather to take traditions to social media platforms. For example, WeChat introduced the virtual red envelope application during the Lunar New Year in 2014. A popular custom during the Lunar New Year in China is for parents to give cash gifts sealed in red envelopes to children. Friends and relatives also sometimes exchange red envelopes. When WeChat introduced its virtual red envelope in 2014, it was an instant hit because of its convenience. On WeChat, you could give virtual red envelopes of small amounts of money to your contacts. You could also hand out red envelopes to your WeChat "circles" for your contacts within the circles to grab. The money is usually in very small amounts, but it is a game of trying out one's luck and of virtually socializing with friends. Once introduced, it was an instant hit and quickly drove up the number of users of WeChat Pay system to rival Alibaba's Alipay system. In this case, a new social media platform increased its market share by appropriating a pre-technological Chinese custom.

The third dimension of state-sponsored platformization is its political logic. Although American platforms like Facebook and Twitter have their own politics,[28] there is a distinct Chinese political logic to platformization in China. In this logic, the bottom line of China's internet politics, like its media politics in general, is the Party line.[29] But as in media politics, the boundaries are fluid and porous, and practices on the ground are often about creative means of negotiation and improvisation.[30] The dialectics of Party-line domination and bottom-up practices are the most fascinating areas for study, as is reflected in the broad range of studies of Chinese internet politics. For example, while some analysts emphasize the authoritarian nature of Chinese internet politics,[31] others stress contestation;[32] some focus on censorship,[33] while others study online activism and citizens' playful appropriation of the internet;[34] still others study issues of internet sovereignty, global internet governance, and the politics of cybersecurity.[35]

Even as the reach of the party-state is ever present, the platformization of the web retains significant technological and commercial logics. In this sense, state-platformization resembles the state corporatist model that was once used to characterize the nature of Chinese nongovernmental organizations,[36] although again, it differs from the state corporatist model because of its entanglements with technological and market logics. That is why I believe the concept of state-sponsored platformization better captures the process of platformization in China,[37] because it captures the complicated layering of state imperatives, market logics, and technological change.

The political dimension of the state-sponsored platformization of the Chinese web entails not only the usual methods of censorship but also a growing repertoire of new tactics and methods. Two of these methods merit emphasis. One is the "civilizing" of the web, meaning using the discourses of civility and civilization to cleanse the web of dissent and criticism. Emotional outpourings of anger at social injustices may thus be cleansed in the name of civility.[38] Instead, only positive emotions producing "positive energy" are encouraged. One recent study of 1,229 short-videos posted by thirteen central government agencies on Douyin, the Chinese version of TikTok, finds that they predominantly convey positive emotions such as pride, joy, and hope.[39]

The other method is the "occupying" of the web, which refers to party-state efforts to manage and shape internet expression by directly participating in it—hence occupying it. These practices include operating official accounts on social media platforms. For example, in September 2010, the Ministry of Public Security held a national conference to promote the use of microblogs by public security agencies. Methods of "occupying" the web also include what Shaohua Guo refers to as "the reinvention of official culture that aims at having a stronger voice online," such as the appropriation of fan culture by the Weibo account of the Chinese Youth League.[40] This latter development is especially important, as we see the CPC trying to consume the once-independent platforms of social media for state purposes.

The political logic of platformization is not necessarily at odds with the market logic. On the contrary, it often incorporates elements of the market logic to enhance its appeal. For example, to grow followers and gain user attention, accounts run by government agencies post sensational headlines in the style typical of commercial accounts. In fact, some of the most influential public accounts on popular platforms are run by official entities. A study by Chinese communication scholar Peng Lan shows that the most popular short videos on the Chinese TikTok platform Douyin for the period May 1 to November 30, 2018, are almost all released by state-owned media agencies, including *Global Times*, Xinhua News Agency, China Central Television (CCTV), and *People's Daily*. A glance at a few titles of these viral videos shows that they are no different from the clickbait titles such as the one about the death of a gifted but poor young man I mentioned at the beginning of this introduction:

> Woman hears strange noise in living room at night. When she checks, she encounters this. Dog saves her life at critical moment.
> (女子深夜感觉客厅有异常，出来查看遭遇这一幕，关键时刻狗狗救了自己)
> A few seconds late, and the result would be unimaginable!!
> (再迟疑几秒，后果不堪设想！！)
> It must be because of divine connection: Guy in search of lost dog fell into a pit only to see his dog there too. (一定是特别的缘分：男子寻狗掉坑里，一看竟然狗子也在坑中)[41]

These are headlines posted by government agencies on their official social media accounts. They pique readers' curiosity, but deliver no news of any social significance. Indeed, partly as a result of civilizing and occupying the web, state-supported platformization has dampened the erstwhile contentious landscape of the Chinese internet.[42]

The ways state-supported platformization have contributed to the depoliticization of Chinese online discourse appear to be a far cry from the seemingly hyper-politicized discourse on American social media platforms. On closer examination, however, there is an eerie connection between the two. Both Trump and his Chinese counterpart Xi see the power of public anger in mobilizing the masses. While Xi suppresses public anger to avoid public mobilization, Trump employs it to appeal to his conservative base and undermine his political opponents. As Chinese social media platforms demobilize radical emotions,[43] American social media platforms have given free rein to Trump's emotional politics in a new media regime which collapses "between news and entertainment, mass-mediated and interpersonal communication, information producers and consumers, and facts, opinions, and beliefs."[44] As Karin Wahl-Jorgensen writes, "the affordances of Twitter facilitate a discursive climate which is more extreme, divisive, and polarized. Trump appears to be a beneficiary of this affective shift by crafting his charged messages on Twitter in a way that spills over into mainstream media."[45] Fred Turner similarly argues that "Trump has married the rostrum-pounding emotionalism of the twentieth century dictator to the interpersonal intimacy of our new media era. On Twitter, his petulance is par for the course."[46] The result is the polarized American social media world inundated by fake news and misinformation.

Organization of the Book and Chapter Summaries

This volume is organized into three parts. The chapters in Part I focus on platforms. They provide evidence and analytical insights for our conceptualization of state-sponsored platformization in China. The first chapter by Yizhou Xu and Jeremy Morris examines mobile radio as both an object and a site where the state, corporate interests, and users wrestle with one another. Since 2013, mobile radio has emerged as a significant cultural practice. Xu and Morris focus on Ximalaya.FM, the most popular mobile radio application. Ximalaya brands itself as a panacea to the frustrations in modern life. It crystalizes a sense of freedom via the individual's use of such an audio application, which diverges from the practice of "collective public listening" in earlier, socialist China. The philosophy of Ximalaya's branding package prioritizes audience reception rather than the content, suggesting that its goal is to establish an individualized, customized, and exclusive "listening" experience. Thus, as radio morphs into podcasting in the social media age, listeners become more segmented for the sake of more effective marketing. For Ximalaya, user attention is data and profits. In addition, Xu and Morris find that Ximalaya extends this business logic to political messaging. By carefully examining the modes of interfacing built into the Ximalaya app, Xu and Morris find that underneath the veil of a sense of community and of user agency in controlling listening, the tension between Ximalaya's commercial interests and the state's intention to direct content and exert ideological influence persists. Ultimately, they argue that instead of promoting new forms of public participation, apps like Ximalaya introduce new forms of media control "where Party governance melts with the logic of the market."

Lin Zhang's chapter studies Alibaba's historical evolution from a quasi-infrastructural e-commerce platform in the late 1990s to a multi-platform ecosystem of infrastructural scale in the late 2010s. She finds that Alibaba positioned itself *against* state infrastructures in the early days as a quasi-governmental alternative while keeping the tensions between public service and profit at bay to prioritize market expansion. In the years following the 2008 global crisis, however, when Alibaba had acquired infrastructural scale and significance, its earlier positioning against the state gradually gave way to a more symbiotic and mutually penetrating relationship with the state. Meanwhile, tensions intensified as Alibaba's profit imperatives began to override quasi-governmental service provisions. Alibaba's evolution into a more symbiotic relationship with the state is telling: it shows how the market and the state are entangled in the process of platformization in China.

The third chapter by Junyi Lv and David Craig offers a comparative study of livestreaming platforms in China and the United States. They argue that China's livestreaming platforms have experienced interplatformization, while US social media entertainment has veered toward intraplatformization. The former refers to strategies through which platforms collaborate with one another to enable cross-platform affordances. These strategies include the invention of the tipping system and the integration of livestreaming platforms with e-commerce businesses. Within the realm of interplatformization, Lv and Craig argue that creators are empowered to produce contents. In contrast, intraplatformization results in "walled gardens," posing obstacles for creators to actively appropriate platforms, thus limiting the success of American livestreaming platforms.

Foreign diplomacy finds new channels of expression on social media, but social media can also be a platform for bringing out the worst of xenophobia and racism. In the fourth chapter, Michelle Murray Yang digs into Donald Trump's barrage of tweets concerning North Korea and China to find out how Trump portrays North Korea and the role of China in the North Korean issue. She finds that the rhetorical style of Trump's tweets exacerbates the negative side of Twitter. Trump's Twitter discourse promotes an outdated Cold War mentality that casts North Korea as an evil state. Trump's blame of China for not solving the North Korean problem mirrors his penchant for scapegoating domestic opponents and eschews the role of the United States in creating the North Korean "problem" in the first place. Her chapter highlights the importance of cultivating "a new kind of Twitter literacy" among citizens to reflectively consume information on social media platforms. Not about state-sponsored platformization in China per se, Yang's chapter nevertheless provides a fascinating comparative angle by showing how social media platforms may be abused by powerful politicians elsewhere, with sobering lessons for understanding the political ramifications of platformization in general. Yang's chapter is particularly salient for our thinking about how social media impacts the US–China relationship, for her analysis of Trump's Twitter feed shows the president marshalling racism, xenophobia, and strident anti-China language, hence souring international relations.

The two chapters in Part II reveal additional layers of state-sponsored plat-formization, especially how state-owned media agencies attempt to expand their influences by incorporating user-generated content or by becoming active users of global social media platforms. Focusing on online short-form news video production, the fifth chapter by Fengjiao Yang and Xiao Li examines the convergence of professionally generated content and user-generated content as well as the cooperation between state-owned news organizations and commercial media platforms. This chapter finds that the news organizations in their study continue to conduct fact-checking, maintain transparency, and add value to information, hence practicing the key norms and basic principles of journalistic professionalism. At the same time, the adoption of user-generated content and cooperation with commercial platforms also impact the content criteria, in essence creating a mixed-media format where traditional journalistic practices are sometimes present but also frequently absent.

Qingjiang Yao's chapter studies how mainstream Chinese news media operate accounts on American social media platforms. Specifically, he examines the non-content techniques used by mainstream Chinese media and their effectiveness. He chooses a range of posting techniques, such as whether a news post uses exclamation marks, emojis, hashtags, or videos. He then tests their relationships with response variables, such as likes, comments, and shares. Among the three types of responses, the audience on Facebook and Twitter makes more likes than shares, and the number of comments was the lowest. Yao concludes that there is a "affective-conative-cognitive" hierarchy in Chinese news media on Facebook and

Twitter. The results also show that posting videos and photos or using exclamation marks tend to attract more audience responses. The study provides an excellent example for a broader inquiry into intercultural and international communication of news media across the world.

As the chapters in Part III show, state-sponsored platformization does not necessarily produce the state's desired outcomes. Far from it. Instead, what we find is an ever-changing terrain of negotiation. For example, the seventh chapter by Wei Wang proposes that new social agents have appeared on Chinese social media to mediate state-society relations. On WeChat, local internet celebrities become famous, sometimes by accident. In one case, one person posted a popular song sung in the local dialect. Seeing that his song went viral among the local WeChat users, he posted more songs in the local dialect and soon became a local internet celebrity. The local internet celebrities studied in Wang's chapter often post government policies on their personal or public WeChat accounts, as well as other social issues and news of local interest. They communicate government policies to local communities and collect public input on government policies. In this way, they serve as digital intermediaries between state and society. Unlike nonprofit or nongovernmental organizations, they operate their WeChat accounts as individuals and have no group affiliation. Their popularity reflects the values of the individualistic culture and the personal branding strategies in the digital age. To the extent that they often proudly work with state agents and serve as communication channels for state policies, they contribute to the agenda of local governance. Their popularity is another manifestation of the multifaceted character of state-sponsored platformization.

Zimu Zhang's chapter studies social media art projects in China. She calls attention to the appearance of new art discourses that lead to new approaches to art, such as "relational art," "participatory art," "community art," and "socially engaged art." While the proliferation of social media has profoundly influenced daily life, it also challenges taken-for-granted perceptions of art practices. Many artists are no longer operating in an ivory tower. Instead, they have assumed the role of mediators or connectors, and become more directly engaged with social issues. The practice of contemporary art has seen a social turn. Analyzing three art projects in mainland China, in which Zhang was personally involved, the chapter contends that contemporary social media art practices express new social visions by pursuing subjects of social concern. Moreover, they do so by relying on artists' own resources and networks, not art institutions such as galleries.

The ninth chapter by Hepeng Jia and his collaborators examines American and Chinese scientists' use of social media for public science communication. It shows that social media help scientists bypass legacy media and reach wider audiences while producing more interdisciplinary collaboration. Scientists strategically choose different social media platforms for their affordability, but their multi-platform social media use is also shaped by contextual factors. Compared with their US counterparts, Chinese scientists try more actively to minimize uncontrollability. However, social media have yet to become a ready tool for public engagement with science. Scientists prioritize their internal networking demands on social media over public engagement. Research institutions and government agencies utilize social media to reach wider audiences without fully considering and responding to public feedback. In light of the COVID-19 crisis in 2020, this discussion of social media and science is particularly significant for thinking about how US and Chinese users learn about and sometimes work with each other across national boundaries.

In the final chapter of this volume, Lei Vincent Huang reports findings from interviews with WeChat users in China to understand why some people feel reluctant to engage in some elements of social media. Although for many users, WeChat's "all in one place" design brings convenience, others find it a constant source of anxiety and therefore manage it carefully. Part of the anxiety derives from the collapsed contexts within the WeChat communication ecology, where one's friends, families, and coworkers may be within the same contact lists, and thus personal life, family relations, and work are all folded into one setting. Yet people are often reluctant to share information intended for families or friends with their coworkers; many prefer to separate their private lives from work. Huang shows how WeChat's integrative design, compounded by cultural norms of online and offline sociality, has led to a degree of reluctance in its use, hence pointing to the crucial question of how privacy is negotiated in a media ecosystem were everything seems to be public.

Taken together, the four chapters in Part III show that state-sponsored platformization is not a tension-free process. Yet friction does not necessarily mean deliberate opposition. Like popular culture—and Chinese internet culture undoubtedly manifests more features of popular culture than official culture—Chinese internet culture is necessarily contradictory. The chapters in Part III show that there is a great deal of what John Fiske might call excorporation, namely, "the process by which the subordinate make their own culture out of the resources and commodities provided by the dominant system."[47] Even those who consciously resist the use of WeChat are selective in their avoidance. But again, to say netizens are "the subordinate" in Chinese internet culture already risks simplification. Artists, scientists, and many WeChat users may not see themselves as subordinate. Nor are all forms of resistance so unambiguously resistant. This volume therefore shows the complex entanglements of state-sponsored platformization and their popular, centrifugal impulses.

Conclusion: State-Platformization and the Mediated US–China Relationship

What are the implications of the state-sponsored platformization of the Chinese internet for US–China relations? As I suggested above, a key element of the commercial logic of platformization is the datafication of personal information through social media platforms.[48] This means that data security and data privacy related to social media platforms are an important issue in US–China relations. In June 2019, as part of its cybersecurity law, China released a draft regulation on the cross-border transfer of personal data.[49] The goal is to enforce more restrictions on transborder data flows. On the US side, the Chinese short video platform TikTok is under national security review due to concerns about data security and surveillance. In the middle of the current US–China trade war and debates about the uncoupling of US–China economies, the global ambitions of major Chinese social media platforms are facing more challenges than ever before. Furthermore, beyond issues of data security and surveillance, longer-term issues of technological competition (such as in the area of artificial intelligence) will continue to trouble US–China relations. We see this already in American media discourses of fear about China's national technology strategies and in concrete policy maneuvers, such as the blacklisting of the Chinese telecommunications company Huawei in the United States. In the age of social media, American discourses of fear about China easily find their way onto Chinese social media platforms, just as Chinese media agencies continue to push their agenda to shape global discourse about China.[50] As social media platforms continue to penetrate all aspects of contemporary life, they will become the "face" of our two nations, and thus bear the brunt of conflicts and interactions in US–China relations at both the elite and grassroots levels. In short, the future of US–China relations will be shaped in large part by intercultural communication taking place on social media and, in China, on social media driven by state-sponsored platformization.

NOTES

1. Transcript of "Younger Waves," May 6, 2020, https://baike.baidu.com/item/ %E5%90%8E%E6%B5%AA/49981848?fr=aladdin#2.

2. Peidong Yang and Lijun Tang, "'Positive Energy': Hegemonic Intervention and Online Media Discourse in China's Xi Jinping Era," *China: An International Journal* 16, no. 1 (2018): 1–22. Zifeng Chen and Clyde Yicheng Wang, "The Discipline of Happiness: The Foucauldian Use of the 'Positive Energy' Discourse in China's Ideological Works," *Journal of Current Chinese Affairs* (February 23, 2020), https://doi.org/10.1177/1868102619899409.

3. China Internet Network Information Center (CNNIC), "Statistical Report on Internet Development in China," July 2018, http://cnnic.com.cn/IDR/ReportDownloads/201911/ P020191112538212107066.pdf.

4. China Internet Network Information Center (CNNIC), "Statistical Report on Internet Development in China," February 2019, http://cnnic.com.cn/IDR/ ReportDownloads/201911/P020191112538996067898.pdf.

5. See, for example, Siva Vaidhyanathan, *Antisocial Media: How Facebook Disconnects Us and Undermines Democracy* (Oxford University Press, 2018). Victor Pickard, *Democracy without Journalism?: Confronting the Misinformation Society* (Oxford University Press, 2019).

6. Jack Nicas, Mike Isaac, and Ana Swanson, "TikTok Said to Be under National Security Review," *New York Times*, November 1, 2019. https://www.nytimes.com.

7. Executive Order on Addressing the Threat Posed by TikTok, August 6, 2020, https://www. whitehouse.gov/presidential-actions/executive-order-addressing-threat-posed-tiktok/. Executive Order on Addressing the Threat Posed by WeChat, August 6, 2020, https:// www.whitehouse.gov/presidential-actions/executive-order-addressing-threat-posed-wechat/.

8. David Kurt Herold, "Introduction: Noise, Spectacle, Politics: Carnival in Chinese Cyberspace," in *Online Society in China: Creating, Celebrating, and Instrumentalising the Online Carnival*, ed. David Kurt Herold and Peter Marolt (London: Routledge, 2011), 1–19.

9. Weiyu Zhang and Taberez Neyazi, "Communication and Technology Theories from the South: The Cases of China and India," *Annals of the International Communication Association* 44 (2020): 41, https://doi.org/10.1080/23808985.2019.1667852.

10. Mike Kent, Katie Ellis, and Jian Xu, eds., *Chinese Social Media: Social, Cultural, and Political Implications* (London: Routledge, 2017).

11. Jacques deLisle, Avery Goldstein, and Guobin Yang, eds., *The Internet, Social Media, and a Changing China* (Philadelphia: University of Pennsylvania Press, 2016).

12. Min Jiang, "The Coevolution of the Internet, (Un)Civil Society, and Authoritarianism in

China," in *The Internet, Social Media, and a Changing China*, ed. Jacques deLisle, Avery Goldstein, and Guobin Yang (Philadelphia: University of Pennsylvania Press, 2016), 28–48.

13. Min Jiang and Ashley Esarey, "(Un)civil Society in Digital China: Inciviliy, Fragmentation, and Political Stability; Introduction," *International Journal of Communication* 12 (2018): 1928–44.

14. Jeroen de Kloet, Thomas Poell, Zeng Guohua, and Chow Yiu Fai, "The Plaformization of Chinese Society: Infrastructure, Governance, and Practice," *Chinese Journal of Communication* 12, no. 3 (2019): 249–56.

15. David B. Nieborg and Thomas Poell, "The Platformization of Cultural Production: Theorizing the Contingent Cultural Commodity," *New Media & Society* 20, no. 11 (2018): 4276, cited in de Kloet, Poell, Zeng, and Chow, "The Plaformization of Chinese Society," 249.

16. de Kloet, Poell, Zeng, and Chow, "The Plaformization of Chinese Society," 252.

17. Jing Wang, *The Other Digital China: Nonconfrontational Activism on the Social Web* (Cambridge, MA: Harvard University Press, 2019).

18. Sally Xiaojin Chen, *Resistance in Digital China: The Southern Weekly Incident* (New York: Bloomsbury Academic, 2020).

19. Luzhou Li, *Zoning China: Online Video, Popular Culture, and the State* (Cambridge, MA: MIT Press, 2020).

20. Marcella Szablewicz, *Mapping Digital Game Culture in China: From Internet Addicts to Esports Athletes* (Palgrave Macmillan, 2020).

21. Silvia Lindtner, *Prototype Nation: China, the Maker Movement, and the Socialist Pitch of Entrepreneurial Living* (Princeton, NJ: Princeton University Press, 2020).

22. Two of their articles are available in English translation. See Lin Chen, "The Performative Space for City Identity Narrative: A Case Study of Suzhou Museum," *Communication and the Public* 2, no. 1 (2017): 52–66. https://doi.org/10.1177/2057047317695813. Zhonghong Ma, "An Online Forum of the Third Type: The Case of Suzhou's Hanshan Wenzhong Forum," *Communication and the Public* 2, no. 1 (2017): 67–83. https://doi.org/10.1177/2057047317698836.

23. Hailong Liu, ed., *From Cyber-Nationalism to Fandom Nationalism: The Case of Diba Expedition in China* (London: Routledge, 2019).

24. Zhong Yong, "The Chinese Internet: A Separate Closed Monopoly Board," *The Journal of International Communication* 18, no. 1 (2012): 19–31.

25. Susan Leong, "Sinophone, Chinese, and PRC Internet: Chinese Overseas in Australia and the PRC Internet," *Digital Asia* 3 (2016): 117–37; and see Guobin Yang, "A Chinese

Internet? History, Practice, and Globalization," *Chinese Journal of Communication* 5 (2012): 49–54.

26. For more discussions of the communication patterns on WeChat, see Eric Harwit, "WeChat: Social and Political Development of China's Dominant Messaging App," *Chinese Journal of Communication* 10, no. 3 (July 3, 2017): 312–27. Also see Yujie Chen, Zhifei Mao, and Jack Linchuan Qiu, *Super-Sticky WeChat and Chinese Society* (Bingley, UK: Emerald Group Publishing, 2018).

27. Jose van Dijck, *The Culture of Connectivity: A Critical History of Social Media* (Oxford University Press, 2013). Alice Marwick, *Status Update: Celebrity, Publicity, and Branding in the Social Media Age* (New Haven: Yale University Press, 2013).

28. Gillespie, for example, draws attention to how platforms shape information policy to seek limited liability for what users say on them. See Tarleton Gillespie, "The Politics of 'Platforms,'" *New Media & Society* 12, no. 3 (2010): 347–64. Schwarz's study of Facebook goes further to argue that digital platforms "engage in intensive legislation, administration of justice and punishment, and develop eclectic governing and legitimation apparatuses consisting of algorithms, proletarian judicial labor and quasiconstitutional governing documents." See Ori Schwarz, "Facebook Rules: Structures of Governance in Digital Capitalism and the Control of Generalized Social Capital," *Theory, Culture & Society* (2019): 117, https://doi.org/10.1177/0263276419826249. For a comprehensive study of the social impact of platforms, see José van Dijck, Thomas Poell, and Martijn De Waal, *The Platform Society: Public Values in a Connective World* (New York: Oxford University Press, 2018).

29. Min Jiang, "Internet Companies in China: Dancing between the Party Line and the Bottom Line," *Asie Visions* 47 (2012), https://ssrn.com/abstract=1998976. Yuezhi Zhao, *Media, Market and Democracy in China: Between the Party Line and the Bottom Line* (Urbana: University of Illinois Press, 1998). For a classic text on Chinese politics, see William A. Joseph ed., *Politics in China: An Introduction*, Third Edition. (Oxford, UK: Oxford University Press, 2019).

30. Maria Repnikova, *Media Politics in China: Improvising Power under Authoritarianism* (Cambridge, UK: Cambridge University Press, 2017).

31. Rebecca MacKinnon, "Liberation Technology: China's 'Networked Authoritarianism,'" *Journal of Democracy* 22, no. 2 (2011): 32–46. Min Jiang, "Authoritarian Informationalism: China's Approach to Internet Sovereignty," *SAIS Review of International Affairs* 30, no. 2 (2010): 71–89.

32. Rongbin Han, *Contesting Cyberspace in China: Online Expression and Authoritarian Resilience* (New York: Columbia University Press, 2018). Guobin Yang, ed., *China's*

Contested Internet (Copenhagen: NIAS Press, 2015).

33. M. E. Roberts, *Censored: Distraction and Diversion inside China's Great Firewall* (Princeton, NJ: Princeton University Press, 2018). Yizhou (Joe) Xu, "Programmatic Dreams: Technographic Inquiry into Censorship of Chinese Chatbots," *Social Media + Society* 4, no. 4 (2018): https://doi.org/10.1177/2056305118808780.

34. Patrick Shaou-Whea Dodge, "Imagining Dissent: Contesting the Facade of Harmony through Art and the Internet in China," in *Imagining China: Rhetorics of Nationalism in an Age of Globalization*, ed. Stephen John Hartnett, Lisa B. Keränen, and Donovan Conley (East Lansing: Michigan State University Press, 2017), 311–38. Ya-Wen Lei, *The Contentious Public Sphere: Law, Media, and Authoritarian Rule in China* (Princeton, NJ: Princeton University Press, 2017). Jing Wang, *The Other Digital China*. Guobin Yang, *The Power of the Internet in China: Citizen Activism Online* (New York: Columbia University Press, 2009).

35. Stephen J. Hartnett, "Google and the 'Twisted Cyber Spy' Affair: U.S.-China Communication in an Age of Globalization," *Quarterly Journal of Speech* 97 (2011): 411–34. Yu Hong and G. Thomas Goodnight, "How to Think about Cyber Sovereignty: The Case of China," *Chinese Journal of Communication* (2019): 1–19, https://doi.org/10.1080/1 7544750.2019.1687536. Min Jiang, "Authoritarian Informationalism." Jinghan Zeng, Tim Stevens, and Yaru Chen, "China's Solution to Global Cyber Governance: Unpacking the Domestic Discourse of 'Internet Sovereignty,'" *Politics & Policy* 45, no. 3 (2017): 432–64. https://doi.org/10.1111/polp.12202.

36. Jonathan Unger and Anita Chan, "China, Corporatism, and the East Asian Model," *The Australian Journal of Chinese Affairs*, no. 33 (1995): 29–53.

37. Plantin and de Seta use "techno-nationalist" to characterize Chinese platforms, but it is debatable that Google and Facebook are not techno-nationalist either. See Jean-Christophe Plantin and Gabriele de Seta, "WeChat as Infrastructure: The Techno-Nationalist Shaping of Chinese Digital Platforms," *Chinese Journal of Communication* (2019), https://doi.org/10.1080/17544750.2019.1572633.

38. Guobin Yang, "Demobilizing the Emotions of Online Activism in China: A Civilizing Process," *International Journal of Communication* 11 (2017): 1945–65.

39. Zhen Zhang and Ziyin Yin, "The Communication of Emotions on Douyin's Governance Accounts" (Chinese), *Press Circle* 9 (2019): 61–69. On the ideology of "positive energy," see Peidong Yang and Lijun Tang, "'Positive Energy': Hegemonic Intervention and Online Media Discourse in China's Xi Jinping Era," *China: An International Journal* 16, no. 1(2018): 1–22.

40. Shaohua Guo, "'Occupying' the Internet: State Media and the Reinvention of Official Culture Online," *Communication and the Public* 3, no. 1 (2018), 19.

41. Peng Lan, "Duan shi pin: Shi pin sheng chan li d 'zhuan ji yin' yu zai pei yu." *Journalism and Mass Communication Monthly* (xin wen jie), No 1 (2019): 34–43.

42. See Guobin Yang, "Demobilizing the Emotions of Online Activism in China."

43. Guobin Yang, "Demobilizing the Emotions of Online Activism in China."

44. Michael X. Delli Carpini, "Alternative Facts: Donald Trump and the Emergence of a New U.S. Media Regime," in *Trump and the Media*, ed. Pablo J. Boczkowski and Zizi Papacharissi (Cambridge, MA: MIT Press, 2018).

45. Karin Wahl-Jorgensen, "Public Displays of Disaffection: The Emotional Politics of Donald Trump," in *Trump and the Media*, ed. Pablo J. Boczkowski and Zizi Papacharissi, 82.

46. Fred Turner, "Trump on Twitter: How a Medium Designed for Democracy Became an Authoritarian's Mouthpiece," in *Trump and the Media*, edited by Pablo J. Boczkowski and Zizi Papacharissi, 149.

47. John Fiske, *Understanding Popular Culture*, 2nd edition (London: Routledge, 1980), 13.

48. See José van Dijck, Thomas Poell and Martijn De Waal, *The Platform Society: Public Values in a Connective World*. Nick Couldry and Ulises A. Mejias, *The Costs of Connection: How Data Is Colonizing Human Life and Appropriating It for Capitalism* (Stanford University Press, 2019).

49. Qiheng Chen, "China's New Data Protection Scheme," *The Diplomat*, July 2, 2019, https://thediplomat.com/2019/07/chinas-new-data-protection-scheme/.

50. On China's strategy to shape the global discourse, see chapters in Daya Kishan Thussu, Hugo de Burgh, and Anbin Shi, eds., *China's Media Go Global* (London: Routledge, 2017). Also see Stephen J. Hartnett, Lisa B. Keränen, and Donovan Conley, eds., *Imagining China: Rhetorics of Nationalism in an Age of Globalization* (East Lansing: Michigan State University Press, 2017).

PART I

Platforms

App Radio

The Reconfiguration of Audible Publics in China through Ximalaya.FM

Yizhou Xu and Jeremy Wade Morris

The period from 2013 to 2017 represents a watershed moment for Chinese mobile radio as several breakout shows such as *Thinking Logically* and the *Guo Degang Comedy Show* became viral topics across the country. Interestingly, this coincided with what critics in the United States have been calling a "golden age of podcasting," fueled by such hit podcasts as *Serial*, *Welcome to Night Vale*, and other highly produced and slickly edited shows.[1] While podcasting's mainstream success in the United States can be traced back to the increasing commercialization and professionalization of already established practices dating back to iPods, RSS feeds, and other web audio experiments since the early 2000s,[2] in China, mobile radio apps and podcasting are relatively new phenomena. This is partially due to the fact that Apple's iTunes—the globally prominent hub for podcast discovery and distribution—was not available in China until 2009 and most Chinese user-generated audio content is not accessible on Western audio platforms because of censorship and strict media controls, which limit users' ability to use and contribute to them. Indeed, such globally prominent platforms as SoundCloud and YouTube are banned in China. Even more so than in the United States then, the rise of internet-based radio and podcasting in China is highly intertwined with the country's rapid smartphone adoption. In 2017, estimates suggest that China has over 717 million smartphone users reflecting a total adoption rate of 51.7 percent,[3] of which 94 percent of those ages 18 to 34 owned a smartphone.[4] Tellingly, the Chinese term for podcasting, *boke*—which loosely translates to audio-blogging—is actually seldom used. Instead, the term *dian tai*, or internet radio, is far more prevalent given its association with internet-enabled phones. The rise of digital radio and on-demand audio in China, in other words, has a different history than in the United States; paying attention to these differences turns media and cultural studies scholars toward culturally specific listening practices, histories, technologies, and state-citizen relations—thus providing a broader understanding of this emerging format.

This chapter contributes to histories of internet radio and podcasting in China by examining one of the most popular contemporary mobile radio apps in China, Ximalaya.FM. In particular, we look at how the app's interface and design contribute to the formation of a listening public as China transitions from socialist to more neoliberal-based politics and practices. Mobile radio in China represents a fruitful site of study because it underscores different modes of reception practices that developed outside of the Western context and offers case studies that transcend the traditional Western focus that drives most histories of the medium.[5] As Rofel suggests, we need to dispel universalizing notions of globalization by demonstrating that neoliberal subjectivities are not homogenous, especially in the case of China, where various disparate state policies and corporate strategies translate into new subjectivities.[6] Indeed, the reconfiguration of the centralized Chinese state media into commodifiable forms of individualized listening highlights the complicated entanglement of post-socialist and neoliberal tendencies. In the early days of Mao-era China, citizens listened to the radio via state-controlled channels, on state-mandated devices, and often in Party-controlled spaces, but auditory life in China has since shifted toward the commodified and individualized listening practices evident today, meaning notions of auditory publics have become increasingly attached to neoliberal sentiments of freedom, privacy, and participation. Additionally, the convoluted relationship between Chinese state and corporate interests adds compounding layers of control and profiteering that may potentially undermine the promotion of public interest and civic participation. By looking at the modes of interfacing built into the Ximalaya app, we argue that contrary to promoting new modes of public participation, apps like Ximalaya largely work to reconfigure media control with the false promise of political participation.

From Collective Listening in Mao-Era China to Contemporary Individualized Listening

To understand the present circumstances of online radio and podcasting in China, we must look back to the historical evolution of the medium and how it differs from radio in the West. As Michele Hilmes points out, broadcast radio is one of the earliest forms of electronic mass media, and it was (and continues to be) crucial in fostering a public sense of nationhood and belonging in the United States.[7] This shares interesting parallels with the development of auditory publics via collective listening practices in socialist China, though the processes of collective listening in the Western context described by Hilmes and other broadcast historians was mainly focused on voluntary listening practices, where people came together as listening publics based on common associations. Kate Lacey, for example, argues this voluntary collective listening is integral in the formation of the public sphere because of its embodied nature, and its role as "a metaphor for an interactive politics."[8] In Mao-era China, on the other hand, collective listening was a mandatory experience. Radio was seen as paramount in exerting state control over China's vast territory. Shortly after the Communist takeover in China, the government built mobile reception stations across China in all public areas such as communes, factories, schools, and work units. This culminated in the creation of radio reception networks (*shouyingwang*) and loudspeakers that have been crucial for the creation of auditory publics in China since 1949.[9] Radio largely became the chief medium by which news, information, and entertainment were communicated to both urban and rural audiences in pre-reform China. These shared listening spaces were so ubiquitous in China that still today, if you wander into an older factory, school, or courtyard, you can find dilapidated speakers hanging from the rafters or sequestered in the bushes. Under this early collective listening regime, public audio spaces were controlled by the Party and listening was both collective and mandatory.

Collective listening was instrumental to the central government's core mission of achieving political legitimacy, garnering popular support, and mobilizing citizens to partake in collective action with and sometimes against others, like in the case of the mass mobilization campaigns around the Cultural Revolution and the Great Leap Forward. Every aspect of auditory consumption was "exercised as a political activity, made obligatory as a form of expression of one's loyalty, and worked to support the Chinese Communist Party–led state."[10] The listening practices in Mao's China occupied all aspects of public and private life and were a fundamental duty of the modern socialist subject. Present-day versions of these older forms of state-imposed collective listening still persist in countries like North Korea.[11]

Since economic liberalization began in China in the 1980s, these state-mandated collective listening practices have become more individualized and privatized. This has coincided with the mobility many citizens have been afforded within a rapidly urbanizing society. Apart from the aforementioned increase in size of China's smartphone market, China also recently surpassed the United States as the largest auto market, providing another highly individualized and mobile space for listening.[12] China's real estate market is also changing rapidly, with millions of citizens moving out of communes and shared living spaces into private apartments.[13] This privatization of space, in cars and in homes, has opened up new outlets for everyday media consumption where the emerging middle class can "engage in conspicuous consumption, and yearn for privacy, comfort, and exclusivity."[14] This connection between mobility, the spatial context of reception, and audible media is certainly not unique to China; Alexander Russo in the United States and Jody Berland in Canada both build on Raymond Williams's ideas of "mobile privatization" in their discussion of radio's ability to extend domestic spaces into public spaces via automobiles (and, in turn, to bring public affairs into private spaces).[15] What is unique, then, is the timing of these developments in relation to the Chinese state's shifting political landscape and to the kinds of technologies many citizens are now making use of on a regular basis.

The ability to create these kinds of "privatized auditory bubbles" is further amplified with the advent of mobile apps that offer users the ability to customize and personalize the media they use to navigate their public surroundings.[16] As a result, there has been significant growth in digital broadcasting in China in the areas of mobile radio, on-demand audio apps, and even WeChat audio messages. These forms of digital audio have become especially important and popular modes of communication for China's burgeoning migrant working class, who face long commutes on a daily basis. The popularity of WeChat's voice message feature, for example, according to Lacey, is precisely due to the ease of recording an audio message compared to text input methods.[17] While the latter tends to be the preferred method of communication for urban citizens on the move using public transit, radio and audio apps are favored by migrant laborers on long commutes and truck drivers because of the affordances of "distracted listening" and hands-free operation while they work.[18] New forms of mobile and digital audio not only provide a respite from the dreariness of long commutes and even longer working hours, but they also play a crucial role in helping migrant workers adjust to new and unfamiliar surroundings. Cara Wallis, for example, argues that mobile phones provide an "immobile mobility" for female rural migrants in China, who negotiate subject formation in their daily work lives in their transplanted and temporary urban spaces.[19] Even though migrant women are often confined within their workplaces and lack the opportunities to advance on social and professional ladders, Wallis argues mobile consumption provides these workers with an outlet for interaction.

In short, while the trends of increased mobility and privatized spaces, and the terms "mobile privatization" and "privatized auditory bubble," can be used to describe podcasting in the West, they also apply in the case of China. Indeed, the persistence of both rural and community radio in the digital age—and the practices of both rural migrant workers and their urban counterparts—reflects the importance of sonic cultures in shaping the emerging neoliberal sensibilities in China. We turn now to look more specifically at mobile radio apps and podcasting in China, and how the Ximalaya.FM app, through its interface design and branding, capitalizes on the privatization of spaces granted by the increasingly mobile population in China.

Ximalaya.FM and the Blurring of State, Private, and Citizen Interests

The Chinese encounter with economic liberalization and neoliberalism reveals how the implementation of market forces into socialist systems can, at times, manifest in complex, asymmetrical, and contradictory ways. Rather than a model where global capital subsumes most aspects of public and private life, the so-called "socialism with Chinese characteristics" presents a hybrid political economic model where Party governance melds with the logic of the market.[20] For example, in looking at the communication industry in China, Yuezhi Zhao contends there is a mutually constitutive relationship between state, communication, and society.[21] The Party regime's response to market liberalization resulted not so much in the loss of state power as in the reconfiguration of centralized power, where the fulcrum of control oscillates between corporate and institutional forces that remain subordinate to the state. In their micro-level analysis of urban media industries, Chin-Chuan Lee, Zhou He, and Yu Huang describe China's media industries as a form of "Party-market corporatism" to emphasize the interplay between the "state-media-capital tripartite."[22] They argue that media companies enter into a kind of patron-client relationship whereby media companies become dependent on the state in a multitude of ways that may not always be consistent or uniform in different regional markets. The loci for control often function in ad hoc and unpredictable ways in response to different and opposing influences from both public and private capital. Within this context, we can think through the case of Ximalaya.FM, which serves as an instructive look at the various tensions between state interests, private capital, and user agency, especially given the important historical role audio and radio, and sonic culture more broadly, has played in China.

Founded in 2013, Ximalaya.FM is the most popular mobile radio app in China with an installed base of 600 million users, accounting for 75 percent of the total on-demand audio market in 2019.[23] Ximalaya is the Mandarin rendition of the Tibetan word "Himalaya," the mountain range, and alludes to the app's attempts to provide the highest level of sound experiences. Unlike podcatching apps that serve as a repository for categorizing and distributing audio via RSS feeds,[24] Ximalaya operates more like an audio distribution service similar to SoundCloud—the Berlin-based sound and social media tool—where users can upload audio directly onto the platform. In fact, Ximalaya and SoundCloud share the same principle early venture capitalist investor, Kleiner Perkins, a major player in incubating start-ups in Silicon Valley. In addition to enabling significant amounts of user-generated content, Ximalaya.FM also syndicates content from national and provincial radio stations, thereby creating a hybrid of state-owned, professionally produced and user-generated audio content. According to a report in 2018, Ximalaya is primarily made up of younger listeners with almost 80 percent of the user base under thirty-five years of age. Additionally, its users generally skew toward the upper middle class and are drawn to high quality content, such as audio books and news. Finally, the core demographic remains heavily urban, with most of the listeners concentrated in the affluent coastal cities in China. This represents a significant departure from prior collective listening practices, which mainly catered toward rural areas, and in turn signifies the shifting modes of audible consumption toward young, mobile, and connected urbanites.

The app positions itself less as a podcasting app and more as an internet/ mobile radio provider; while this distinction between *boke* and *dian tai* may seem minor, it reveals how the role of sound is positioned in China. The existing literature on podcasting in Western contexts features debates on the "radioness" of podcasts and whether podcasts are categorically different than radio, or simply radio remediated.[25] But in these debates, regardless of what scholars call it, the emerging format represents a challenge to the heavily regulated and high-cost broadcast sector by allowing for an increase in user participation and production, and, in theory, a greater diversity of voices in the public sphere. In the Chinese context, the attachment to the term "radio" signifies a set of institutional differences in how radio evolved as China transitioned to a market economic system. Here the separation between internet radio and amateur podcasts reflects a wider debate surrounding the publicness of traditional radio and the private modes of individualized listening. The distinction between mobile radio and podcasting is an important one because the history of digital audio and sonic reception in China follows a different trajectory than in the United States. Given that the authoritarian state played such a determining role in shaping the practices of radio listening in Mao-era China, the choice to emphasize radio over podcasting in how mobile apps are described highlights how on-demand audio in China is framed as an activity in which the state still plays a central role. This complicates some of the typical emancipatory narratives around podcasting and mobile apps that accompanied the rise of podcasting in the United States, where the trend was pushed by commercial entities emphasizing the values of consumer choice and freedom.

How then does Ximalaya.FM work to categorize and curate content via its app interface and design? How does the app foster modes of reception that serve to reconfigure auditory publics in China? How does the app, and the private company behind it, negotiate the divergent interests of state control, advertiser interests, and user participation? Such questions provide a useful framework for understanding how the platform's architecture contributes to the formation of culturally specific listening experiences. To answer these questions, we undertake a discursive interface analysis that explores the affordances, interfaces, and user-inputs of the app in an attempt to "interpret the embedded assumptions about its own purpose and appropriate use."[26] We are particularly interested in how the spaces of consumption are codified within the paratextual elements of the app and in asking how these cultural, corporate, and state-influenced transformations reflect wider political changes in China. We also draw on the walkthrough method to explore the spatial logic of "app-as-infrastructure" and to address how interface design reveals how users make sense of an app and the implicit assumptions of developers on how the app *should* be used.[27] Our analysis therefore builds on Ramon Lobato's call to recognize the importance of "platform space," where modes of organization and categorization of media serve as the framework for "programming and, by extension, audience reception."[28] We also draw upon Andreas Fickers's insights about the affordances of radio dials, which are heavily influenced by the government's regulation of frequencies and thus produce a form of interfacing through which users make sense of their sonic experiences.[29] We focus heavily, then, on what Ben Light, Jean Burgess, and Stefanie Duguay call the "environment of expected use"—how an app developer anticipates the app will be received, succeed, and regulate user activity—and focus on how the form of Ximalaya.FM's design and content directly shapes how an ideal listening public is imagined.[30]

We recognize that interface analyses and walkthroughs are limited in their scope. Apps are often "lures" designed to "trick users and draw their attention from the network's algorithm architecture to entertaining and user-friendly opaque screens."[31] Moreover, these interfaces are largely abstractions meant to "present that which is otherwise unpresentable."[32] Apps are dynamic texts that change frequently (as Ximalaya has done during the period of our analysis), making it difficult to draw conclusions that aren't obsolete by the next update. With this in mind, we have also augmented our walkthrough with an archival analysis of past versions of the app to look at how Ximalaya.FM's interface has changed over time, thus tracing different moments during its development cycle. Using sites like APKMirror or APKHere to source older versions of the app's installation file and running these through an Android emulator, we hope to track how developer intentions may have changed as the app evolved.[33] This method allows us to track the precise design and content-related changes through each succeeding update. In doing so, and much like Duguay's analysis of the links between Tinder's changing features and media perceptions as the app gained popularity, we seek to highlight how the app is not a static object but is constantly being refined, based on changing developer intent and user expectations.[34] We also draw from news reports, advertising, and white papers as "semi-embedded industry texts" to look at the conversation surrounding the reception of the app.[35] By combining a walkthrough of the current app with analysis of previous versions and other paratextual materials, we hope to excavate the ways the app has positioned itself as facilitating either public or private listening experiences and what this might mean for the changing role of radio and audio media in light of China's transition from socialist to market-driven media industries.

Ximalaya.FM: Interface, Advertising, and Feature Walkthrough

Ximalaya.FM reconfigures the notions of the auditory public through its deliberate design, messaging, and advertising. The tagline "anytime, anywhere; listen to anything I want" is the fixture within the app text and its associated paratextual promos. Ximalaya.FM is available from the Google Play store, but as a Chinese app—and due to the censorship of Google services in China—its main point of distribution is from domestic Chinese vendors like Tencent's MyApp.[36] Accordingly, updates to Ximalaya.FM will generally appear sooner on Chinese app stores than in Google's, but the app description and associated preview images remain the same. For example, the following app store description is repeated throughout its preview and advertising videos in both Tencent's and Google's stores:

> —Waiting in line, doing housework . . . bored? Listen to Ximalaya, make boredom fun.
> —Annoyed while driving? Listen to Ximalaya, you might fall in love with getting stuck in traffic.
> —Missing something before bed? Listen to Ximalaya, let the soothing sounds put you to sleep.
> —Want to improve yourself? Listen to Ximalaya, let the experts make you soar.
> —Time is scarce, space is limited. Listen to Ximalaya, seize your chance, and make every moment precious.[37]

In these excerpts from Ximalaya.FM's advertisements and press releases, the app is presented as a sort of panacea to the boredom associated with everyday routines (i.e., housework, traffic, queuing, etc.), even if such moments of boredom are merely symptoms and byproducts of contemporary life under neoliberal modernity. The app promises to address the symptoms, if not the causes, to help users milk more productivity, joy, or efficiency out of every moment. The boredom of chores won't be boredom any longer; chores plus Ximalaya will be "fun," the taglines promise. The chores, of course, remain, as do the demands they make on a user's time and energy. Apps like Ximalaya ask users to think of those demands as ones that can also be tolerable and enjoyable. Wendy Chun argues that this is a common trope of many "new" media: they form a perpetual network of constructed crises which can only be resolved via regular updates.[38] Similarly, Ximalaya.FM presents these mundane everyday activities as problems that can only be solved through the individualized listening experiences of the app. Ximalaya therefore promotes mobile listening to help users negotiate the varying spatial limits of their urban lives, various demands on their time required by modern work life, and the constant neoliberal pressures to improve oneself.

Many of Ximalaya.FM's features and content are directly targeted at groups such as white-collar workers, truck drivers, homemakers, and students, all of whom share similar mobile listening practices rooted in their daily activities and spaces of consumption. Here, the company frames the affordances of the isolated listening experience as an escape from the cacophonies of the everyday and presents public spaces such as buses and parks—and the public life they bring with them—as places of nuisance that the app can solve. In line with neoliberal tendencies to conflate branding, marketing, and public interest in ways that shift governance toward corporations and private spheres, Ximalaya.FM equates a user's individual choice over, and access to, sonic media with the liberating affordances of mobile app consumption.[39] Collective public listening, and the interaction with public life this entails, is de-emphasized in favor of individual choice, personal enjoyment, and increased productivity. Since the economic reforms of the 1980s, the Chinese regime has aggressively marketed the notion of "socialism with Chinese character- istics" as an exceptional model of economic development, yet here we encounter what feels more like the end of socialism altogether, as marketing, anomie, and self-improvement merge in a mediated effort to "make boredom fun."

Unlike traditional state-run radio, which places the content of the broadcast at the center of its concerns, Ximalaya.FM emphasizes audience reception as the primary selling point of the app. The app logo for Ximalaya.FM is the Chinese character *ting* or "listen." When a user first launches the app, they are greeted by a splash screen that highlights some of the intended usages of the app, such as "listen to books," "bored while working out?" and "make housework more interesting." United States–based podcasting apps seldom have these kinds of splash screens, but for Ximalaya.FM, these introductory images act as an important framing device. Because the splash screen is the first page users encounter, it provides valuable real estate for developers to set the tone for how the developers envision the app, thus establishing the "environment of expected use." The splash screens change with each major update of the app, usually indicated by a change in version number (i.e., version 1.00 to version 2.00), indicating a variety of branding and design tactics that both retain old users and attract new ones. For example, early versions of the app included splash screens that focused on how, when, and where users should use the app (i.e., jogging, commuting, etc.) while more recent versions focus more on specific content offerings, such as audiobooks. While earlier iterations of the interface seemed designed to introduce users to the benefits of mobile listening, later iterations emphasize the listener's agency in terms of constructing media content by utilizing individualized and customized content offerings.

On the front page of each respective section, users are given the choice of subject matter they can pursue, such as "listen to books," "listen to news," "listen to history," etc. Within these genre categories, user-generated content (UGC) and community participation are heavily promoted across the app interface. For example, a dedicated menu enables users to record podcasts on the fly; the comment visualization feature encourages users to interact with each other by leaving comments for other listeners and the audio hosts (this function is similar to SoundCloud's annotation feature, except it occurs in real time). By presenting listening as a user's individual choice and giving greater agency to users both to listen to and to create audio, Ximalaya.FM attempts to create a sense of community within what might otherwise be an isolating and individualized listening experience.

This is not necessarily to suggest that Ximalaya.FM's encouragement of user-generated productions and community interaction is somehow altruistic; as José van Dijck warns, user agency in the context of digital media is always ambiguous, given that any valorization of "active" users is also dependent on the "role a site's interface plays in maneuvering individual users and communities."[40] The prevalence of user-centric features, as in other forms of social media, act as a form of "free lunch" that entices the users with the user-friendly features for making media and community interaction while they also perform labor for the platform by creating much of its content and by generating actionable data from social interactions with other users.[41] In other words, while there are certainly a number of features that, on the surface, signify podcasting (*boke*) and echo the rhetoric of disrupting traditional broadcasting, underneath many of these features lies a more traditional enterprise-based conception of the role of radio (*dian tai*): to segment users into distinct groups for the purposes of marketing, sales, or as we'll argue below, political messaging.

When comparing early versions of the app to the present one, we find a significant overhaul to the app interface, especially with respect to the number of categories from which users can choose. Unlike United States–based podcatching apps (i.e., PocketCast, OverCast, etc.), Ximalaya.FM offers a specific breakdown

TABLE 1. Categories within version 5.4.45.9 released in June 2017; the categories appear in the order in which they appeared in the app's interface. (ASMR stands for autonomous sensory meridian response, a physical tingling sensation that can occur from hearing certain vocal delivery styles, like whispers.)

Audiobooks	Relationship advice	Foreign languages	Radio drama	Anime
Children	Culture	Business	Chinese opera	Online courses
Standup comedy	Talk show	Health	Radio	Party history
Music	Entertainment	National studies	Technology	Film
History	English	3D audio/ASMR	Gaming	Lifestyle
	Education	News	Automobile	Poetry

of niche genres, such as ASMR and anime, while also including Chinese-specific programming, such as national studies and Chinese comedy. Each category leads to further submenus providing even more specific breakdowns based on individual interests. For example, under the ASMR menu there is an entire section dedicated to spooky Halloween/horror sounds that dares the users to listen at night. Beyond the categories, Ximalaya.FM's interface also includes a recommendation tab/link that offers individual suggestions based on previous listening history along with countless app-curated "top 10" recommendations and "must listen" lists. While these options underscore neoliberal sensibilities of accumulation, individualism and personal choice in matters of consumption, this "fantasy of abundance" also belies a mode of company-controlled categorization and hierarchization of information based on the app's interface.[42] For example, many of the top lists in Ximalaya.FM are not so much based on user popularity (or play counts or number of listeners) as they are based on contracts Ximalaya has negotiated with hosts it promotes. Likewise, the recommendation tab always directs users to paid subscriptions of premium content as opposed to free content. The app's interface presents suggestions that seem tailored and specific to any given user, but they often represent a series of other interests, investments, and relationships that Ximalaya.FM has in its content. Not unlike apps in the United States, then, we conclude that behind the façade of user-generated content and individualized usages, Ximalaya.FM manifests consistent corporate interests.

Despite Ximalaya.FM's desire to reframe its auditory public toward private listening experiences and user participation, state radio nevertheless occupies a prominent position in the app's interface. A centrally located "radio" tab/link in the middle of the screen contains the categories "national stations," "provincial stations," "local stations," and "web stations," all of which are controlled by state-run media.[43] The two main bodies of China's state-owned radio—China National Radio and China Radio International—produce the bulk of content that users can find in this section. Much like Mao-era radio programming, CNR and CRI act as the official outlets for news and entertainment that filter down to the provincial and local stations as well. This reassertion of state media in a mobile app advertised as a place for user participation may seem contradictory at first, but upon closer inspection of the content on the platform, it becomes clear this decision is key to the app's monetization efforts, and thus often takes precedence over user-generated content or community building. For example, Ximalaya.FM has recently embraced its corporate branding to promote the government's bottom-line. In 2018, the company introduced a tailor-made version of the XiaoYa AI speaker—a voice activated home speaker like Alexa or Google home, but complete with the hammer and sickle branding—for Communist Party members to study Communist doctrines and to "help more people to better understand the Party's thinking through content provided by the Communist Party and Communist Youth League in China."[44] This outreach/branding effort shares some strategies with promotional culture in the West, as Laurie Ouellette has shown in terms of the increasing "convergence between governing and branding strategies" in the United States in the form of corporate social responsibility and public outreach campaigns.[45] But while in the US context, such promotional culture tends to focus on notions of "self-branding,"[46] the case of Ximalaya.FM demonstrates the renewed primacy of "Party-branding" as the central aim of the state-corporate regime within an app that otherwise positions itself as place for user-generated content and user interactions.

Another worrying example of state influence within the app can be seen in Ximalaya.FM's gradual shift away from user-generated content to professionally generated content as a means of generating subscription revenues, as well as a general promotion of safe and censored content rather than user-generated audio. For instance, Ximalaya.FM has increasingly been promoting programming from influencers and "public intellectuals," many of whom are mobilized by the state to shape public opinion in promoting politically correct (i.e., in line with the Communist Party ideas and ideals) discourse.[47] Similarly, in 2015, Ximalaya set up a 300-person content moderation team to filter content across user-generated shows in a comprehensive effort to remove subversive content that ran afoul of State censorship policies. Estimates suggest that close to 10,000 user-generated "podcasts" were deleted each day.[48] Ximalaya also has exclusive agreement with the largest online publisher in China, China Literature Limited. They control over 70 percent of the audiobook market, and most of the books are already pre-censored by the publisher making it easier content for Ximalaya to manage.[49] As a final example, Ximalaya.FM has recently geo-blocked its popular built-in recording function to prevent users from outside China recording audio and sharing content on the app. Considering the prevalence of dissent in China's vast expatriate communities in Singapore, Taiwan, America, and elsewhere, this geo-blocking amounts to a new layer of international censorship.

Thus, despite building a platform to promote open participation, users are actually extremely constrained on account of the heavily regulated media environment in China. We know from recent research on United States–based platforms that one of the key components of any platform, as "custodians of the Internet," is that they moderate; they take an active role in shaping what content is deemed acceptable and what content is banned, or what content is prioritized and monetized and what content is buried and hidden.[50] These decisions, in the United States, are often made for the sake of profit, appeasing advertisers, or in reaction to controversy (e.g., YouTube's recent attempts to adjust to concerns around their kids' content/videos). Like Ximalaya.FM, United States–based platforms and social networks employ content moderators, technological controls (e.g., YouTube and ContentID), and internal content policies to shape and curate content in ways, and for reasons, that are not transparent. For Ximalaya.FM, there's also the key role of the state to consider, and the various tensions between users, advertisers, and government policy. In other words, the Chinese state works to de-centralize and de-emphasize its power by diffusing it across private corporate media platforms, like Ximalaya. FM, hence underscoring why we argue that China's culturally specific audio context offers fresh opportunities for studying the relationships between neoliberal and post-socialist logics.[51]

Thus, rather than providing a liberating and potentially subversive listening experience, Ximalaya.FM largely reconfigures the existing structures of power by diffusing and normalizing processes of control. By promoting isolated, individualized listening experiences, and offering the veneer of user-generated content and community while simultaneously downplaying these features in its interface, Ximalaya.FM presents itself as a potential alternative to state-run media even as it actively works to support the state's political objectives. While Lee, He, and Huang argue that the diversity of power within the state/media patron-client relationship "may collectively help loosen the rigid Party ideology in the long run,"[52] we take a more pessimistic view of the challenges to power and media diversity that new media like Ximalaya.FM might present, especially in light of the reassertion of state power via tighter supervision and oversight of the corporate media industries that has taken place in China in recent years.

Conclusion: From "Making Boredom Fun" to New Forms of State Power

In December 2017, Ximalaya released a localized, English version of the app on the Google Play Store, called "Himalaya—Free Podcast Player & Audio App." It is a more conventional podcatching app, designed for the United States market, that allows users to subscribe to podcasts and receive recommendations based on their previous usage. Notably, the title of the US version emphasizes the word "podcast" in a way that its Chinese counterpart does not. And while the app's description claims that the app is also "a family for podcast creators" (Google Play Store, 2018), there's no recording feature in the app and no easy way for users to upload content without going through the Ximalaya.com website. The localized version also omits the splash screens, provides simplified menus, and offers fewer options than the Ximalaya.FM app, resulting in a fairly typical podcasting app for finding, organizing, and listening to podcasts. While these changes to the Chinese version might seem to result in an app with reduced potential compared to the original, the localized version perhaps represents the culmination of the complex negotiations taking place among competing interests (i.e., state, user, corporate) that the original app has endured. Indeed, the need for localization is indicative of how Ximalaya's original app is unsuitable for the US app, not just through its affordances and design, but because of its content, censorship, and data collection practices. This is not surprising, as other Chinese platforms such as the massively popular TikTok (the glocalized version of the Chinese app Douyin) has come under increasing scrutiny from US regulators over its content regulation and potential national security risk. Such contentions are echoed in the Sino-US trade war, which many pundits label a "tech cold war,"[53] wherein US–China tensions are not merely about technological dominance but divergent interpretations of what constitutes publicness and openness in the digital age.

As our breakdown of Ximalaya.FM's features and platform infrastructure has demonstrated, the abundance of choice, user participation, and interaction with audio media may not be what it seems at the level of the interface. The promotion of user-generated content is offset by the profusion of state and corporate media within the app, leaving only a veil of community and participatory culture in a highly curated media environment. While many US platforms that emerged in the wake of Web 2.0 display similar kinds of "politics" that place corporate interests above those of users,[54] Ximalaya.FM introduces the added complexity of the state and its political goals. This is where the distinction between *boke* and *dian tai* comes to matter again. The disjuncture between podcasting and radio in China is not just a debate of semantics, as it sometimes can be in discussions of podcasting in the West, but rather it stands in for a longstanding conflict between authoritarian control and economic liberalization of media in general, and audio communication more generally. State media control in this instance is reconfigured into multi-nodal sites of control where individual corporations take the reins over the processes of content filtering and the enforcement of censorship policies. For Lacey, the shift to digital audio also entails a shift from radio listening as a public and collective activity for civil purposes—what she calls "listening out"—to the widespread privatization and domestication of personal and privatized listening, or "listening in."[55] While post-socialist China did bring about increased personal freedom and choice in regard to citizens' media consumption practices, the subtle reconfiguration of listening as a political obligation through a more private, consumptive process demonstrates how the state and the country's emerging businesses view the collective public as an entity to be divided into manageable units defined by their individual class, status, and taste. As Wei Lei and Wanning Sun argue, "what has emerged is not an autonomous and independent space of public communication, whereby individuals can freely access radio as a public good and become members of the mediated public. Instead, radio-sound in post-Mao-era China serves more as a force of exclusion, producing a range of social spaces whose boundaries are based on socioeconomic status."[56]

Given its history of state-directed public listening, followed by an extended period of economic liberalization where private companies expanded citizens' listening possibilities, what defines contemporary listening in China is ultimately an incongruous set of values and uses. The case of Ximalaya.FM illustrates on one hand the individualized, personalized, and private aspects of listening as envisioned by a private company looking to market user-generated content and to collect data and profit from everyday listening practices. On the other hand, the app also shows the ongoing tensions between state and private companies and the persistent desire of the state to manage channels of communication with its citizens. As a result of these tensions between the state and the companies that work within it, Ximalaya.FM complicates podcasting's promises of user-generated content and user agency. Despite Ximalaya's marketing materials, which emphasize users' role in controlling their listening experiences, the app's features and interface situate users rather precariously. The affordances and constraints of the app's interface put users squarely in between Ximalaya's interests, which direct the flow of user interaction in ways that commodify listening, and the state's interest, which hinges on managing new listening publics so that even individualized users become ideal political subjects. Ultimately, then, we conclude that Ximalaya.FM extends state-directed messaging in the digital age.

NOTES

1. Eric Blattberg, "The Podcast Enters a New Golden Age," *Digiday Nielsen*, November 19, 2014, https://digiday.com/media/nielsenes-rise-podcast/; Kevin Roose, "What's Behind the Great Podcast Renaissance?," *New York Magazine*, October 30, 2014; Lene Bech Sillesen, "Is This the Golden Age of Podcasts?,"2014\n 236\n 478\n 9\nMobile-Nielsen-banner (1 *Columbia Journalism Review*, November 24, 2014. https://archives.cjr.org/behind_the_news/is_this_the_golden_age_of_podc_1.php?page=all#sthash.BZ1312b8.dpuf.

2. Jonathan Sterne, Jeremy Wade Morris, Michael Baker, and Ariana Moscote Freire, "The Politics of Podcasting," *Fibreculture*, no. 13 (2008); Andrew Bottomley, "Podcasting: A Decade in the Life of a 'New' Audio Medium; Introduction,"the New Oxford American Dictionary (NOAD *Journal of Radio & Audio Media* 22, no. 2 (2015): 164–69.

3. Newzoo, "Top 50 Countries by Smartphone Users and Penetration," demography, online population, and inequality. These estimates are benchmarked with our clients in the industry along with third-party reports and institutions. *Newzoo Website*, 2017, https://newzoo.com/insights/rankings/top-50-countries-by-smartphone-penetration-and-users/.

4. Jacob Poushter, "China Outpaces India in Internet Access, Smartphone Ownership," *PEW Research Center for Internet and Technology*, March 16, 2017, https://www.pewresearch.org/fact-tank/2017/03/16/china-outpaces-india-in-internet-access-smartphone-ownership/.

5. Richard Berry, "A Golden Age of Podcasting? Evaluating *Serial* in the Context of Podcast Histories," *Journal of Radio & Audio Media* 22, no. 2 (July 3, 2015): 170–78; Richard Berry, "Will the iPod Kill the Radio Star? Profiling Podcasting as Radio," *Convergence: The International Journal of Research into New Media Technologies* 12, no. 2 (2006): 143–62."; Sterne et al., "The Politics of Podcasting." The author argues that *Serial* is a significant moment in the history of podcasting. Recent trends have shifted podcasts from iPods to networked screen-based mobile devices in smartphones and connected dashboards, locations where global brands enjoy a significant advantage. It is in this context that the author places Serial as cultural object.

6. Lisa Rofel, *Desiring China: Experiments in Neoliberalism, Sexuality, and Public Culture* (Durham: Duke University Press, 2007).

7. Michele Hilmes, *Radio Voices: American Broadcasting, 1922–1952* (Minneapolis: University of Minnesota Press, 1997).

8. Kate Lacey, *Listening Publics : The Politics And Experience of Listening in the Media Age* (Malden, MA: Polity Press, 2013), 159.

9. Wei Lei and Wanning Sun, "Radio Listening and the Changing Formations of the Public in China," *Communication and the Public* 2, no. 4 (2017): 320–34.

10. Lei and Sun, "Radio Listening and the Changing Formations of the Public in China," 330.

11. Daniel Byman and Jennifer Lind, "Pyongyang's Survival Strategy: Tools of Authoritarian Control in North Korea," *International Security* 35, no. 1 (Summer 2010): 54.

12. Patricia Jiayi Ho, "China Passes U.S. as World's Top Car Market," *Wall Street Journal*, January 12, 2010, https://www.wsj.com.

13. Wade Shepard, "China Now Has an Answer to Its Housing Crisis—It's Called Rent," *Forbes*, October 29, 2019, https://www.forbes.com.

14. Li Zhang, *In Search of Paradise: Middle-Class Living in a Chinese Metropolis* (Ithaca, NY: Cornell University Press, 2010), 3.

15. Jody Berland, "Locating Listening: Technological Space, Popular Music, and Canadian Mediations," in *The Place of Music*, ed. Andrew Leyshon, Davide Matless, and George Reveill (New York: Guilford Press, 1998); Alexander Russo, *Points on the Dial: Golden Age Radio beyond the Networks* (Durham, NC: Duke University Press, 2010).

16. Michael Bull, "No Dead Air! The iPod and the Culture of Mobile Listening," *Leisure Studies* 24, no. 4 (2005): 344.

17. Kate Lacey, "Smart Radio and Audio Apps: The Politics and Paradoxes of Listening to (Anti-) Social Media," *Australian Journalism Review* 36, no. 2 (2014): 77–90.

18. Minghe Hu, "China's Podcast King Yu Jianjun Rides Smartphone Wave to Build Ximalaya FM," *South China Morning Post*, August 30, 2019, https://www.scmp.com/tech/start-ups/

article/3024942/chinas-podcast-king-yu-jianjun-rides-smartphone-wave-build-ximalaya.

19. Cara Wallis, *Technomobility in China: Young Migrant Women and Mobile Phones* (New York: New York University Press, 2013).

20. Minxin Pei, *China's Trapped Transition: The Limits of Developmental Autocracy* (Cambridge, MA: Harvard University Press, 2006).

21. Yuezhi Zhao, *Communication in China: Political Economy, Power, and Conflict* (Lanham, MD: Rowman & Littlefield, 2008). See also: Jing Wang, *Brand New China: Advertising, Media, and Commercial Culture* (Cambridge, MA: Harvard University Press, 2009). Chin-Chuan Lee, Zhou He, and Yu Huang, "'Chinese Party Publicity Inc.' Conglomerated: The Case of the Shenzhen Press Group," *Media, Culture &Society* 28, no. 4 (2006): 581; Anthony Fung, "'Think Globally, Act Locally': China's Rendezvous with MTV," *Global Media and Communication* 2, no. 1 (2006): 71; M. Keane, "Once Were Peripheral: Creating Media Capacity in East Asia," *Media, Culture & Society* 28, no. 6 (2006): 835.

22. Chin-Chuan Lee, Zhou He, and Yu Huang, "Party-Market Corporatism, Clientelism, and Media in Shanghai," *International Journal of Press/Politics* 12, no. 3 (2007): 24.

23. Sohu, "Ximalaya Industry Production Report," Market Research, Sohu, August 21, 2017.

24. Jeremy Wade Morris and Eleanor Patterson, "Podcasting and Its Apps: Software, Sound, and the Interfaces of Digital Audio," *Journal of Radio & Audio Media* 22, no. 2 (2015): 220–30.

25. Berry, "Will the iPod Kill the Radio Star?"; Lacey, "Smart Radio and Audio Apps"; Eleanor Patterson, "This American Franchise: This American Life, Public Radio Franchising and the Cultural Work of Legitimating Economic Hybridity," *Media, Culture & Society* 38, no. 3 (2016): 450–61.

26. Mel Stanfill, "The Interface as Discourse: The Production of Norms through Web Design," *New Media & Society* 17, no. 7 (2015): 1059–74.

27. For information on the walkthrough method, see Ben Light, Jean Burgess, and Stefanie Duguay, "The Walkthrough Method: An Approach to the Study of Apps," *New Media & Society* 20, no. 3 (2018): 881–900. For information on apps-as-infrastructure, see Finn Brunton, "WeChat: Messaging Apps and New Social Currency Transaction Tools," in *Appified: Culture in the Age of Apps*, ed. Jeremy Wade Morris and Sarah Murray (Ann Arbor: University of Michigan Press, 2018), 179–87.

28. Ramon Lobato, "Streaming Services and the Changing Global Geography of Television," in *Handbook on Geographies of Technology*, ed. Barney Warf (Cheltenham, UK: Edward Elgar, 2017), 178–93.

29. Andreas Fickers, "The Radio Dial as Mediating Interface," https://github.com/citation-style-language/schema/raw/master/csl-citation.json"} in *The Oxford Handbook of Sound*

Studies, ed. Trevor Pinch and Karin Bijsterveld (Oxford University Press, 2012), 411–39.

30. Light, Burgess, and Duguay, "The Walkthrough Method."

31. Svitlana Matviyenko and Paul D. Miller, *The Imaginary App* (Cambridge, MA: MIT Press, 2014), 4.

32. Branden Hookway, *Interface* (Cambridge, MA: MIT Press, 2014).

33. We had to rely on emulators because many older versions of Android apps are incompatible with the latest versions of the Android platform. Whereas emulators can simulate the working environment of past versions. The reason we are using Android as opposed to iOS is due to the overwhelming dominance of Android over iOS in terms of installed base, with nearly 75 percent of the smartphone market in China made up of Android users. "APK Mirror," http://apkmirror.com, accessed March 21, 2019. "APK Here," https://www.apkhere.com/app/com.ximalaya.ting.android, accessed July 22, 2020.

34. Stefanie Duguay, "Tinder-Swiped: A Focal Gesture and Contested App Visions," in *Appified: Culture in the Age of Apps*, ed. Jeremy Wade Morris and Sarah Murray (Ann Arbor: University of Michigan Press, 2018).

35. John Caldwell, *Production Culture: Industrial Reflexivity and Critical Practice in Film and Television* (Durham, NC: Duke University Press, 2008).

36. Nina Li, "Tencent MyApp (Yingyong Bao) Android App Stores and the Appification of Everything," in *Appified: Culture in the Age of Apps*, ed. Jeremy Wade Morris and Sarah Murray (Ann Arbor, MI: University of Michigan Press, 2018), 42–50.

37. Ximalaya.FM description in Google Play App Store, https://play.google.com/store/apps/details?id=com.ximalaya.ting.himalaya&hl=en; and in the Tencent App Store, https://android.myapp.com/myapp/detail.htm?apkName=com.ximalaya.ting.android.

38. Wendy Chun, *Updating to Remain the Same: Habitual New Media* (Cambridge, MA: MIT Press, 2016).

39. Laurie Ouellette, "Citizen Brand: ABC and the Do Good Turn in US Television," in *Commodity Activism: Cultural Resistance in Neoliberal Times*, ed. Roopali Mukherjee and Sarah Banet-Weiser (New York, NY: Routledge, 2012), 57–75.

40. José van Dijck, "Users Like You? Theorizing Agency in User-Generated Content," *Media, Culture & Society* 31, no. 1 (2009): 45.

41. Dallas Smythe, "On the Audience Commodity and Its Work," in *Media and Cultural Studies: Keyworks*, ed. M. G. Durham and Douglas Kellner, 1st ed. (Oxford: Blackwell, 2001), 253–79; Mark Andrejevic, "'Free Lunch' in the Digital Era: Organization Is the New Content," in *The Audience Commodity in a Digital Age: Revisiting a Critical Theory of Commercial Media*, ed. Vincent Manzerolle and Lee McGuigan (New York: Peter Lang, 2013), 25–30.

42. Jodi Dean, "Communicative Capitalism: Circulation and the Foreclosure of Politics," *Cultural Politics* 1, no. 1 (2005): 51–74.

43. "Web stations" may seem redundant since all of the categories are digital radio stations, but in this case, it refers to web stations owned by universities and other organization that are managed by the state. "APK Mirror," http://apkmirror.com.

44. Li Tao, "Audio Sharing Platform Ximalaya FM Launches Smart Speaker to Aid Communist Party Members with Studies," *South China Morning Post*, September 1, 2018.

45. Ouellette, "Citizen Brand," 58.

46. Alison Hearn, "Structuring Feeling: Web 2.0, Online Ranking and Rating, and the Digital 'Reputation' Economy," *Ephemera* 10, no. 3/4 (2010): 421–38.

47. Wen-Hsuan Tsai, "How 'Networked Authoritarianism' Was Operationalized in China: Methods and Procedures of Public Opinion Control," *Journal of Contemporary China* 25, no. 101 (2016): 731–44.

48. Sina, "Chong Hundun Au Dao Fengkou: Yidong FM de Wunian Zhizheng [From Chaos to Mainstream: The Tumultuous 5 Years in Mobile FM App Development]," Sina.com, March 3, 2018, http://tech.sina.com.cn/i/2018-03-03/doc-ifyrztfz6954433.shtml.

49. David Paulk, "This Un-American Life: China's Struggling Podcast Industry," *Sixth Tone*, January 26, 2017, http://www.sixthtone.com/news/1872/this-un-american-life-chinas-struggling-podcast-industry.

50. Tarleton Gillespie, *Custodians of the Internet: Platforms, Content Moderation, and the Hidden Decisions That Shape Social Media* (New Haven, CT: Yale University Press, 2018).

51. Zhao, *Communication in China*.

52. Lee, He, and Huang, "Party-Market Corporatism, Clientelism, and Media in Shanghai," 39.

53. Alexei Oreskovic, "The Tech Cold War: Everything That's Happened in the New China-US Tech Conflict Involving Google, Huawei, Apple, and Trump," *Business Insider*, July 29, 2019, https://www.businessinsider.com/us-china-tech-cold-war-everything-that-has-happened-2019-5.

54. Tarleton Gillespie, "The Politics of 'Platforms,'" *New Media & Society* 12, no. 3 (2010): 347–64.

55. Lacey, *Listening Publics*.

56. Lei and Sun, "Radio Listening and the Changing Formations of the Public in China," 330.

Assembling Alibaba

The Infrastructuralization of Digital Platforms in China

Lin Zhang

"Platform studies" have emerged in the past decade in response to the rapid expansion of various "platforms" (e.g., Facebook, Amazon, YouTube, Google, and Uber) to theorize the dynamic interactions between technological affordances and human agency.[1] More recently, the increasing domination of platforms in our social, economic, and cultural life, especially regarding the controversies surrounding the roles of social media platforms like Facebook and Twitter in the 2016 US presidential election, has prompted both fear about their monopoly and debates on government regulation or even nationalization.[2] Responding to these trends, a new line of research has emerged, looking at existing internet companies as hybrid entities of platforms and infrastructures, or "infrastructuralized platforms."[3] This shift speaks to scholarly efforts to situate discussions about monopolizing digital platforms in culturally and historically specific contexts, seeking to explore what happens when digital platforms' technical properties and profit imperatives converge or clash with the public service responsibilities associated with their now infrastructural scale and function?

Building on this "infrastructuralized platforms" perspective, I take an "assemblage" approach to platforms and their infrastructuralization in order to highlight the culturally/nationally specific experiences of technological transformations, albeit without essentializing culture or falling into the techno-determinist trap.[4] Empirically, I will use the Chinese e-commerce giant Alibaba as a case study. In doing so, I echo the call of Poell et al. for a "more relational approach" to Chinese social media studies that pays attention to the intertwining of technical and non-technical features and their reconfiguration through complex associations.[5] I argue that scholarly discussions of digital platforms can benefit from treating platformization and infrastructuralization not as static concepts but as a constantly transforming assemblage of heterogeneous forces, actors, traditions, and institutions. These assemblages include aspects that are both human and nonhuman, that are both historical and emerging, and that have impacts on both global networks and local communities.

As the world's largest e-commerce company and retailer, Alibaba has garnered enormous media attention, especially after its high-profile NYSE IPO in 2014.[6] While the English-language media had been obsessed with the company's legendary CEO Jack Ma and its stock market performance, the majority of academic literatures published in English on Alibaba or Chinese e-commerce in general are in business management or economics.[7] Scant attention has been devoted to unpacking Alibaba's enormous and growing social, cultural, and political impacts. This is an unfortunate oversight in our collective scholarly effort, for since its emergence in 1999, Alibaba has evolved from a start-up founded in Jack Ma's apartment in Hangzhou to a public-listed, multi-platform, e-commerce corporation of immense size. Especially in the past decade, following the 2008 global crisis, the corporation has achieved and consolidated its monopoly in China. By 2018, Alibaba, with nearly 550 million active mobile users per month, dominated the "iron-triangle" sectors of e-commerce, digital finance/payment, and logistics in China. With a rapidly expanding "eco-system" of subcontractors, affiliated companies, and invested high-tech firms, the corporation is making fierce inroads into new growth areas like cloud computing, digital mapping and navigation, online-offline hybrid stores, and entertainment industries. Alibaba is also trying to promote its overseas presence in regions like Southeast Asia and Australia. Meanwhile, the corporation enjoys immense support from both the central and local governments of various levels in China as governments rely on the company to spearhead the on-going economic restructuring and ease unemployment pressure. In short, Alibaba has evolved into a startling new form of international capitalism: it is part independent corporate entity and part quasi-official infrastructure taking up public service functions in collaboration with the state, part an online social-media monopoly yet also an on-the-ground seller of goods and services.

Given Alibaba's platform-to-infrastructure evolution in the past two decades, I ask how is this process similar and different from those experienced by its Western counterparts? What are the social and political implications of Alibaba's infrastructuralization? What are the sites of tensions? And how does an assemblage approach to the Chinese experiences of platformization and infrastructuralization help us reconceptualize platform studies? Weaving together materials about Alibaba and Chinese e-commerce collected between 2009 and 2017 through ethnographic fieldwork, interviews, and industry analyses, I argue that the historical evolution of Alibaba resembles the "platformization-to-infrastructuralization" trajectory taken by its Silicon Valley counterparts, like Facebook and Google, as documented by Plantin and his colleagues.[8] However, what this veneer of sameness conceals is the culturally and historically specific "assembling" of heterogeneous forces that constituted the two-phase transformation of Alibaba. Specifically, during the early years of its platformization, between the 1990s and mid-2000s, Alibaba positioned itself *against* state infrastructures as an alternative form of capitalism, while managing the tensions between its public services and profit motive. In the years following the 2008 global crisis, however, when Alibaba acquired infrastructural scale and significance, its earlier alternative positioning against the state gradually gave way to a more *symbiotic* relationship with the state. Meanwhile, tensions intensified as Alibaba's profit imperatives began to override its quasi-governmental service provision, as was captured by the two "Anti-Taobao" campaigns (to which I turn below). Small and medium-sized sellers, feeling betrayed and marginalized by Alibaba's prioritization of established and branded businesses, deployed networked technical means to momentarily disrupt the smooth running of the platforms in order to voice their discontents, demand government and public intervention, and hold Alibaba accountable to its infrastructural role.

The expansion of Alibaba from an alternative platform to government-dominated infrastructure had indeed opened up many opportunities for small entrepreneurs during its more public-oriented years when it was relatively marginalized by the state and aspired to infrastructural scale. Ironically, its public service role became compromised in the past decade as Alibaba grew more discriminating against small and medium-sized sellers after it had achieved infrastructural importance and established closer ties with the state. This tracing of the historical evolution of Alibaba from an assemblage perspective problematizes dichotomous constructions of state vs. corporation, profit-driven platform vs. public-oriented infrastructure, and China as recipient/appropriator of Western technologies vs. the West as innovator and creator. Instead, I argue for a dynamic model of technological and cultural transformations that treats platformaization and infrastructuralization as historically and culturally specific processes and relations constituted by constantly shifting and interacting heterogeneous forces.

Platforms, Infrastructures, and Assemblages

Platform studies emerged in the latter half of the 2000s as part a rising tide of scholarly voices critical of web 2.0 media corporations' profit-driven logic of encouraging social media interactivity. Crucially, platform studies drew attention to the increasingly significant role that "nonhuman" algorithmic agents were playing in mediating the interactions and negotiations between corporations and users. Equally important is their emphasis on the performative and relational dimensions of platform-mediated power. For instance, Gillespie analyzed how social media companies like YouTube deploy the discourse of "platform" to negotiate and conceal tensions between their populist image and their business and marketing appeal. Van Dijck portrayed platforms as a "set of relations that constantly needs to be performed" to maintain a delicate balance between the commercial, creative/ expressive, and legal demands of various agents.[9] A more recent development in the field of platform studies underlined the convergence between platforms and infrastructures.[10] According to these scholars, digital platforms, relying on technical properties of platformization such as participation, programmability, and datafication, have evolved to reach a scale and social utility typical of infrastructures traditionally operated by government or quasi-governmental corporations. Like Facebook or Amazon in America, Alibaba too has evolved from being an online social media and consumer-services business to something more like a quasi-governmental entity, providing a wide range of services not embedded in other state institutions yet reaching hundreds of millions of daily users.

The convergence of platform studies and infrastructural studies therefore reflects two main concerns within and beyond platform studies. First, continuing from platform studies' sensitivity to technology-mediated power relationships, these scholars explore the shifting power dynamics facilitated by the infrastructuralization of platforms. That is, what does the privatization and deregulation of public service–oriented infrastructures and the subjectification of infrastructures to the logics of corporate-run and profit-driven monopoly digital platforms mean for society? For instance, using Google Maps as an example of new cartographic infrastructure, Plantin argued that while the early platformization of maps in the mid-2000s decentralized mapping capacities, the recent infrastructuralization of Google Maps amounted to a "recentralization around private interests."[11] Second, the growing interest in infrastructuralized platforms coincides with the global expansion of Western digital platforms and the rise and global ambition of monopoly digital platforms in non-Western regions like China. These trends have prompted scholars to situate digital platforms historically while becoming more sensitive to platforms' interaction with different cultural and national contexts. These trends have led scholars to ask how do tensions generated by the convergence between platforms and infrastructures play out in historically and culturally specific ways as they intersect with different economic systems, labor traditions, business-state relations, and user habits?

Of these two trends, the former is represented by Nick Srnicek's *Platform Capitalism*, which situates the contemporary proliferation of different types of platforms within the history of capitalism, and hence as an evolution in dynamics of labor extraction, market creation, and profit motivation. According to him, while platform capitalism deepened the post-1970s trend toward neoliberalization, it is also distinguished from pre-existing formations of capitalism by the centrality of data in the valorization process.[12] The latter trend intersects with another emerging set of literature that attempts to bring postcolonial studies into dialogue with platform, software, and media studies.[13] One representative work in this area is Thomas Lamarre's recent article on platformativity, where he describes the "infra-individual intra-actions between platform and human, and individual and collective," arguing that new modes of power are generated as a result of the operation of media infrastructures "alongside and through national and regional forms."[14] From this perspective, the histories of platformization loosely mirror the course of colonialism and postcolonialism, thus mapping onto long struggles for national independence.

The current chapter builds on this merging of platformization and infrastructuralization, and deploys the theoretical and methodological lens of assemblage to analyze the case of Alibaba. While inspired by both Deleuze and Guattari and actor-network theory (ANT),[15] I find Bucher's approach to assemblage most relevant. Following her, I use assemblage as "an overall heuristic that allows for thinking more broadly about the co-functioning and productiveness of heterogeneous elements."[16] The perspective of assemblage, I argue, offers a productive site to draw on both platform studies' analytical focus on the interactions between algorithm and human agency, and the postcolonial sensitivity to historical and cultural specificities as emphasized by the recent attention to the infrastructuralization of platforms. This assemblage approach theorizes platforms and their infrastructuralization without essentializing culture or reifying technologies. I mean to trace, analyze, and depict the *process* of how heterogeneous agents—a web of global and local, human and nonhuman, historical and emerging entities—work together, in harmony or cacophony, in shaping specific experiences and formations. As McFarlane argues, "assemblage thinking is concerned with how different spatio-temporal processes are historically drawn together at a particular conjuncture." [17] This focus on the process of assembling offers a dynamic model of both technological change and cultural/national transformation. That is, assemblage thinking problematizes not only the binaries of Western technology/theory vs. non-Western culture/case, but also the very idea of culturally homogeneous nation/region.

This assemblage methodology enabled me to ask what platformization and its infrastructuralization mean for China, and what China means for our thinking (and rethinking) about the convergence between platforms and infrastructures? Instead of thinking about China as a passive recipient or appropriator of Western technology and capitalism, I see China as an active participant/actor in shaping platform capitalism, including its technical, economic, legal, and cultural properties.[18] In the following section, I will take the assemblage approach to address Alibaba's rise and evolution, hence depicting the Chinese experiences of platformization and infrastructuralization. I then discuss the sociopolitical implications of the convergence of platformization and infrastructuralization in China.

(Dis)Assembling Alibaba: When Platformization Meets Infrastructuralization

From Alibaba to Taobao

The first phase in the genealogy of the Alibaba empire was bookended by the genesis of its business-to-business (B2B) e-commerce platform, Alibaba.com in 1999, and the market domination achieved by its consumer-to-consumer (C2C) platform, Taobao.com, in the mid-2000s. While Silicon Valley platforms emerged and expanded with the "splintering" of the "modern infrastructural ideal" in the West since the late 1980s,[19] Chinese digital platforms like Alibaba unfolded in the same period of time in parallel to the expansion of state-led capitalism.[20] In these early days, Alibaba took on a quasi-infrastructural role by positioning itself against state infrastructures as a more participatory, accessible, and efficient alternative to government-operated trading channels. This quasi-governmental "alternative" positioning was achieved partially by leveraging platform properties like participation, interactivity, programmability, and multiplication, which foster user labor, with the process financed by the global expansion of venture capital following the bust of the dot-com bubble. However, despite its alternative positioning against the state, Alibaba also reaped the fruit of state-led, export-oriented capitalism while riding on the development of state infrastructures like telecommunication and transportation. Prioritizing market expansion and user growth in the early days, Alibaba was able to manage the tensions between its profit incentive and its public-serving ambition by targeting small and marginalized business owners. This blurring between profits and public service came to define Alibaba's brand and corporate image and gave the company—likes it counterparts in America—the appearance of being both pragmatically useful for users and somewhat rebellious.

The broader force at play here was the development of state-led capitalism since the 1980s, resulting in the expansion of an export-oriented and manufacturing-based economy. This model, after all, was a post-socialist reinvention and revival of China's centuries-old "petty capitalist" tradition, in which small family-based commodity producers prospered but were prevented from expanding into full-blown capitalism by the extractive and paternalistic power of the state.[21] At the turn of the new millennium, when Alibaba kicked off its e-commerce sites targeting small and medium-sized enterprises (SMEs), the tensions between petty entrepreneurs and different levels of government remained true, if not more complicated. Two decades after the initiation of China's post-socialist reform, the expansion of an export-oriented regime had fostered a vast and growing base of SMEs, serving as subcontractors and engaging in labor-intensive manufacturing for foreign corporations. Many were concentrated in the southern and southeastern coastal regions. While some started out as state-owned township and village enterprises (TVEs) in the late 1970s and 1980s, most became privatized in the 1990s as more private-owned businesses emerged in the decade of growing foreign direct investment (FDI) and export.[22] Alibaba's rise thus coincides with the epic transformation of China from a

Mao-style command economy into a hybrid, post-socialist economy led by capitalist corporations with varying connections to the state.

Under this transformation, different levels of governments became active participants, not just in regulating but also in running the economy via practices like operating state-owned enterprises, leasing out land, and forming patronage relationships with business people.[23] As a result, the relationships between governments and small businesses were often ambiguous: while governments invested in building basic infrastructures like transportation and telecommunication networks, and promoted small businesses to create employment and boost GDP growth, they also curbed their expansion when SMEs threatened governmental economic monopoly and political control. Jack Ma, having grown up in one of the most entrepreneurial Chinese provinces as a small business owner with a humble family background, knew only too well the government's dilemma and the needs of those small businesses. Small businesses had limited means to secure export deals and expand production—they often lacked the scale and connections to be able to trade through state-owned export middlemen and found it costly and inconvenient to travel to trade shows like the Canton Fair.[24] Governments, bogged down in bureaucratic intricacies and conflicting logics, are inefficient in creating alternative trading channels. Therefore, Jack Ma positioned Alibaba.com as a private-owned trading platform for Chinese SMEs to bypass state-owned middlemen by directly finding overseas outlets for their products. Exploiting tensions within state-business relations in post-socialist China, Alibaba rode on the state-commanded export-oriented economy and governmental investment in infrastructures while trumpeting the platform's quasi-infrastructural role as a more democratic, accessible, and participatory alternative to state infrastructures.

Alibaba's quasi-infrastructural ambition in the early days was apparent from the numerous speeches that Jack Ma delivered. At one occasion, he said, "If you divide enterprises into rich people and poor people, the Internet is a realm for poor people . . . the price for a web page is basically the same. I want to enable poor people to use this tool to rise in a kind of revolution."[25] Evoking techno-utopian discourse, particularly referencing the participatory property of the platform as offering market opportunities with low-threshold entry costs, Jack Ma positioned his platform as an alternative infrastructure for the poor. On another occasion, he reiterated Alibaba's quasi-infrastructural ambition by invoking the metaphor of grains of sand united by the platform to rival big stones, highlighting the platform's technical feature of multiplication, where small businesses were empowered by networking effect:

> Small and medium-sized enterprises are like grains of sand on a beach. The Internet can glue them together. It can make them into an invincible force that is able to go up against the big stones. The virtue of the Internet is that it uses small to compete with big, it uses fast to compete with slow.[26]

While emphasizing Alibaba's public service function, Jack Ma was intentionally vague about its profit motive. If anything, he shunned talking about profits when he commented in an interview with China Central Television (CCTV) that "no matter what you are doing, material gain should not be your main motivation."[27] What he also downplayed in all these public remarks was the fact that the platform's accessibility to SMEs was made possible by a series of inflow of venture capital money that Alibaba had secured from global venture investors like Goldman Sachs and Softbank between 1999 and 2001, before the company became profitable for the first time in December 2001. The assembling of a set of intersecting forces—such as the platform's technical properties, the small entrepreneurs' participation and labor, China's petty capitalist residuals revived by the state-commanded export-production regime, and the expanding global venture capitalist regime—constituted Alibaba's quasi-infrastructural positioning in the early days.

This quasi-infrastructural role was only strengthened with the emergence of its C2C/B2C platform, Taobao.com. Launched in May 2003, Taobao.com expanded Alibaba's quasi-infrastructural function by drawing more people to set up e-shops on its platforms and creating an alternative online shopping channel with more diverse choices and lower cost, and thus boosting domestic consumption. This expansion, on the one hand, intersected with the Chinese government's post–World Trade Organization policy shift to boost domestic consumption and digital and cultural industries.[28] The local Hangzhou municipal government and the Zhejiang provincial government, in particular, having realized Alibaba's potential in tax contribution and driving their local economies, grew increasingly supportive of its expansion. It also coincided, on the other hand, with global venture capitalists' post-dot-com-bubble enthusiasm about the Chinese internet industry. Since the early 2000s, the Chinese IT industry turned out to be a more exciting new site for global venture capital in the aftermath of the high-tech boom and bust in the 1990s.[29] This optimism about the Chinese market and industry was translated into a constant inflow of venture capital investment into Chinese tech companies. Both trends facilitated Taobao's technical and business innovation strategies, which strengthened Alibaba's quasi-infrastructural role.

One central technical innovation that Taobao implemented to stimulate and channel seller and consumer participation and free labor is AliWangWang—the embedded IM system that allowed shoppers and shop owners to virtually replicate the bazaar-style haggle and banter familiar to Chinese people. The informal bargaining and chatting are reminiscent of the face-to-face communication between sellers and shoppers at local food markets, bazaars, and night markets occupied by small-business owners. In an informal market with no fixed price and formal product quality guarantee mechanism, the sellers and shoppers communicated with each other via instant messaging to quickly establish trust, negotiate a fair price, and sometimes form lasting friendships. While virtual chatting compromised the immediacy and transparency of face-to-face contact, AliWangWang created a set of expressive built-in emoticons to partially make up for this loss. This technical innovation not only helped establish "swift trust" in an unfamiliar virtual market perceived by many Chinese at that time as risky, it also functioned to improve the platform's "stickiness" and enhance users' sense of community.[30]

Another winning strategy that Taobao adopted to set itself apart from other competing platforms, especially its biggest rival, eBay China, was to play the "non-fee" card. In 2003, when Taobao initially launched the website, it was free for sellers to register, list products, and sell online. In contrast, eBay China pushed for eBay's global "formula" with "insertion fees, final-value fees, and features fees, though at a lower level."[31] eBay's senior vice president for international business, William C. Cobb, justified the company's implementation of this standard fee structure in the Chinese market as a way to "train the community in how they can have the most vibrant marketplace possible."[32] This fee-based model of platform economy prevailed in the United States and other Western developed regions following the bust of the dot-com bubble in the early 2000s when venture capital money shrank, and the tech-scene was dominated by the few monopoly players who had survived the crisis. However, the situation on the ground in China was different than in the West. Taobao's free model turned out to be an irresistible attraction to Chinese petty sellers who usually had little, if any, start-up investment to begin with. Many of the early Taobao sellers, as I encountered during my fieldwork, were young people from ordinary, if not disadvantaged, family backgrounds, whose lack of personal connection and/or educational credentials made them less competitive in the formal white-collar job market. It was typical for an entrepreneurial young couple or two college friends to get started by moonlighting on Taobao in addition to their day-time job or college education, sourcing commodities from local wholesale markets during the weekend and dropping off delivery packages on their way to work in the morning. As business expanded and became steadier, some sellers might quit their formal job to become full-time small-business owners. Thanks to global venture capital firms' optimism about the Chinese market, Taobao was able to sustain its "no fee" strategy for a prolonged period of time in its battle with eBay.[33] Taobao triumphed over eBay China by the end of 2005 with a market share of 67 percent vs. eBay's 29 percent. By 2006, Taobao had achieved domination of China's e-commerce market by virtually driving eBay out of China.[34]

What's ironic here was how inter-platform competition backed by venture capital helped sustain, if not strengthen, Alibaba's quasi-infrastructural role and public service–oriented corporate image—a phenomenon frequently replicated in the following years as start-up digital platforms pursued the "growth-before-profit" model. If anything, Taobao.com's success had only rendered Jack Ma more assertive in publicizing Alibaba's social values and infrastructural ambition. Speaking at a 2005 economic forum in Shanghai, Ma justified Taobao's free model saying that his purpose of doing business was not to "win the competition," but to "create social value."[35] He was quoted in a 2008 speech explaining why Taobao stuck to its no-fee model, saying Alibaba's "mission" was not to "make some money," but to "create one million job opportunities and change the fate of numerous people."[36]

Taobao Village and Post-2008 Rural Expansion

Situations started to shift gradually when the Alibaba ecosystem/platforms reached an infrastructural scale and criticality around 2008, converting millions of more people into its army of e-commerce entrepreneurs. Entering its second phase of expansion, the Alibaba empire witnessed exponential growth between 2008 and 2014 and saw its annual revenue skyrocket from around 0.29 billion USD in 2007 to 8.05 billion USD in 2014, leading up to its high-profile IPO in 2014 at the New York Stock Exchange.[37] While numbers matter, Alibaba's increasingly important role in China's state-championed economic restructuring, which was itself a primary component of the post-crisis global recovery, appears to be crucial to the consolidation of its status as an infrastructuralized platform. Two new characteristics distinguished this new phase of development. A deepened mutual penetration between Alibaba and the various levels of governments in China led to a more symbiotic and collaborative corporate-state relationship, which departed from Alibaba's prior alternative positioning. In comparison to its growing affinity to the Chinese state, its relationship with sellers, especially the small and medium-sized sellers that Alibaba had claimed as its primary consumers, became strained as the tensions between the platform's profit and social service orientations grew with its size.

Following the 2008 global financial crisis, a sudden contraction in overseas demand for made-in-China commodities forced export-oriented businesses to look inward toward China's own rapidly expanding domestic consumer market to ease the pressure of over-production. And so the Chinese state ramped up its new millennial ambition to restructure the export-oriented developmental model. Technological innovation, creativity, and entrepreneurship emerged as the new visions through which the nation reimagined itself in the post-2008 global world.[38] Despite its efforts, the central government found it hard to overcome the inertia of an old economic model built on export and fixed asset investment. As the pressure of unemployment and underemployment ran high, Alibaba became one of the biggest beneficiaries of the crisis. Not only did it serve as a bridge between factories seeking new outlets for their products and a growing number of domestic e-commerce consumers, it also helped generate employment and self-employment opportunities to absorb surplus labor from traditional industries.

The group that was hit hardest by the crisis was migrant workers who had been shuffling between cities and their rural homes for temporary work opportunities. Many had no choice but to return to their home villages due to factory labor cuts or shutdowns. However, once back home, they were often confronted with rural China's dire reality of lack of economic opportunities. As it did with the export-oriented small businesses in 1999 and the growing number of eager small-business owners and online shoppers in 2003, Alibaba seized the 2008 global crisis as an opportunity to expand its business empire into rural China and to recruit migrant workers and farmers onto its platform as both laborers and consumers.

A changing set of forces constituted the new terrain on which the post-2008 infrastructuralization of digital platforms has played out. Alibaba's growing capacity in the extraction, analysis, and monetization of its increasingly rich platform-based user data—and its pre-IPO imperative to expand user base and market—aligned with the central and local governments' eagerness to revitalize rural economies, ease unemployment pressures, and facilitate economic restructuring. These technical and policy shifts also intersected with Chinese peasants' desire for village-based entrepreneurial economic opportunities that would allow them to earn a decent living while staying rooted in the countryside.

Platform-based datafication and participation worked together with non-technical forces of governments, media, academia, and entrepreneurs in shaping the assemblage of infrastructuralized platforms in this new phase of state-led capitalist restructuring, wherein corporate, governmental, and entrepreneurial ambitions converged. Departing from Alibaba's earlier alternative positioning, its infrastructuralized platforms bespeak the changing regime of technology-mediated governance and state-business relations in China, where governments and monopoly digital firms become increasingly symbiotic and mutually penetrating with the convergence of platforms and infrastructures. In particular, Aliresearch, the e-commerce research institute directly serving the interests of the Alibaba Group, played an instrumental role in weaving together a web of media, scholars, governmental agencies, and peasant entrepreneurs to create the so-called "Taobao village" phenomenon.

The concept of the "Taobao village" was initially coined by Aliresearch in late 2010 to describe three villages where e-commerce self-employment had become a dominant profession among villagers. The attention-grabbing stories of Chinese peasants on computers were soon picked up and widely circulated by media. In September 2010, Alibaba Group crowned the most well-known of the first three Taobao Villages, Shaji village,[39] with the title of "Best Cradle for E-commerce." Not coincidentally, in December of the same year, a research team from the state-owned Center for Information Study (CIS) visited Shaji and released a report on Aliresearch's website.[40] Titled "Shaji Model and Its Significance," the report compared Shaji to Xiaogang village, which is widely known as the "birth place of post-socialist reform." It also eulogized rural e-commerce as the triumph of information technology and market forces—a grassroots-initiated "bottom-up" path of informationalization.[41] On December 18, immediately following the release of the report by Aliresearch, a group of "high level experts" (Gaoceng Zhuanjia) from governmental and academic agencies, such as the Development Research Centre of the State Council, the Ministry of Agriculture, and the Ministry of Industry and Information Technology, convened in Shaji to "discuss the significance of the Shaji model" as "a new path for rural development."[42]

In a more detailed report released in 2014, the same team from CIS celebrated

"Taobao village" as a solution to China's "rural problem" and an alternative path of urbanization.[43] It was said that the internet had made it possible for small household-based production to directly reach the global market without the intermediary of big companies. Compared to TVEs in the 1980s, e-commerce was more effective in absorbing rural surplus labor, driving the modernization of rural China and democratizing opportunities to participate in economic activities, and thus had helped restructure rural economies to make rural society more just and "harmonious."[44] Taobao village was thus endowed with the same significance that TVEs enjoyed two decades ago when the post-socialist market reforms were initiated in rural China. Thus, in contrast to the United States, where e-commerce tended to facilitate opportunities in major urban areas, Alibaba managed to deploy e-commerce for the advantage of rural users.

At the village level, Alibaba cultivated representative villages and individual entrepreneurs through a combination of data and media management. Alibaba's big-data team generated visualization of e-commerce businesses on its platform by tracking shop owner's IP addresses. Once they identified a heavy concentration of businesses in one rural area, they would dispatch a team of Alibaba employees to cultivate relations with the local government and peasant shop owners. To bring visibility to the selected village, the company would invite journalists from various media outlets to carry reports on the village and peasant entrepreneurs. To attract more peasants into e-commerce, Alibaba would sometimes pick one representative peasant inside the village to create a "success story." One way to do so was by channeling more advertising traffic to the selected peasant entrepreneur's business. This was often achieved through technical means such as bumping up their product listing ranks and offering them more opportunities to participate in the various promotional activities that the platform hosted periodically. As one of the peasant entrepreneur interviewees that I met during my fieldwork in Shandong explained to me: "They will let this person get rich quickly, get a car, and buy a new house. Then villagers will follow his footsteps in the hope of replicating his success story. It's all the same trick if you observe the adjacent villages in this area."[45] This algorithmic promotional cherry-picking strategy was usually supplemented with media publicity of the entrepreneur, hence spreading his/her success stories for others to emulate. While I conducted my fieldwork in the same Taobao village in rural Shandong, I spent a couple of weeks at the family shop of a local "model entrepreneur." I quickly noticed that his schedule was filled with either receiving visitors accompanied by local cadres who had come to "learn from his success," or interviews by media outlets from across the country and occasionally from overseas media as well. In this way, Alibaba's e-commerce strategies were deeply indebted to its aggressive marketing.

Between 2010 and 2015, as the concept of "Taobao village" was gaining traction through media coverage and expert endorsement, rural e-commerce began to garner support from different levels of government. In 2012, Alibaba proposed a new "Suichang model" of Taobao villages based on its collaborating experience with the Suichang County government (Zhejiang Province). Emphasizing the functional role of local government, this move hinted at a stronger tie between the e-commerce giant in search of new markets and local governments eager to boost economic growth and earn political cache. This merging of the corporate goal of market expansion with local governmental interests through media publicity and academic endorsement is at heart of the making of the Taobao village phenomenon. The mechanism came into maturity in late 2013 at the "First Taobao Village Summit"—a ritualistic ceremony that I attended during my fieldwork in China. Cohosted by Aliresearch and a municipal government in Zhejiang, and attended by journalists, scholars, and peasant representatives from fourteen Taobao villages, the event was nothing short of a staging of the different forces that had cocreated the Taobao village phenomenon.

At the central level, Alibaba's lobbying efforts had materialized into proposals conceived by various parliamentary representatives calling on the Chinese state to spearhead rural e-commerce at annual parliamentary sessions. Pressured by a slowdown in economic growth, the Chinese state had issued a series of documents to encourage peasant digital entrepreneurship. In November 2014, the Chinese Premier Li Keqiang visited Qingyanliu, the so-called "No. 1 Taobao village" in Zhejiang before giving a speech at the World Internet Conference. It turned out that he was just sending out political signals for his major policy initiatives of "Internet Plus" (*Hulianwang Jia*) and "Mass Entrepreneurship and Innovation" (*Wanzhong chuangye*). Released in his March 2015 government work report, both were designed to restructure the Chinese economy, with the former emphasizing the informationalization of existing manufacturing and agricultural industries and the latter aiming at rendering the current economic system more participatory and less centralized. These new governmental initiatives aligned perfectly with Alibaba's stress on peasant internet entrepreneurship and the digitalization of traditional rural industries and agriculture. Meanwhile, Alibaba increased its counting of the number of Taobao villages to 212 following its NYSE IPO at the "Second Taobao

Village Summit" in late 2014. Faced with competition from other Chinese e-commerce corporations like the JD Group, Alibaba was making further inroads into rural China by supplementing its Taobao village project with a new "A Thousands Counties and Ten Thousand Villages" (*Qianxian Wancun*) campaign. Launched in October 2014, the campaign intended to collaborate with local governments to build rural e-commerce infrastructure, such as village-based package delivery stations and an e-commerce "innovation park." Thus leading the post-crisis restructuring of Chinese capitalism, Alibaba turned the crisis into a new site of business expansion.

As Alibaba had reached infrastructural scale and significance, we witnessed a more collaborative and mutually penetrative relationship between the state and digital platforms. Departing from Alibaba's earlier quasi-infrastructural positioning as a more efficient, accessible, and participatory alternative to governmental infrastructures, we witnessed a convergence of corporate and governmental forces in shaping infrastructuralized platforms. Alibaba effectively leveraged its economic and political power to cultivate intimate ties with both the central and local governments in China, which had cleared the decks for its further expansion. The rapidly expanding group of e-commerce businesses, some of which had grown into big firms, with hundreds or even thousands of employees over the years, but most of which stayed small, constituted a new entrepreneurial class in China with shared interests, aspirations, and concerns. However, within this new entrepreneurial class, new hierarchies began to form. As Alibaba became increasingly discriminating against small and medium-sized sellers, after it had achieved monopoly status in China, it's not surprising that disadvantaged and disgruntled sellers rose in protest to hold Jack Ma accountable for Alibaba's now-broken public-serving promises. The two "Anti-Taobao Campaigns" launched by some discontented small and medium-sized shop owners on Taobao in 2011 and 2013 respectively, as I will show, represented two such moments of disruption. In each case, disaffected actors hijacked Alibaba's own algorithmic machines to "disassemble" Alibaba, disrupting the smooth running of the platform to get their voices heard.

Tensions and Disruptions

While Taobao's "free model" was crucial to its rapid market expansion in the early days, especially in its battle with eBay in the mid-2000s, it became a liability after the corporation had secured about 90 percent of China's C2C e-commerce market share following the 2008 crisis. On the one hand, a large number of low-quality commodities sold by small sellers were knockoffs of branded products, posing both quality control and legal challenges for Alibaba. On the other hand, the fact that Taobao was not generating sufficient profit for Alibaba, despite its high volume of transactions, discouraged the company's investors and employees—both were anxiously waiting to cash in on its long overdue IPO. In response to mounting pressure, Jack Ma's first move was to launch a fee-based B2C site, Tmall.com, which was linked with the original Taobao.com, and encouraged bigger businesses on Taobao to migrate to Tmall. As an incentive, Tmall shops received preferential treatment, which ranged from better customer service to more advertising traffic. This move rendered the Taobao/Tmall platform immediately profitable in 2009, yet it also sowed the seeds of dissatisfaction among the small and medium-sized shops on Taobao.

Apart from the launch of the new fee-based B2C site, Alibaba also created new embedded advertising and marketing applications on Taobao to boost revenue. One of the most profitable but notorious apps, known among shop owners as the "blood-sucking" Zhitongche, is a paid search ranking system that charges shop owners based on the number of user clicks. Another advertising mechanism, Taobaoke, consists of a network of freelancing social media marketers who are paid by commission fee in direct proportion to the number of transactions generated for businesses on Taobao. These new applications and other subtler changes in the platform's algorithmic design tilted the website toward big sellers with more start-up funds and financial backing, while making it increasingly costly for small shops to generate profit. Adding fuel to the fire, Alibaba decided to push the monetization process even harder in October 2011 by announcing two new changes. First, the company increased Tmall's annual technology and service fee from 6,000 RMB to two new levels of 30,000 and 60,000 RMB. Second, it bumped the one-time security deposit charge up to three new levels of 50,000 RMB, 100,000 RMB, and 150,000 RMB respectively. This announcement immediately caused an uproar among the small and medium-sized shop owners who had long felt marginalized and unfairly treated by the platform's profit-driven transformations. In short, Alibaba had adopted more traditionally corporate, profit-driven practices—and its users were soon in rebellion

Following the release of the policy, disaffected shop owners immediately gathered together for discussion, using the group chat function of Taobao's embedded IM tool AliWangWang while posting comments on Taobao's internal forum to express their anger. When the night fell, a small group gathered in a virtual chatroom on YY—a popular Chinese video-based social networking platform—to avoid being monitored by Alibaba. In the following day, anger escalated as the size of the group quickly ballooned from a few dozens to more than fifty thousand people. Meanwhile, the name of the virtual chatroom switched from "Meeting to Discuss Tmall's New Policy" to "Anti-Taobao Price Increase Coalition," and then to "E-commerce Businesses' Rights-Defending Channel." Participants queued up in the chatroom to vent their frustration, some broke into tears while recollecting how hard they and their families had worked to make a living on Taobao, and others called on the participants to launch virtual attacks at big sellers on Taobao.[46] One of the protestors argued:

> Why don't we just leave Taobao? Putting aside personal feelings, consumer base and traffic are the key. Our small and medium-sized sellers have spent seven to eight years, selling high-quality products, working day and night, investing hard labor, and even sacrificing our health. It is us who have toiled to help Taobao accumulate such a huge consumer base and volume of traffic, sending Taobao to its monopoly position today. Why do we have to leave now? Who would compensate for our loss if we move to another platform?[47]

Another protestor had just moved from Taobao to Tmall but was intimidated by the impending fee hike. He protested:

> Why don't we want to return to Taobao? If we could still maintain a decent living, as they told us to "realize our dream" on Taobao, then who wants to make a fuss by moving to Tmall? The answer is simple. Businesses on Tmall are like children of the first wife's who are always spoiled no matter what they do. In comparison, those on Taobao are treated like adopted children. Alibaba neglects us and leaves us with little traffic and customer attention.[48]

The night following the release of the new policy, protestors from the YY chatroom began to launch organized attacks at big Tmall shops. They swarmed into the online stores of a few targeted big sellers, placed a large number of orders, left negative ratings and comments, but refused to finalize the payment process. They gamed the platform's algorithm to paralyze the operation of the targeted big sellers. By October 17, one week after the announcement of the new policy, 112 big Tmall shops were attacked, 5,599 people participated in the attack, and 7,230 null orders were placed, causing a damage of 94.55 million RMB.[49] In the evening of October 21, under the slogan of "ants eat up the elephant," a wordplay with Taobao's brand mascot "Taotao the ant," a new round of virtual attack was launched targeting Alibaba's payment system, Alipay. They called on dissatisfied sellers to empty their Alipay account by transferring the money out into their bank accounts.

In parallel to the online protest and virtual attack, some sellers organized offline campaigns to protest in front of Alibaba's Hangzhou headquarters. The YY-based coalition also donated money to send a group of representatives to protest in Hong Kong's Time Square. During the protest, a theatrical moment struck when the protesters set up a "mourning hall" for the very-much alive Jack Ma to express their disappointment in this cultural icon of grassroots IT entrepreneurship. The 2011 Anti-Taobao campaign went so belligerent that the Chinese Ministry of Commerce had to step in as an arbitrator between Alibaba and the protesting businesses. In the end, Jack Ma was forced to make a concession with the protestors. He spent 1.8 billion RMB to subsidize qualified small businesses on Tmall and help smooth the migration from Taobao to Tmall.[50]

Two years later, in December 2013, the "anti-Taobao" coalition launched another protest when Alibaba suddenly went on a campaign to penalize the much-tolerated practices of faking transactions and ratings, intentionally targeting small and medium-sized shops while turning a blind eye to big businesses engaged in the same practices. By 2013, competition grew so fierce on Taobao and Tmall that faking transactions had become a commonly practiced trick among businesses of all sizes to improve shop ratings and artificially drive up product page rankings. If anything, a new underground industry of third-party businesses had emerged in China to cater to Taobao shops' growing demand for faking transactions and customer comments and ratings. It was generally known that Alibaba had tolerated such practices because they helped boost the platform's transaction volume. So when the company suddenly decided to get tough on selected businesses, it was widely believed among Taobao shop owners to be a coordinated effort to crack down on unwanted small businesses so as to clear the way for its upcoming global IPO.

This time, the small business owners on Taobao organized under the slogan of "Anti-Monopoly." They appealed to Alibaba with eight clearly-stated demands, asking for a more democratic and fair online trading environment that respected the rights of the small players. To make their campaign more effective, the coalition again resorted to technical means. This time, they decided to hijack the much-hated "blood-sucking" advertising application Zhitongche. The strategy was to keep clicking on the targeted big businesses' product listing pages without placing an order, causing them tons of wasted advertising money while lowering their "click-to-purchase conversion rate" (Zhuanhuanlv)—a key algorithmic criterion by which the platform calculates shops' reputation scores.[51] Offline protests were again staged in front of Alibaba's Hangzhou headquarters but met stronger confrontation from the local Hangzhou municipal police, who were acting on behalf of their biggest taxpayer to muffle resistance against its monopoly. Compared to the 2011 anti-Taobao campaign, the 2013 protest subsided more quickly without much compromise from Alibaba, which could partially be explained by the corporation's stronger ties with both the central state and the Hangzhou provincial government. The transformation is therefore remarkable: from standing as a rebellious and user-friendly alternative to the state in its early days, Alibaba was now relying upon the police to break up protests while paying off its critics.

Conclusion: "Alibaba Neglects Us" and the Evolution of Platforms

Alibaba's expansion in the past two decades has opened up new economic opportunities for small-business owners in China who had been marginalized by state-operated infrastructures. Its success rendered it an indispensable technological and social infrastructure in China, straddling the corporate and public realms. This assemblage approach to the history of Alibaba represents my modest attempt at seeking an alternative theoretical and methodological route to both the techno-determinist and cultural essentialist accounts of Chinese internet studies. I hope that I have demonstrated how we could approach technological changes and national/cultural transformations, here captured through the lenses of platformization and infrastructuralization, as intertwining processes constituted by heterogeneous forces that could be technological or cultural, global or local, historical or emerging.

The evolution of Alibaba since the late 1990s from an e-commerce startup to a multi-platform ecosystem of infrastructural scale and significance resembled the process of platformization and infrastructuralization as experienced by digital platforms in the West. However, while the Western story of platformization and its infrastructuralization unfolded with the splintering of the "modern infrastructural ideal" and the retreat of government from the digital economy, a closer examination of Alibaba's history using the assemblage approach reveals a more ambivalent relationship with the state, characterized by its quasi-infrastructural positioning *against* the state until the mid-2000s, when Alibaba shifted into a more symbiotic relationship with the state following the 2008 global crisis.[52]

Ironically, as a quasi-infrastructural platform in the early days, Alibaba fared better at managing the tension between its profit imperative and its public service ambition of providing nondiscriminatory service. Despite the deepening mutual penetration between Alibaba and various levels of government in China, the tension intensified after the corporation reached a monopoly scale and infrastructural significance in the late 2000s, resulting in growing discontents coming from its small and medium-sized sellers and a series of seller-initiated protests and attacks on the platform. This story about Alibaba's evolution challenges dichotomous conceptualization of public vs. private, governmental infrastructure vs. corporate platform, local culture vs. global technologies. However, we are just beginning to grasp the profound but also constantly shifting implications of the convergence and blurring of these forces.

A 2014 *New York Times* article, quoting Duncan Clark, the chairman of the Beijing-based consulting firm BDA China, humorously referred to this "Taobao Empire" as a "constituency" with Alibaba's CEO Jack Ma as its captain: "a politician with a small 'p'" who "effectively represents millions of people who now depend on Alibaba for their livelihood."[53] In an interview with *60 Minutes* correspondent Lara Logan on September 28, 2014, when asked about Alibaba's relationship with the Chinese government, Jack Ma stated that "they [Chinese politicians] care that I can stabilize the country. I told the government, 'if people have no jobs, you are in trouble—the government will be in trouble.' My job is to help more people have jobs."[54]

By this time, Ma sounded less like a tech-driven rebel than the unofficial minister of finance. However, it would be important to ask what kinds of jobs the e-commerce platforms are creating now that they have become infrastructuralized, absorbing labor from traditional industries and governmental sectors—as a result of, but also further facilitating, the shrinking of those sectors with the deepening of China's economic restructuring. If platform-based flexible "employment" and self-employment are going to be normalized, how can we ensure that the workers'/ entrepreneurs' rights are protected? These questions are beyond the scope of this paper, but it's certainly both ironic and alarming to see the increasingly unequal profit-driven and algorithm-mediated distribution of resources on Alibaba's platforms, particularly as they become infrastructuralized and are thus more and more entwined in daily life in China.

The resistance staged and disruptions generated by technically equipped small and medium-sized sellers give us some hope about collective bargaining. However, the deployment of user data and the manipulation of platform ranking systems to serve corporate expansion appear particularly disturbing given the direct or indirect roles that governments and state-owned media and academic institutions play in promoting the expansion of the platform-based regime of accumulation in post-2008 China. Looking ahead, it's likely that small and medium-sized sellers will find it increasingly difficult to survive on Alibaba's platforms given policies and algorithms favoring big players and established brands. It's urgent that we call for a "reassembling" of the different forces that constitute infrastructuralized platforms—governmental and grassroots, technological and social, domestic and abroad—to reorient the platformization and its infrastructuralization to a more sustainable and socially responsible direction.

NOTES

1. For representative works on platform studies, refer to Tarleton Gillespie, "The Politics of Platforms,'" *New Media & Society* 12, no. 3 (2010): 347–64; Ganaele Langlois and Greg Elmer, "The Research Politics of Social Media Platforms," *Culture Machine* 14 (2013): 1–17; José Van Dijck and Thomas Poell, "Understanding Social Media Logic," *Media and Communication* 1, no. 1 (2013): 2–14.

2. See Nick Srnicek, "We need to nationalize Google, Facebook and Amazon," The Guardian, August 30, 2017, https://www.theguardian.com/commentisfree/2017/aug/30/nationalise-google-facebook-amazon-data-monopoly-platform-public-interest; Adam Thierer, "10 reasons why nationalizing Facebook would be ridiculous," *Forbes.* August 17, 2012 https://www.forbes.com/sites/adamthierer/2012/08/17/10-reasons-why-nationalizing-facebook-would-be-ridiculous/#17d2a7724760.

3. For discussion on the infrastructuralization of platforms, see Thomas Lamarre, "Platformativity: Media Studies, Area Studies," *Asiascape: Digital Asia* 4, no. 3 (2017): 285–305; Ani Maitra and Rey Chow, "'What's "in"? Disaggregating Asia through New Media Actants'." in *Routledge Handbook of New Media in Asia*, ed. Larrisa Hjorth and Olivia Khoo (London: Routledge, 2015), 17–27; Jean-Christophe Plantin, "Mapping Platforms as Infrastructures: Participatory Cartography, Enclosed Knowledge," *International Journal of Communication* 12 (2018): 489–506; Jean-Christophe Plantin, Carl Lagoze, Paul N.

Edwards, and Christian Sandvig, "Infrastructure Studies Meet Platform Studies in the Age of Google and Facebook," *New Media & Society* 20, no. 1 (2018): 293–310. Nick Srnicek, *Platform Capitalism.* (New Jersey: John Wiley & Sons, 2017); José Van Dijck, Thomas Poell, and Martijn De Waal, *The platform Society: Public Values in a Connective World.* (New York, NY: Oxford University Press, 2018).

4. For discussion on assemblage and assemblage theories, please refer to Taina Bucher, "The Friendship Assemblage: Investigating Programmed Sociality on Facebook," *Television & New Media* 14, no. 6 (2013): 479–93; Félix Guattari and Gilles Deleuze, *A Thousand Plateaus: Capitalism and Schizophrenia,* (London: Athlone Press, 2000). Bruno Latour, *Reassembling the Social: An Introduction to Actor-Network-Theory* (Oxford University Press, 2005).

5. Thomas Poell, Jeroen de Kloet, and Guohua Zeng, "Will the Real Weibo Please Stand Up? Chinese Online Contention and Actor-Network Theory." *Chinese Journal of Communication* 7, no. 1 (2014): 1–18.

6. Nicole Bullock, Alibaba hits record $25bn. *Financial Times.* September 22, 2014 https://www.ft.com/content/0f97cc70-4208-11e4-a7b3-00144feabdc0.

7. A few recent exceptions of works about Alibaba published outside of economics and management include: Linliang Qian, "The 'Inferior' Talk Back: Suzhi (Human Quality), Social Mobility, and E-commerce Economy in China." *Journal of Contemporary China* 27, no. 114 (2018): 887–901; Michael Keane and Haiqing Yu "Communication, Culture, and Governance in Asia: A Digital Empire in the Making; China's Outbound Digital Platforms." *International Journal of Communication* 13 (2019): 18.

8. Plantin, "Mapping Platforms."

9. José Van Dijck and Thomas Poell, "Understanding Social Media Logic," *Media and Communication* 1, no. 1 (2013): 2–14.

10. Lamarre, "Platformativity"; Maitra and Chow, "*Asiascape*"; Plantin et. al., "Infrastructure Studies Meet Platform Studies"; Srnicek, *Platform Capitalism.*

11. Plantin, "Mapping Platforms," 501.

12. Srnicek, *Platform Capitalism.*

13. Lilly Irani, Janet Vertesi, Paul Dourish, Kavita Philip, and Rebecca E. Grinter, "Postcolonial Computing: A Lens on Design and Development," in *Proceedings of the SIGCHI Conference on Human Factors in Computing Systems* (ACM: 2010), 1311–20.

14. Lamarre, "Platformativity," 285.

15. See Manuel DeLanda, *Assemblage Theory* (Edinburgh University Press, 2016), and Bruno Latour, *Reassembling the Social: An Introduction to Actor-Network Theory* (Oxford University Press, 2007), for more information about assemblage and ANT.

16. Bucher, "The Friendship Assemblage," 481.

17. Colin McFarlane, "Assemblage and Critical Urbanism," *City* 15, no. 2 (2011): 209.

18. Michael Keith, Scott Lash, Jakob Arnoldi, and Tyler Rooker, *China Constructing Capitalism: Economic Life and Urban Change* (London: Routledge, 2013).

19. Steve Graham and Simon Marvin, *Splintering Urbanism: Networked Infrastructures, Technological Mobilities and the Urban Condition* (London: Routledge, 2002).

20. See Yuezhi Zhao, "China's Pursuits of Indigenous Innovations in Information Technology Developments: Hopes, Follies and Uncertainties," *Chinese Journal of Communication* 3, no. 3 (2010): 266–89. Since the 1980s until the mid-2000s, the Chinese state had followed a path of gradual and partial privatization, setting the nation on the developmental track of an export-driven accumulation regime, embracing foreign direct investment (FDI) while maintaining control of commanding heights sectors like telecommunication infrastructures.

21. Hill Gates, *China's Motor: A Thousand Years of Petty Capitalism* (Ithaca, NY: Cornell University Press, 1996).

22. Yasheng Huang, *Capitalism with Chinese Characteristics: Entrepreneurship and the State* (Cambridge, UK: Cambridge University Press, 2008).

23. You-tien Hsing, "No Crisis in China? The Rise of China's Social Crisis," in *Aftermath: The Cultures of the Economic Crisis*, ed. Manuel Castells, Joao Caraca, and Gustavo Cardoso Oxford University Press, 2012), 251–77.

24. Duncan Clark, *Alibaba: The House That Jack Ma Built* (New York: HarperCollins, 2018).

25. Shiying Liu and Avery Martha, *Alibaba: The Inside Story Behind Jack Ma and the Creation of the World's Biggest Online Marketplace* (New York: Harper Collins, 2009).

26. Shiying Liu, *Shui Renshi Mayun 2* [Who knows Jack Ma 2] (Beijing: China Friendship Press, 2012).

27. Alibaba, *Mayun Neibu Jianghua* [Jack Ma's talks given inside the company] (Zhejiang: Hongqi Publishing House, 2010), 21.

28. Michael Keane, *Created in China: The Great New Leap Forward* (London: Routledge, 2007).

29. Lianrui Jia and Dwayne Winseck, "The Political Economy of Chinese Internet Companies," *International Communication Gazette* 80, no. 1, 30–59.

30. Carol Xiaojuan Ou and Robert M. Davison, "Technical Opinion–Why eBay Lost to TaoBao in China: The Global Advantage," *Communications of the ACM* 52, no. 1 (2009): 145–48.

31. "Online Extra: eBay's Patient Bid on China," *Bloomberg Businessweek*, March 15, 2004, https://www.bloomberg.com/news/articles/2004-03-14/online-extra-ebays-patient-bid-on-china.

32. "Online Extra: eBay's Patient Bid on China."

33. While in 2003 eBay claimed 90 percent of the Chinese C2C market share, Taobao was able to grab 9 percent of the market by early 2004 when SoftBank replenished its investment. In October 2005, emboldened by a new round of venture capital injected by Yahoo!, Taobao announced an extension of its no-fee plan for three additional years, following which it received a mass migration of customers from eBay China.

34. Shiying Liu, *Shui Renshi Mayun 2.*

35. Cuodao Jin, *Mayun Guanli Riji* [Jack Ma's management diary] (Zhejiang, China: Zhejiang University Press, 2013).

36. Alibaba, *Mayun Neibu Jianghua.*

37. Darryl Date-Shappard, "Alibaba Can Supply Huge China Consumer Demand with U.S. Businesses on Tmall, Taobao," *Seeking Alpha*, June 11, 2015, https://seekingalpha.com/article/3252045-alibaba-can-supply-huge-china-consumer-demand-with-u-s-businesses-on-tmall-taobao.

38. The export-driven model on the exploitation of cheap manufacturing labor, over-capacity, and fixed-asset investment was often blamed for contributing to the country's foreign dependency, growing social and regional disparities, and environmental crisis.

39. Located in Jiangsu province.

40. An academic institute affiliated with the Chinese Academy of Social Sciences or CASS.

41. Aliresearch, *Shaji Moshi Jiqi Yiyi* [Shaji Model and Its Significance], 2010, http://www.aliresearch.com/blog/article/detail/id/12574.html.

42. Lin Shan and Congqi Xiao, "'Taobao cun' yinglai gaoceng zhuangjia tansuo nongcun fazhan xinlujing—Shaji, wangluo shidai de 'xiaogangcun'" ["Taobao village" has attracted top-level experts to explore new path of rural development—Shaji, the Xiaogang village of the networked era], *Xuzhou Daily*, December 21, 2010, 1.

43. Xiangdong Wang, Qiping Jiang, and Xiumin Ye, *Hexie Shehui Yu Xinxihua Zhanlue* [Harmonious society and the informationalization strategy] (Beijing: The Commercial Press, 2014).

44. Xiangdong Wang, Qiping Jiang, and Xiumin Ye, *Hexie Shehui Yu Xinxihua.*

45. Personal interview, 2014.

46. Personal Interview, 2014.

47. Personal Interview, 2014.

48. Personal Interview, 2014.

49. Cuodao Jin, *Mayun Guanli Riji.*

50. Cuodao Jin, *Mayun Guanli Riji.*

51. Chunhui Zhuang, "Taobao Zhengzhi Xujia Jiaoyi Bufen Maijia Wangshang Kangyi"

[Taobao got tough on fake transactions and some sellers protested online], *Dongfang Daily*, December 9, 2013, http://tech.sina.com.cn/i/2013-12-09/07598987781.shtml.

52. Stephen Graham and Simon Marvin, *Splintering Urbanism: Networked Infrastructures, Technological Mobilities and the Urban Condition* (London: Routledge, 2001).

53. Neil Gough and Alexandra Stevenson, "The Unlikely Ascent of Jack Ma, Alibaba's Founder," *New York Times*, May 7, 2014, http://www.nytimes.com/2014/05/08/technology/the-unlikely-ascent-of-jack-ma-alibabas-founder.html?_r=0.

54. Lara Logan, "Jack Ma Brings Alibaba to the U.S.," CBS News, September 28, 2014, https://www.cbsnews.com/news/alibaba-chairman-jack-ma-brings-company-to-america/.

Firewalls and Walled Gardens

The Interplatformization of China's Wanghong Industry

Junyi Lv and David Craig

Over the past century, Hollywood has benefitted from first-mover advantage by advancing control over media distribution and entertainment IP around the world. Earlier communication and media scholars framed these conditions of American cultural and media imperialism as a "one-way street"[1] or a "patchwork quilt,"[2] although more nuanced accounts of media globalization have advanced more complex and dynamic flows of media power. China's efforts to thwart, if reverse, cultural imperialism have proved limited, despite the arguments by policy advisors like Li Wuwei that "movies, plays, and novels that are engaging have proved to be more effective in disseminating Chinese culture than diplomatic delegations."[3] While experiencing vast growth in their domestic cultural and legacy media industries, Chinese entertainment IP has rarely succeeded at going "over the wall."

History may be repeating in the twenty-first century through the rise of US-owned streaming video and social media platforms operating globally. The international domination outside of China by the FANGs (Facebook, Amazon, Netflix, and Google) has further advanced claims by critical communication scholars like Fuchs and Jin of American platform imperialism.[4] However, the rise of China's digital economy, nurtured by their tech policy and BATs digital champions

(Baidu, Alibaba, and Tencent), is "challenging the platform imperialism thesis."[5] China's investment in and protection of their own tech industry, including digital and social media platforms, pose a threat to American global media incumbency.

These developments toward competing systems reflect the advance of China's parallel social media platform strategies. This has been evidenced by the newest B in the BATs system, Bytedance, which has accelerated the development of a diverse array of rapidly scaling social media platforms within China, including Douyin, Toutiao, Vigo, and Huoshan, along with a complimentary set of international platforms, like TikTok. As Keane and Su argue, these developments indicate how "China Inc. is directly pitted against Silicon Valley."[6]

As described in this chapter, one of the factors in the success of China's digital and platform economy is the rapid growth of China's social media entertainment industry, labelled *wanghong*. This industry has been propelled by the dynamism between cross-integrated social media platforms operating collectively to advance China's technological power and the rise of a class of new cultural producers—social media entrepreneurs—harnessing these platforms to advance their entrepreneurial and cultural ambitions. As argued here, China's platform economy has secured fast-mover advantage by fostering collaborative, cross-integrated platform practices that have empowered a new class of cultural producers, wanghong creators with varying degrees of opportunity, precarity, and sustainability.

The term "wanghong" literally means "internet red," but translates into "internet famous" or "internet celebrities." Compared with Western terms like "creators" and "influencers," wanghong refers more specifically to social media entrepreneurs, whether commercializing livestreamers, beauty and lifestyle vloggers, short-video content creators, micro-bloggers, gameplayers, or other online micro-celebrities who secure fame and profit through their social media practices. The prominence of these social media entrepreneurs signals why wanghong has more broadly been used to refer to the rapidly emerging Chinese cultural industry. Thus the wanghong industry harnesses Chinese social media platforms to aggregate and engage affinity communities that can be converted into cultural, communicative, and commercial value. There are wanghong platforms, wanghong creators, and a wanghong industry.

China's wanghong industry, while a relatively nascent concept in Chinese area and media studies, has grown at an accelerated pace seemingly overnight. While the first-generation wanghong platforms like Youku and Weibo date back to the mid-2000s, around the same time as the launch of YouTube and Twitter, the rise of social media entrepreneurs harnessing these platforms for profit notably accelerated with the launch of short-video and livestreaming social media apps such as Miaopai and Meipai around 2013. Within a few years, the industry had eclipsed China's domestic box office and, as of 2018, is estimated to be worth over 18 billion dollars.[7] Recent estimates suggest that as many as 21 million wanghong creators are operating in China, albeit at different degrees of influence and viability.[8]

Nurtured by the Great Chinese Firewall, the wanghong industry has emerged as an alternative and likely competing industry to what Cunningham and Craig refer to as the West's "social media entertainment," or SME.[9] SME is distinguished by social media entrepreneurs, or creators, harnessing US-based platforms globally, with the exception of China and a few other countries. Both SME and the wanghong industry operate differently from legacy media industries by functioning outside of the conventional control of IP content and distribution. These industries are bounded by the technological means afforded by social media platforms and informed by institutional factors from markets to governance, while representing alternative means for cultural production and reception.

While the wanghong industry is comprised of multiple platforms and creators, operating with diverse forms of modality like photography, text, and recorded video, livestreaming platforms and creators have especially flourished. In 2016, there were as many as one thousand livestreaming platforms in China,[10] although the number has since subsided due in part to platform consolidation and competition.[11] Outside China and within the global-scaling social media entertainment industry, livestreaming platforms have either struggled or failed.[12] First-generation livestreaming websites like Stickam died in the wake of second-generation mobile livestreaming apps like Meerkat,[13] which, in turn, survived less than a year due to competition and other market conditions.[14] Pre-existing platforms like Facebook, Instagram, and YouTube have integrated livestreaming functions as added features, and these services have garnered great controversy from the broadcast of sexual acts to homicides and terrorism, including the Christchurch massacre in 2019.[15] For those few independent livestreaming apps operating outside of China, they have struggled for solvency. Some have been forced to rely on rounds of investment capital, including revenues from Chinese tech firms, like Cheetah Mobile's investment in the platform Live.me.[16] The most successful Western platform, Amazon's Twitch, has flourished in the West, but languished in comparison to Chinese platforms, and failed to extend beyond the niche of gaming or integrating online payment or e-commerce services, even within their own Amazon platform.[17]

This chapter contrasts the platform strategies in relation to creator practices between China's wanghong industry and the global-scaling, US-based social media entertainment industry (SME). Our analysis of platforms engages with the concept of affordances to account for the material relationship between humans and technology and between users and platforms. Our research distinguishes those strategies of interplatformization in Chinese wanghong industry from intraplatformization in US social media entertainment. Interplatformization refers to how China's wanghong platforms operate more collaboratively and contribute to a more competitive landscape while advancing social media entrepreneurialism within China's emerging digital economy.[18] In contrast, Western intraplatformization refers to how social media entertainment is dominated by competing US-owned platforms, like Google's YouTube and Facebook, which are rapidly advancing toward their own closed platform ecosystems, or "walled gardens." In the intraplatformization system, creators yield comparatively less influence or value when compared to the more open and fluid situation enabled by China's interplatformization.

We adopted mixed methodologies, including the walkthrough method, to understand the user interface and cross-platform integration of the commercializing and communicative features and affordances of social media platforms.[19] We also gathered empirical data from nearly one hundred ethnographic interviews with platform executives, livestreamers, investors, and media scholars in Beijing, Shanghai, and Guangzhou in China over the past three years. Interviewees were either contacted through social media platforms such as LinkedIn and Weibo, or introduced by other interviewees and connections.

We seek to understand the underlying structural and material reasons why Chinese platforms have managed to foster greater wanghong creator entrepreneurialism at an even more accelerated rate relative to Western-based SME platforms. In Cunningham, Craig, and Lv,[20] we previously accounted for the politics and precarity of Chinese platforms and wanghong, including recognition of the fluid and contingent nature of state-based interventions around platforms and creators designed to secure commercial advantage but maintain social control. Here we extend our considerations of platform strategies within and between these competing industries, moving beyond political economic concerns to consider issues of governance around platform power and social control. We share the goals expressed by Wang and Lobato around their study of Chinese streaming platforms:

> Our aim is not to approach the Chinese cases as exceptions to Western models, as though they require a separate platform area studies. On the contrary, we explore

the possibility that analysis of Chinese services may provide important opportunities for theory-building around platforms in general, and thus an opportunity for Chinese media studies expertise to feed more directly into global media studies debates.[21]

China's internet has been "localized to the extent that it is now possible to talk about the 'Chinese Internet' as opposed to the Internet in China."[22] In our approach, we take up the call from Yang to consider the distinct Chinese ideals and practices that have shaped the Chinese internet, inclusive of wanghong platform strategies and wanghong creator practices, to also account for markets, management, cultural production, and technological innovation alongside critical cultural concerns over governance and power.[23] As we strive to demonstrate here, China's interplatformization strategies have nurtured the accelerated growth of China's wanghong industry, thus helping to distinguish and advance China's internet and digital economy. Domestically, these developments have social and cultural impact especially in encouraging micro-creativity and entrepreneurship as resistance to the hegemonic power-money-intellect alliance and forming the "new normal" of the public-private alliance.[24] Internationally, China's booming wanghong industry signals not only the emerging global competition between these cultural industries but also challenges notions of unilateral Western platform imperialism, posits the advance of Chinese soft tech power, and anticipates the decentralization of the internet.

Platformization, Infrastructure, and Affordances

In this section, we consider the concepts of platformization and affordances in order to contribute to our understanding of the dynamic and contingent relational environments between wanghong and SME platforms and creators. These are concepts developed within the emerging subfield of platform studies, which "investigate the relationships between the hardware and software design of computing systems (platforms) and the creative works produced on those systems, which include but are not limited to video games—digital art, electronic literature, recreational and playful programs, and virtual environments."[25] These frameworks inform the distinctions we will map between the Western-based strategies of intraplatformization within SME and Chinese interplatformization strategies.

As social media platforms are vital to the growth of wanghong, platforms have become increasingly central to the function of cultural industries.[26] A platform can be defined as "an infrastructure to build applications on."[27] Thus, platforms have become the primary means by which netizens access the internet. Whereas once users accessed the worldwide web, increasingly the most viable means to harness this technology is through platforms, whether via browsers or social media. This turn has generated the concept of platformization, which embodies an emerging platform-dependent phenomenon in cultural production and consumption.[28] As further detailed by platform scholars, platformization describes "the penetration of economic, governmental, and infrastructural extensions of digital platforms into the web and app ecosystems, fundamentally affecting the operations of the cultural industries."[29] Helmond uses platformization "to refer to the rise of the platform as the dominant infrastructural and economic model of the social web and the consequences of the expansion of social media platforms into other spaces online."[30] While, as Hilmes points out, platforms are sites that provide the means for commercializing cultural production,[31] critical platform scholars like Gillespie have shown that platforms reinforce hierarchies of power, lack transparency, accountability, and self-regulation, and violate normative values of freedom of speech and rights to privacy.[32]

Focusing more notably on the platformization of cultural production, Nieborg and Poell engaged with a mix of business studies, political economy, and platform (or software) studies to provide an "institutional" account. Beyond platforms and users, they argue that cultural production involves "penetration of economic, governmental, and infrastructural extensions of digital platforms into the web and app ecosystems, fundamentally affecting the operations of cultural industries."[33] Both in the West and in China, platformization "is reconfiguring the production, distribution, and monetization of cultural content in staggering and complex ways" and contributing to "key shifts in practices of labor, creativity, and citizenship."[34]

While their focus is on underlying structural and material conditions that influence how cultural production operates on platforms, platformization is deeply informed by the dynamic practices of users, creators, and other stakeholders. Here we re-engage with the familiar, if often overdetermined and multivalent concept of "affordances." While earlier scholars have mapped the role of affordances more broadly to describe how users interact with technology,[35] Bucher and Helmond describe the "relational and multi-layered" affordances of social media, which create platform environments wherein users operate as actors and stakeholders.[36] As detailed in the next section, these platform environments comprise sites and applications in which walled and communal gardens have been built, removed, renovated, and broached, particularly by SME and wanghong creators.

Scholars have introduced diverse accounts of affordance to describe how social media platforms facilitate or limit social networking and communication. Postigo coins the term *social affordance*, distinguishing it from the technical affordances of social media platforms.[37] Whereas technical affordances describe platforms' technical functions, such as uploading and sharing videos, social affordances enable platform users to interact and connect with "the social structures that take shape in association with a given technical structure."[38] For instance, vloggers may appear in the videos of other vloggers, or two vloggers might create content together, forming a mutually beneficial relationship. Similarly, Hutchby describes *communicative affordance* as the "possibilities for action that emerge from . . . given technological forms."[39]

Noticeably, platforms not only afford users social networking and communication, but also generate possibilities for commercialization. Van Dijck and Poell discuss how platforms' social-technological affordances link content creation to users and advertisers.[40] Focusing more on the world of gameplay, Postigo examines how the socio-technological architecture of YouTube allows creators to secure "pay for play."[41] Humphreys considers how the commercial affordances of platforms offer the possibility of the co-existence of "financial and social economies."[42] Although commercial affordances may have been underdetermined and poorly theorized as pure business logics, as we argue, commercial affordances connect the political economy, technology, and social-cultural values of platforms within the SME and wanghong industries.

These conceptual frameworks of platformization and affordances inform our account of how creators harness platforms for commercial, cultural, and communicative value. Numerous terms and concepts have been used to describe this process, from "produsage"[43] to "co-creation"[44] to "vernacular creativity."[45] Cunningham and Craig coin the term *social media entertainment* to distinguish this emerging industry from legacy media through the rise of social media entrepreneurs operating on and across the social media platforms.[46] These same frameworks and concepts help to illuminate how wanghong are harnessing Chinese social media platforms to cultivate and aggregate communities and convert them into multiple revenue streams.

Informed by platformization and affordances theories, we contrast the United States' and China's livestreaming platform landscapes and evolution. Our research considers how US platforms have veered toward more intraplatformization, whereas China's platforms reflect greater interplatformization. We define intraplatformization as the siloing of platforms, colloquially referred to as walled gardens. This model fosters oligopolistic control by platforms and the tech owners, while often impeding access and affordances for users and creators. Alternatively, interplatformization represents a more collaborative approach in which platforms allow access and foster better integration of cross-platform features and affordances. These strategies have contributed not only to a more competitive platform landscape, but also fostered a more profitable environment for the wanghong industry and creators to flourish. These conditions are mutually constitutive of the power that wanghong creators have secured at competing platforms, where they seek to integrate features that allow them to garner greater commercial, communicative, and cultural value.

Western Intraplatformization

SME has been dominated by US-based platforms owned by tech behemoths engaging in strategies of intraplatformization. Amazon, Google, and Facebook have increasingly veered toward building walled gardens, whether acquiring or launching new platforms or integrating new features and services exclusively within their own platforms, often emulating those offered by other services. These strategies have hindered the growth of their livestreaming platforms and features, as well as the viability of livestreaming SME creators operating across them. Western livestreaming has featured standalone apps like Twitch and added features like YouTube Live and Facebook Live. For the latter, these features have not become effective means of acquiring more viewers or subscribers. To stream live on YouTube involves a complex set of instructions including opening a creator account, downloading encoded software, and verifying age limits around the content and monetization of the video. Around gameplay, the most popular form of livestreaming, YouTube previously launched a separate livestreaming platform designed to compete with Twitch. However, the platform did not gain much popularity and was integrated into the YouTube main platform.[47] This integration has inhibited the remuneration and viability of YouTube gameplayers, subject to YouTube's ever-changing creator partnership and monetization agreements limited primarily to advertising revenue.

Whereas YouTube secures 44 percent of gameplay viewers, Twitch delivers 54 percent of gameplay revenue,[48] which features multiple revenue streams including subscriptions, advertising, and virtual gifts. Facebook Live has similarly struggled as an added feature on the platform, while experiencing a backlash from having aired a series of live murders and crimes.[49]

Next-generation platforms developed for mobile use, like Instagram and Snapchat, have also moved toward similar practices of insulating users and creators. Instagram is well-integrated with its sister platform, Facebook, but does not allow posters to include other URLs or links to other sites in their Instagram posts. As a platform encouraging users to upload high-resolution pictures, their livestreaming feature has a high threshold for Instagrammers to create content and gather followers with less seamless interoperability than the Chinese platforms TikTok and Kuaishou. Snapchat has never facilitated cross-platform use, including Instagram, which has repeatedly emulated Snapchat's features like filters and stories to secure competitive advantage.[50] The remarkable success of Chinese-owned TikTok apps, both the non-Chinese version and the Chinese Douyin version, can be attributed to its blend of short recorded video and livestreaming features. While the non-Chinese platform does not offer monetization to its native creators or the ability to link to their other sites, the Chinese version Douyin introduced a shopping cart logo into their interface, which allows wanghong creators to link to their Taobao stores.[51]

Western platforms do not allow cross-platform integration unless these platforms are owned by the same company, as with Facebook–Instagram, Twitter–Periscope, and Amazon–Twitch. Creators' choices are limited, whether sharing and spreading content, or providing alternative means for commercialization through cross-platform integration. For instance, Facebook posts cannot be shared readily with other platforms and, as of 2018, tweets can no longer be auto-posted on Facebook.[52] YouTube provides the means to post links to other sites underneath in descriptions but eliminates their annotations, which creators could post on end cards that allow them to drive fans to their other sites, like the creator-focused subscription site Patreon.[53] Facebook owns Instagram, which allows photos, but not livestreams, to be shared across both platforms. Instagram does not allow their own posts or stories, much less other content, to be shared or integrated from competing platforms.

Blocked from integration across other platforms, Twitter launched its own livestreaming function while also integrating its standalone Periscope livestreaming app, which was purchased in 2014. Neither platform livestreaming strategy has proven successful for either the platform or creators in generating revenue, securing users, or growing followers.[54] Meanwhile, Twitter's creator program for monetization still lags far behind other platforms, requiring a complex set of conditions for creators such as signing up for their Twitter-owned Niche advertising platform. Even Twitter acknowledges that creators use the platform to engage community but not to generate revenue.[55] With the exception of Twitch, none of the livestreaming platforms mentioned above provides e-commerce capabilities or virtual tipping systems for creators to monetize their streams.

As previously mentioned, Twitch is the most successful stand-alone livestreaming app outside of China, where it was banned in 2018.[56] Launched around the same time as YouTube, Twitch was originally called Justin.tv, which was designed for online broadcasting of conventional television formats, followed by other livestream platforms like livestream.com. Renamed Twitch in 2011, it has survived the collapse of other livestreaming competitors, in part due to deep capitalization once it was purchased by Amazon for 1 billion dollars in 2014. At that time, critics wondered, "Why Amazon would spend so much cash for Twitch was a real head-scratcher—live game broadcasts via the Internet isn't exactly what you would call core to Amazon's retail business."[57] Nonetheless, Twitch has proven successful in growing its platform into the lucrative, if limited, niche of gameplay, in what has emerged as a "gold rush" for gameplayers.[58] Within the platform, Twitch has introduced multiple revenue streams from advertising, subscriptions, and virtual goods. Their success has spawned a series of competitors, including YouTube gaming, which has since folded. In late 2019, Microsoft-owned Mixer, a gameplay-focused livestreaming platform, began offering exclusive deals with top Twitch gameplayers like Ninja.[59]

The rise of gameplay livestreaming platforms in the West has lagged compared to their counterparts in China. Since 2017, "gaming platform wars" between platforms like Douyu, Huya, and the now defunct Panda TV emerged, before the platforms expanded into new vertical and cross-platform integration. Twitch creators and their communities are not supported to venture off the platform, and only a rare few are afforded fees to remain exclusively. In contrast, the Chinese gameplay platforms encourage cross-platform practices to appeal to broader audiences or otherwise offer fees to remain exclusively on their gameplay platform. While Twitch has failed to integrate even with its very own Amazon e-commerce platform, these Chinese platforms allow wanghong creators to promote their own e-commerce sites and stores like Taobao and Tmall while integrating online payment systems Alipay and WeChat Pay that belong to their competitors.

As mentioned in the introduction, other Western livestreaming platforms like Stickam and Meerkat have struggled to secure market share while some have been dependent upon investor funding, including Chinese-owned Cheetah Mobile's investment in Live.me.[60] The Western platform strategies of intraplatformization provide one explanation for their failure to perform comparable to the wanghong platforms. Through their "walled garden" competitive practices, these platforms have inhibited the growth of SME creators, who rely on cross-platform strategies to aggregate and engage with their fan communities as well as diversify their business portfolios in pursuit of greater sustainability. In contrast, China's wanghong platforms have pursued the alternative approach of interplatformization, which has empowered the entrepreneurialism of their wanghong creators.

Chinese Interplatformization

As Bryan Shao, an executive at Youku, described in our interview, "They can kill us, and we can kill them. So we need to stay together so we can both grow faster." This comment alludes to how China's wanghong industry has been nurtured by strategies of interplatformization, most notably across livestreaming platforms. These strategies include encouraging greater collaboration across platforms, thus fostering a more competitive platform landscape featuring greater diversity of content and more features for monetization. In turn, these strategies are empowering livestreaming wanghong to build their own brands. The following pages map the accelerated evolution of wanghong livestreaming platforms, their strategies of interplatformization, and the affordances that have empowered wanghong creators.

Based on these transformations, the year 2016 was named "the year of livestreaming" by the Chinese press.[61] By June 2018, China had 425 million livestreaming users, representing more than half of the 802 million Chinese netizens.[62] The 2018 annual revenue of this industry increased 32 percent compared to 2017, reaching US$4.4 billion.[63] As for wanghong, in 2017, the top commercializing livestreamers could make more than 1 million RMB (around US$145 thousand) monthly and 10 million (about US$1.45 million) yearly, although the vast majority of wanghong remain hobbyists while struggling to secure a sustainable living.[64] According to the news site Zhibobang, "livestreaming is steadily becoming a basic service of the Internet. Such popularization is gradually eliminating prejudice against the industry."[65]

As discussed in our earlier article,[66] state-based policy interventions have exerted an ever-accelerating degree of governance and oversight that reflects regressive and censorious social and cultural control. Sexual content, soft porn, violence, and other "over the line" content have burdened this industry with a constant struggle of regulation and censorship. The Chinese government has banned content that may "harm social morality" not once but many times over.[67] In 2016, the State Administration of Press, Publication, Radio, Film and Television (SARFFT) shut down a female livestreamer's account for five days because of her "erotic banana-eating" behavior.[68] In 2017, seventy-three platforms and 1,870 livestreamers were banned permanently.[69] In 2018, 370 livestreaming apps were removed from app stores because they did not "comply with regulations."[70] In total, more than four hundred platforms have been shut down since 2017 because of "violence, pornography, gambling, superstition, and other values harmful to public morality."[71] Most recently, Hubei province issued their own set of standards for livestreaming, which include banning scandalous and sexy attire.[72] Facing pressure from regulations and fierce competition, some small platforms such as Quanmin TV and Netease's Bohe livestreaming did not survive.[73] Even larger platforms like Douyu had to fire employees to cut their budgets in response to the costs for moderating content across these livestreaming channels and as a consequence of declining revenue.[74]

In response to these policy regulations, the industry has been forced to pursue strategies and practices designed to accommodate policy concerns in pursuit of sustainability. For example, to address the concerns around gendered performance, more diverse content genres have been incubated and nurtured. YY supports multiple verticals of livestreaming such as eating, outdoor traveling, wild surviving, and selling agricultural products. Platforms have also developed different commercial strategies designed to generate greater profits, accommodate wanghong creators, and manage risks from government regulatory oversight. One strategy includes "going out" with parallel or non-Chinese platforms, like the aforementioned dual platform strategy of Bytedance's TikTok platforms. YY, which owns a number of wanghong platforms including the gameplay platform Huya, has invested in non-Chinese platforms such as BIGO Live. The livestreaming app integrates game and pan-entertainment livestreaming with social networking and has more than 200 million registered users primarily in Southeast Asia.[75] Pursuing cross-platform integration, the platforms have adopted localization strategies around content while featuring comparable monetization strategies around advertising, virtual goods, and e-commerce. The latter has helped to expand Chinese online mobile payments services Alipay and WeChat Pay abroad,[76] while Alibaba has invested heavily in e-commerce platforms like Lazada in these same territories.[77] As Yu remarks, this international platform strategy aligns with China's Digital Silk Road initiatives and soft power economic and cultural ambitions.[78] However, the dual platform strategy continues to constrain wanghong creators (and their cultural influence) behind the wall while forcing the platforms to secure and grow new creators locally.

Apart from diversifying content and attracting overseas users, platforms provide commercial affordances for livestreaming wanghong to generate revenue. The primary source of revenue for both livestreaming platforms and wanghong is from users' virtual tipping.[79] As a Huya's manager informed us, "Platforms mainly rely on tipping revenue. Some livestreamers will open their Taobao store, have advertising sponsors, or have some offline performance activities, but most revenue comes from audiences' tipping." Bobby Kiki, a livestreamer operating across multiple platforms, commented that "my revenue comes from fans' tipping. It is based on luck. If I have good luck, I can earn 10,000 to 20,000 RMB (US$2,000 to 3,000) a day. But if I have bad luck, I can only make a few dozen RMB (US$10–15)."

The tipping system exemplifies the success of an interplatformization strategy that includes near frictionless integration with online payment platforms owned by competing tech firms. Using online payment platforms such as Alipay and WeChat Pay, livestreaming users can buy virtual gifts within a few clicks. Virtual gifts are a premium currency that can be exchanged without users having to inconveniently log in and out of platforms.[80] On the one hand, integrating different platforms and simplifying the payment process encourage, if not seduce, users into tipping as a means of bolstering revenue.[81] On the other hand, the affordance provides users with a smoother user experience while also enabling wanghong to spend more time on the platforms to generate more tips.

Another kind of interplatformization is the integration of China's livestreaming platform with e-commerce platforms. As livestreamers sell products in livestreaming rooms, viewers can click the links near the livestreaming window, which will direct them to e-commerce sites such as Tmall and Taobao to buy products immediately. These sites are owned by Alibaba, but are often integrated into livestreaming platforms run by competing tech firms such as YY and Momo. Cheese, a livestreamer on YY, explained the affordance of e-commerce and livestreaming integration: "Below the livestreaming room, there is a small shopping cart (logo), which links to Taobao. Fans can buy things via the link, and I can get revenue share."

Some platforms have launched their own e-commerce stores, which may resemble Western strategies of intraplatformization. Douyu has launched Yugou Online Shopping Mall to sell game-related products, game equipment, and snacks.[82] The shopping mall collaborates with stores on Taobao, Netease, and JD.com, thus giving users the experience of watching livestreaming and buying products in a few clicks. Users can reach Taobao stores through the online shopping mall. As our interviewee, Feng Dou, the leader of Douyu's Beijing Office, said: "We (Douyu) cooperate with Alibaba currently. Douyu has e-commerce as a revenue model. Every position of our livestreaming rooms can be distributed. . . . Every livestreaming room has four to five products-selling positions. When you click them, you will be directed to Douyu's Shopping Mall, which is like buying Taobao stuff on Douyu. Then we share the revenue with Taobao."

In addition, e-commerce platforms like Taobao and JD.com have added livestreaming functions, while continuing to be integrated across other competing livestreaming platforms. One of the most successful fashion influencers and Taobao store owners, Zhang Dayi, brought 170 million RMB revenue for Taobao on the Double Eleven Festival (Chinese version of Black Friday and Cyber Monday) in 2017.[83] Livestreaming can stimulate users' purchasing practice far more than other modalities such as texts or images. The leader of the e-commerce department of Mogujie, an online shopping platform, commented:

> A customer on Mogujie needs to view two to three hundred webpages to finish shopping. In this process, it is very difficult for her to actually buy something. But livestreaming is like face-to-face (communication). It is like a fashion expert telling you what suits you best face-to-face . . . so many people buy immediately.[84]

The tech giants in China, the so-called BAT (Baidu, Alibaba, and Tencent), have also invested in livestreaming platforms, either creating their own livestreaming platforms or adding livestreaming functions to their original platforms.[85] Theoretically, these would have allowed these firms to merge their e-commerce and mobile payment services and emulate the walled garden strategies of the West. However, as in the case of Western tech titans such as Google and Facebook, these strategies have proven relatively unsuccessful. Tencent has added livestreaming functions to its social media QQ Zone and Tencent News with limited appeal. Although its largest social media platform, WeChat, does not include a livestreaming function, users can livestream through other platforms and connect the content to WeChat public accounts for fans to watch.[86] Tencent has developed three livestreaming platforms (Huayang livestreaming, Tencent Livestreaming, and Now), but none has secured strong positions in the market. Tencent has also invested in Douyu and Huya, which have been successful in game livestreaming.[87] Tencent's strategies emulate what Postigo said of YouTube, "YouTube (or any platforms that invite UGC for its inventory) is not unlike a bettor at a roulette table who is in the happy position of betting on all the numbers, where the payout, while low in aggregate, outweighs what appears to be an otherwise wild investment."[88]

Alibaba has deployed an array of livestreaming strategies, while continuing to integrate its e-commerce and online payment systems throughout the platform landscape. Although it does not have any self-developed livestreaming platform, Alibaba has invested in Momo, one of the most successful social livestreaming platforms, as well as YouKu's Laifeng Livestreaming and Yi Live.[89] Further, Alipay, Alibaba's online payment platform, is alpha-testing a livestreaming function on the platform.[90] Compared with Alibaba and Tencent, Baidu's strategy is more conservative, veering from a multi-platform strategy to focus more on developing artificial intelligence.[91] Baidu previously developed the Baixiu and Ala livestreaming platforms, and has invested in iQiyi's Qixiu Livestreaming.[92] Qixiu and iQiyi are rather independent from Baidu's system. Xu Songsong at Qixiu told us: "Qixiu does not really belong to Baidu. iQiyi is actually quite independent from Baidu's system. Qixiu is a livestreaming branch of iQiyi."

While the BATs have cultivated diverse livestreaming strategies with mixed results, the platform landscape has remained competitive with new entrants, nurtured by these strategies of interplatformization. The livestreaming company YY went public in 2012 and does not rely on any BAT investment. Its mother company, YY Inc., received initial investment from Lei Jun, the founder of Xiaomi Corporation, a technology company that mainly develops smartphones. In 2018, YY and Xiaomi Live, a livestreaming platform of Xiaomi, signed a contract of cooperation, which may generate deeper platform integration.[93]

As of 2020, livestreaming continues to be a dominant player in the wanghong industry, while a new wave of platformization is emerging. These platforms feature alternative modalities, formats, and affordances, while also benefiting from interplatformization that commercially empowers their native wanghong. Bytedance, the parent company of the dual TikTok and Douyin platforms, has developed a multi-platform strategy aimed at making the company "the world largest content ecology."[94] In addition to the aforementioned Douyin and TikTok platforms, Bytedance owns Today's Headline (the news distribution platform with livestreaming function), Huoshan (short video platform with livestreaming function), and Xigua (longer short video platform with livestreaming function). Interplatformization strategies incorporating platforms and services from competing tech firms have fueled their growth, as with the near frictionless access to either WeChat Pay or Alipay to buy virtual gifts and tip livestreamers on Douyin and Xigua.[95]

These platform strategies are mutually constituted by the demands and agency of wanghong creators. Like their Western counterparts, wanghong creators harness multiple platforms for their commercial and communicative affordances, which allow them to aggregate and engage fan communities and convert them into cultural and commercial value. One model of livestreamer–fan interaction is the livestreaming platform functioning alongside other social media apps such as WeChat and Weibo. Livestreamers spend hours on livestreaming platforms to directly talk and perform in front of their fans. They spend even longer hours on WeChat groups chatting with their fans when they are not livestreaming. Moreover, Weibo serves as a picture curating medium, where fans can follow the livestreamers and watch them post pictures of their daily lives.

Even though some top livestreamers may sign exclusive deals with livestreaming platforms for commercial partnerships, they are still encouraged to use multiple platforms to engage with their communities. Wanghong creator Bobby Kiki's platform practices are a model of interactivity replicated by many wanghong creators interviewed in our research. She said:

> My interaction with fans can be divided into "online" (when livestreaming) and "offline" (not livestreaming). When I am livestreaming, I talk with them and perform my talent. For offline interaction, my family (of fans) has a WeChat group, in which I will post some of my daily activities. For instance, when I go out, I will post a picture of mine. . . . We talk about daily things, like what I eat that day. Then they will discuss what food is good for my health, what food will make me fat. When I fall sick, they will remind me to take medicine. They will tell me what medicine I should take and ask me to see a doctor. Every day, they will say hello to me. Everyone will post "good night" every evening and "good morning" every morning. For Weibo, I post lots of pictures and interesting short videos as much as I can. I need to make various content to attract my fans on Weibo—otherwise, I may lose them. But I do not have to do that in the livestreaming room. My fans in the livestreaming room

are not there for my talent or outward appearance, it is more like a spiritual or emotional companionship.

As Bobby Kiki's experience illustrates, multi-platform strategy facilitated by China's interplatformization has provided affordances for wanghong creators to deeply engage in fan communities and strengthened the social bonds between community members, generating diverse community cultures.

Above all, at the individual level, China's interplatformization empowers creators to become entrepreneurs and develop more sustainable business models with creativity and agency. At the community level, interplatformization provides a broader space for communication between wanghong and fans and among fans themselves, forming and circulating participatory cultures.[96] At the industry level, platforms collaborate with each other as one of the different strategies to survive and thrive, in response to government's cracking-down and political precarity.

Beyond Walled Gardens and Firewalls

In this chapter, we mapped the different platformization strategies used by Chinese and American livestreaming platforms. Western platforms dominated by the US tech behemoths are advancing oligopolistic strategies of intraplatformization, fostering walled gardens within their owned-and-operated platforms or companies. In addition to the balkanization of users, the consequence has been limited competition from upstart platforms. Although Western creators continue to pursue cross-platform strategies, compared to their Chinese wanghong counterparts, they are not able to monetize their platforms as effectively through integrated e-commerce and online payment platforms. In contrast, China's livestreaming platforms have nurtured strategies of interplatformization. These strategies have fostered a more competitive platform landscape, particularly among livestreaming platforms. Wanghong, especially on livestreaming platforms, have benefited from these strategies, as have the platforms, by fostering cross-platform features and commercial and communicative affordances.

Previous studies of China's internet development and cyberspace have discussed the possibility of increased civic participation and rising nationalism.[97] Whether these developments point toward utopia or dystopia, there is no doubt that China is playing an important role in international communities and overlapping cultural spheres.[98] The combination of platform interoperability and creator agency may also align with China's soft power aspirations, fostering yet another Chinese "dream" of the future. In this case, Xi Jinping's "China Dream" narrative is advanced through technological developments, which are being used to spread China's economic, political, and cultural influence. Yet as critics worry, this techno-version of the "China Dream" is ratcheting up tensions between America and a rising Chinese exceptionalism.[99]

NOTES

This research was funded by an Australian Research Grant secured by Queensland University of Technology and the USC-SJTU Institute for Cultural and Creative Industries at Shanghai Jiao Tong University.

1. Kaarle Nordenstreng and Tapio Varis, *Television Traffic—a One-Way Street? A Survey and Analysis of the International Flow of Television Programme Material* (Paris: UNESCO, 1974), 1.

2. M. Tracey, "Popular Culture and the Economics of Global Television," *Intermedia* 16, no. 2 (1988): 19–25, 9.

3. Li Wuwei, "The Challenges of China's Culture 'Going to the World,'" *The Handbook of Cultural and Creative Industries in China*, ed. Michael Keane (Cheltenham, UK: Edward Elgar, 2016), 116.

4. Christian Fuchs, *Social Media: A Critical Introduction* (Los Angeles: SAGE, 2014). Dal Yong Jin, "The Construction of Platform Imperialism in the Globalization Era," *Communication, Capitalism & Critique* 11, no. 1 (January 1, 2013): 145–72.

5. Haiqing Yu, "Beyond E-commerce: The Social Case of China's Digital Economy," *China Perspectives*, no. 4 (October 1, 2017): 3.

6. Michael Keane and Guanhua Su, "When Push Comes to Nudge: A Chinese Digital Civilisation In-the-Making," *Media International Australia* 173, no. 1 (November 2019): 3–16, 2.

7. Grace Tsoi, "Wang Hong: China's Online Stars Making Real Cash," *BBC News*, August 1, 2016, https://www.bbc.com. "What's the Difference Between a KOL and a Wanghong," *eMarketer*, August 2, 2018, https://www.emarketer.com.

8. Julie Wernau, Stu Woo, "China's Influencers—Moms, Farmers and Even Dogs—Hawk Their Wares on Live Streams," in *The Wall Street Journal*, December 8, 2019. Available on https://www.wsj.com

9. Stuart Cunningham and David Craig, *Social Media Entertainment: The New Intersection of Hollywood and Silicon Valley* (New York: New York University Press, 2019).

10. Yueshi Shen, "Comparing the Live Streaming Industries of China & The United States," *Heavybit Industries*, August 10, 2017, https://www.heavybit.com.

11. Amanda Lee, "China's Booming Live Streaming Industry May Have Reached its Peak," *South China Morning Post*, December 18, 2017, https://www.scmp.com.

12. Nathan McAlone, "Facebook Is Running into a Problem that has Plagued Live Video since 2007," *Business Insider*, June 21, 2016, https://www.businessinsider.com.

13. Zack Zarrillo & friends, "Stickam Closing Down Tonight after Seven Years of Service," *Property of Zack*, January 31, 2013, https://propertyofzack.com.

14. "Meerkat Live-Streaming App 'Dead,'" BBC News Technology, October 4, 2016, https://www.bbc.com.

15. Ian Sherr, "Livestreaming on Facebook, Twitter and YouTube Needs Radical Change," *Cnet*, March 15, 2019, https://www.cnet.com.

16. "Cheetah Mobile Responds to Recent Allegations," Cheetah Mobile, October 27, 2017, http://ir.cmcm.com.

17. Matt Weinberger, "Amazon's $970 Million Purchase of Twitch Makes So Much Sense Now: It's All about the Cloud," *Business Insider*, March 16, 2016, https://www.businessinsider.com.

18. Hong Yu, *Networking China: The Digital Transformation of the Chinese Economy* (Urbana: University of Illinois Press, 2017).

19. Ben Light, Jean Burgess, and Stefanie Duguay, "The Walkthrough Method: An Approach to the Study of Apps," *New Media & Society* 20, no. 3 (March 2018): 881–900.

20. Stuart Cunningham, David Craig, and Junyi Lv, "China's Livestreaming Industry: Platforms, Politics, and Precarity," *International Journal of Cultural Studies* 22, no. 6 (November 2019): 719–36.

21. Wilfred Yang Wang and Ramon Lobato, "Chinese Video Streaming Services in the Context of Global Platform Studies," *Chinese Journal of Communication* 12, no. 3 (July 2019): 356–57.

22. Luzhou Nina Li, "Rethinking the Chinese Internet: Social History, Cultural Forms, and Industrial Formation," *Television & New Media* 18, no. 5 (July 2017): 394. Guobin Yang, "A Chinese Internet? History, Practice, and Globalization," *Chinese Journal of Communication* 5, no. 1 (March 2012): 49.

23. Guobin Yang, "The Return of Ideology and the Future of Chinese Internet Policy," *Critical Studies in Media Communication* 31, no. 2 (March 2014), 109–13.

24. Haiqing Yu, "Beyond E-commerce: The Social Case of China's Digital Economy," *China*

Perspectives, no. 4 (October 1, 2017): 3–8. Yuezhi Zhao, *Communication in China: Political Economy, Power, and Conflict* (Lanham, MD: Rowman & Littlefield, 2008). Angang Hu, "Embracing China's 'New Normal': Why the Economy Is Still on Track," *Foreign Affairs* (May/June 2015), https://www.foreignaffairs.com/articles/china/2015-04-20/embracing-chinas-new-normal.

25. Ian Bogost and Nick Montfort, "Platform Studies: Frequently Questioned Answers," *UC Irvine: Digital Arts and Culture* (December 12, 2009): 6, http://www.escholarship.org/uc/item/01r0k9br.

26. David. B. Nieborg and Thomas Poell, "The Platformization of Cultural Production: Theorizing the Contingent Cultural Commodity," *New Media & Society* (April 2018): 4276–7.

27. Anne Helmond, "The Platformization of the Web: Making Web Data Platform Ready," *Social Media + Society* (July-December 2015): , doi:10.1177/2056305115603080sms. sagepub.com; Tarleton Gillespie, "The Politics of 'Platforms,'" *New Media & Society* 12 (February 2010), 347–64, doi:10.1177/1461444809342738.

28. Nieborg and Poell, "The Platformization of Cultural Production," 4275–92.

29. Nieborg and Poell, "The Platformization of Cultural Production," 4276.

30. Helmond, "The Platformization of the Web," 5.

31. Michele Hilmes, "Nailing Mercury: The Problem of Media Industry Historiography," *Media industries: History, Theory, and Method* (Malden, MA: Wiley-Blackwell, 2009), 21–32.

32. Tarleton Gillespie, "The Politics of 'Platforms,'" *New Media & Society* 12, no. 3 (May 2010): 347–64, doi:10.1177/1461444809342738.

33. David B Nieborg and Thomas Poell, "The Platformization of Cultural Production: Theorizing the Contingent Cultural Commodity," *New Media & Society* 20, no. 11 (November 2018): 4276.

34. Brooke Erin Duffy, Thomas Poell, and David B. Nieborg, "Platform Practices in the Cultural Industries: Creativity, Labor, and Citizenship," *Social Media + Society* (October 2019), doi:10.1177/2056305119879672.

35. Ann Majchrzak, Samer Faraj, Gerald C. Kane, and Bijan Azad, "The Contradictory Influence of Social Media Affordances on Online Communal Knowledge Sharing," *Journal of Computer-Mediated Communication* 19, no. 1 (October 2013): 38–55. Donald Norman, "Affordance, Conventions, and Design," *Interactions* 6, no. 3 (May 1, 1999): 38–43.

36. Taina Bucher and Anne Helmond, "The Affordances of Social Media Platforms," in *The SAGE Handbook of Social Media*, ed. J. Burgess, T. Poell, and A. Marwick (New York: SAGE,

2017), 16.

37. Hector Postigo, "The Socio-Technical Architecture of Digital Labor: Converting Play into YouTube Money," in *New Media & Society* 18, no. 2 (February 2016): 332–49.

38. Postigo, "The Socio-Technical Architecture of Digital Labor," 336.

39. Ian Hutchby, *Conversation and Technology: From the Telephone to the Internet* (Cambridge, UK: Polity, 2001): 30. Bucher and Helmond, "The Affordances of Social Media Platforms," 10.

40. José van Dijck and Thomas Poell, "Understanding Social Media Logic," *Media and Communication* 1, no. 1 (January 1, 2013): 8.

41. Postigo, "The Socio-Technical Architecture of Digital Labor," 339.

42. Sal Humphreys, "The Economies Within an Online Social Network Market: A Case Study of Ravelry," (paper presented at ANZCA 2009 Annual Conference: Communication, Creativity and Global Citizenship, Queensland University of Technology, Brisbane, Australia, July 8–10, p. 2).

43. Axel Bruns, *The Key Characteristics of Produsage, Blogs, Wikipedia, Second Life and Beyond: From Production to Produsage* (London: Peter Lang, 2008), 1.

44. John Banks and Sal Humphreys, "The Labour of User Co-Creators: Emergent Social Network Markets?," *Convergence* 14, no. 4 (November 2008): 401–418.

45. Jean Burgess, "Vernacular Creativity and New Media" (PhD dissertation, Queensland University of Technology, 2007).

46. Cunningham and Craig, *Social Media Entertainment*, 1–368.

47. Tim Peterson, "YouTube Gaming's Shutdown Could Be an Attempt to One-Up Twitch," *Digiday,* September 25, 2018, https://digiday.com.

48. "2019 Video Game Industry Statistics, Trends & Data," *WEPC*, November 2019, https://www.wepc.com.

49. Gina Tron, "The Most Disturbing Facebook Live Videos of 2017 So Far," *Oxygen,* April 24, 2017, https://www.oxygen.com.

50. "Why Instagram Steals Ideas from Snapchat," *Cave*, https://www.cavesocial.com.

51. Elijah Whaley, "Douyin Announces E-commerce Linking Taobao," *Parklu*, March 23, 2018, https://www.parklu.com.

52. Andrew Hutchinson, "Facebook API Changes Mean You Can No Longer Auto Post Tweets to Facebook," *Social Media Today*, August 3, 2018, https://www.socialmediatoday.com.

53. Nick Statt, "YouTube to Discontinue Video Annotations Because They Never Worked on Mobile," *The Verge,* March 16, 2017, https://www.theverge.com.

54. Kerry Flynn, "As Twitter Stock Soars, its Video App Periscope Is Suffering from Neglect," *Mashable Asia*, February 9, 2018, https://mashable.com.

55. Tyler Vaught and Meghann Elrhoul, "The Power of Creators on Twitter," *Blog, Twitter,* June 21, 2018, https://blog.twitter.com.

56. "China Blocks Twitch Game-Streaming Service," *BBC News,* September 21, 2018, https://www.bbc.com.

57. Matt Weinberger, "Amazon's $970 Million Purchase of Twitch Makes So Much Sense Now: It's All about the Cloud," *Business Insider,* March 16, 2016, https://www.businessinsider.com.

58. Mark R Johnson and Jamie Woodcock, "'It's Like the Gold Rush': The Lives and Careers of Professional Video Game Streamers on Twitch.tv," *Information, Communication & Society* 22, no. 3 (February 2019): 336–51.

59. Kevin Webb, "Ninja's Move to Mixer Brought More Streamers to Microsoft's Platform—but Not More Viewers," *Business Insider,* October 5, 2019, https://www.businessinsider.com.

60. Cheetah Mobile, "Cheetah Mobile Responds to Recent Allegations," October 27, 2017, http://ir.cmcm.com.

61. Eva Yoo, "China's Top Social Apps All Owe Thanks to Live Streaming," *Technode,* January 26, 2017, http://technode.com.

62. Chijixianyu, "Banshu beidiaocha de zhubo doushi benke yishang xueli [Half of the livestreamers being surveyed hold bachelor degrees or above]," *Zhibobang,* January 9, 2018, p. 1.

63. Frank Lavin, "China's Live-Streaming Industry Is Booming—Here's How It Works," *Forbes,* June 19, 2018, https://www.forbes.com.

64. QQ News. "Dianjing zhubo diyi tidui nianshouru yiguo qianwan, wanghong baiwan qibu [The first annual revenue of the gaming team has over ten million dollars]," *QQ News,* June 05, 2017, https://news.qq.com. Netease, "Zhubo shouru paihangbang, Feng Timo yueru 157 wan cheng zhibo yijie [Revenue ranking of livestreamers: Feng Timo made 1.57 million monthly, becoming number 1 of livestreaming]," March 31, 2018, https://3g.163.com.

65. Chijixianyu, "Banshu beidiaocha de zhubo doushi benke yishang xueli [Half of the livestreamers being surveyed hold bachelor degrees or above]," 1.

66. Chijixianyu, "Banshu beidiaocha de zhubo doushi benke yishang xueli [Half of the livestreamers being surveyed hold bachelor degrees or above]," 11–13.

67. Josh Horwitz, "China's Crackdown on the Country's Livestreaming Craze Is Getting More Intense," *Quartz,* June 23, 2017, https://qz.com.

68. Tom Phillips, "Gone Bananas: China Bans 'Erotic' Eating of the Fruit on Live Streams," *The Guardian,* May 9, 2016, https://www.theguardian.com.

69. Xinhua, "Live Streaming Revenue Exceeds 30b Yuan in China in 2017," *The State Council, The People's Republic of China*, January 21, 2018, http://english.gov.cn.

70. Pang-Chieh Ho, "China Removes 370 Live-Streaming Apps, Cracks Down on Online Games," *Technode*, April 18, 2018, https://technode.com.

71. Pang-Chieh Ho, "China Removes 370 Live-Streaming Apps, Cracks Down on Online Games," 1.

72. Michelle Wong, "Cover Up! Chinese Female Live-Stream Performers Banned from Wearing Skimpy Clothes," *South China Morning Post*, January 30, 2019, https://www.msn.com.

73. Yu Su, "Duojia zhibo pingtai caiyuan daobi, hangye 'handongqi' mianlin qiusheng kunjing [Many livestreaming platforms are laying off or closing; the industry is facing "the winter and struggle to survive]," *Qiaobao Wang*, December 15, 2018, http://www.uschinapress.com.

74. Yu Su, "Duojia zhibo pingtai caiyuan daobi, hangye 'handongqi' mianlin qiusheng kunjing," 1

75. "Interview with Bigo: How a Chinese Live Streaming Service Successfully Replicated Itself in Southeast Asia Aarkets," *KrASIA*, June 6, 2018, https://kr-asia.com.

76. Chris Donkin, "WeChat Pay Chiefs Unveil Global Expansion Strategy," *Mobile World Live*, March 2019, https://www.mobileworldlive.com.

77. Jon Russell, "Alibaba Doubles Down on Lazada with Fresh $2B Investment and New CEO," *Techcrunch*, March 1, 2018, https://techcrunch.com.

78. Haiqing Yu, "China's 'Social+' Approach to Soft Power," *East Asia Forum*, June 27, 2019, https://www.eastasiaforum.org.

79. Tracey Xiang, "Virtual Gifts Are Still the Top Earner in China's Live Video Streaming Market," *Technode*, May 5, 2016, https://technode.com.

80. Ramin Shokrizade, "The Top F2P Monetization Tricks," *Gamasutra*, June 26, 2013, http://www.gamasutra.com.

81. Shokrizade, "The Top F2P Monetization Tricks," 1.

82. Douyu, "Douyu shangcheng shangxin la; dingzhi haoli dengni na [Douyu Mall has been online: Customized gifts are waiting for you]," May 28, 2017, https://www.douyu.com.

83. Sohu, "Wall Street Modern News WeChat Public account Shuangshiyi ri ru 1.7 yi. Zuilihai taobao wanghong dianzhu zhengzai choubei meiguo shangshi [Making 170 million daily at Double Eleven Festival: The best Taobao influencer is preparing for IPO in the U.S.]," November 16, 2018, http://www.sohu.com.

84. Changfan Zhou, "Zhibo zhege bianliang huigei dianshang shijie dailai shenme [What will livestreaming bring to e-commerce]," *36Kr*, June 3, 2016, https://36kr.com.

85. Liebaoquanqiuzhiku, "BAT zhibo lingyu zhanshu touxi, kan zhepian guoneiwai zhibo hangye zuiquan baogao [To know BAT's strategies in livestreaming, read this report about domestic and international livestreaming industries]," September 10, 2016, http://www. tmtpost.com.

86. Liebaoquanqiuzhiku, "BAT zhibo," 1.

87. Liebaoquanqiuzhiku, "BAT zhibo," 1. Binansuoxiaozi, "Huya zhibo fumei IPO, shi tengxun geile ta shangshi de yongqi [Huya went IPO in the U.S. does Tencent give it courage to do so]," April 10, 2018, https://www.huxiu.com.

88. Postigo, "The Socio-Technical Architecture of Digital Labor," 346.

89. Liebaoquanqiuzhiku, "BAT zhibo," 1.

90. Hexunwang Cailianshe, "Zhifubao gongneng shangxian, hangye cuisheng qianyi shizhi gongsi [Alipay's livestreaming function is going to be online: The industry might create billion-level companies]," *Ebrun*, September 10, 2016, http://www.ebrun.com.

91. Xiao Lu, "Baidu zhuanxing rengong zhineng [Baidu is pivoting to artificial intelligence platform]," *Sina*, September 22, 2018, http://finance.sina.com.cn.

92. Liebaoquanqiuzhiku, "BAT zhibo," 1.

93. Luochao pindao, "YY he xiaomi zhibo qianshou zhibo hangye mataixiaoying jiang jinyibu zengqiang [YY and Xiaomi Live have successfully held hands! The Matthew Effect in livestreaming industry is increasing further]," November 14, 2018, https://36kr.com.

94. "Zhang Yiming: Jinri toutiao dazao quanqiu zuida neirong shengtai. Qixia chuangzuozhe guoyi [Zhang Yiming: Today's Headline is developing the world largest neirong shengtai, having more than 100 million content creators]," *Xihua News*, November 23, 2017, http:// www.xinhuanet.com.

95. "Xigua shipin zhong chongzhi zuanshi de juti buzhouYesky [How to buy virtual diamond on Xigua video]," *Yesky*, May 23, 2018, http://mydown.yesky.com.

96. Henry Jenkins, Mizuko Ito, and danah boyd, *Participatory Culture in a Networked Era: A Conversation on Youth, Learning, Commerce, and Politics* (Cambridge, UK: Polity Press, 2015).

97. Stephen J. Hartnett, Lisa B. Keranen, and Donovan Conley, *Imagining China: Rhetorics of Nationalism in an Age of Globalization* (East Lansing, MI: Michigan State University Press, 2017).

98. Guobin Yang, "The Internet and the Rise of a Transnational Chinese Cultural Sphere," *Media, Culture & Society* 25, no. 4 (July 2003): 469–90.

99. William A. Callahan, *China Dreams: 20 Visions of the Future* (Oxford, UK: Oxford University Press, 2013).

This Is Not How a US President Should Behave

Trump, Twitter, and North Korea in Rhetorical Constructions of US–China Relations

Michelle Murray Yang

President Donald Trump appeared genuinely wowed by his November 2017 state visit to China. During his visit, Trump marveled at the grandeur of the Forbidden City, was honored by an opera performance at the Pavilion of Pleasant Sounds, and dined on sumptuous dishes at a state banquet held in his honor. He described the visit as "absolutely terrific" during his speech at the Great Hall of the People.[1] The president's glowing assessment of his time in China translated into positive discourse on controversial topics. Even on historically contentious issues in US-Sino relations such as North Korea, the US president adopted a more conciliatory tone. Trump asked President Xi to "act faster and more effectively" in his dealings with North Korea. He expressed faith in the Chinese president, reassuring listeners that if Xi "works on it [North Korea] hard, it will happen. There is no doubt about it."[2] Trump expressed a similar sentiment on Twitter, his preferred communication channel. Just days after his visit to China, he tweeted, "President Xi of China has stated that he is upping the sanctions against #NoKo. Said he wants them to denuclearize. Progress is being made."[3]

However, Trump's optimistic rhetoric regarding China would not last. In December 2017, the president tweeted that China was "caught RED HANDED" allowing oil to be transported to North Korea.[4] A South Korean newspaper reported that US forces had apprehended Chinese ships transporting oil to North Korean vessels. According to the report, the ships were suspected of making thirty oil deliveries since October 2017. The Chinese foreign ministry denied the accusations, describing them as "hyped-up media reports."[5] However, South Korean officials divulged that they had captured a Hong Kong vessel that was suspected of transporting "600 tons of refined petroleum to North Korea" in late November,[6] violating United Nations Security Council sanctions designed to punish North Korea for its nuclear weapons and ballistic missile program. In response, the CPC mouthpiece, *Global Times*, disputed the veracity of South Korean and US satellite imagery and criticized the US president for falsely accusing China "before the truth was clarified."[7] Not unlike Trump, the CPC has adopted this strategy of parrying unwelcome facts by simply claiming they are false. Thus admonishing Trump while mimicking one of his central strategies of deflection, the *Global Times* declared, "This is not how a U.S. president should behave."[8]

This project analyzes the complicated role of North Korea in US–China relations. It does so by analyzing President Trump's Twitter discourse concerning the intersection between US–China relations and North Korea from the 2016 US presidential campaign through the second year of his presidency. A rhetorical approach is beneficial for this endeavor as it allows scholars to examine "discourse microscopically—at the level of the sentence, phrase, word, and syllable."[9] I argue that Trump's Twitter discourse illustrates how Cold War characterizations of North Korea continue to be revived, revised, and re-appropriated in US political discourse. In turn, Trump's Twitter rhetoric perpetuates the outdated assumption that China can and should solve problems associated with North Korea. Such rhetoric significantly constrains ways of seeing and understanding North Korea and its role in US–China relations. Additionally, it is important for scholars, political leaders, journalists, and citizens to carefully reconsider the role of Twitter in diplomacy, as the platform becomes an increasingly important tool for articulating and circulating transnational rhetoric regarding the relationships between the United States, China, and North Korea.

For the international community, North Korea poses complex challenges encompassing competing interests and conflicting fears. While the United States, South Korea, and Japan insist on North Korea's denuclearization, Russia and China are wary of measures that may result in the dissolution of Kim Jong Un's regime.[10] In turn, North Korea views its nuclear proliferation program as non-negotiable, with Kim claiming North Korea needs nuclear weapons in order to safeguard itself from a possible invasion by the United States.[11] Despite heightened UN sanctions and Trump's blustery warnings, North Korea has made significant advances in its nuclear capabilities, including conducting its sixth nuclear weapons test and its first intercontinental ballistic missiles test in 2017.[12] During the first year of Trump's presidency, North Korea conducted over a dozen missile tests; then in early August 2017, North Korea threatened to strike Guam.[13] Late in November 2017, North Korea announced it had successfully developed an intercontinental ballistic missile with nuclear capabilities that could hit the continental United States.[14] Despite Trump's threats, then, North Korea has continued to make steady progress in expanding its nuclear capabilities.

Trump and Kim have done little to de-escalate tensions in East Asia. The leaders have infamously engaged in an escalating war of words.[15] For Trump, Twitter has been the site of some of his most heated rhetoric regarding North Korea, including ridiculing Kim, calling him "little rocket man."[16] While John Delury likens Trump and Kim to "professional wrestlers who go round after round, with plenty of trash talk . . . but never really come to blows," he warns we must "remember that these two characters are commanders in chief of real armies." He concludes, "In these conditions of mutual hostility and ignorance, things could go wrong, fast."[17] While some may dismiss Trump's Twitter discourse as mere bluster, the president's tweets can have significant implications for US foreign relations in East Asia and across the globe. In this regard, it is terrifying to think that the future of US–China relations hinges in part on dueling insults getting hurled across Twitter.

North Korea is a particularly contentious issue in US–China relations. US politicians and journalists routinely claim China can end the threat posed by North Korea. For instance, former CIA officer Craig Osth asserts, "Certainly China can end this threat [North Korea] by working with the U.S., South Korea and Japan. And certainly China will not."[18] US political leaders and journalists often describe China as North Korea's "enabler."[19] Despite increasing frustration with North Korea's contentious behavior and lack of economic reform, China retains diplomatic and economic ties to the country. China is North Korea's largest foreign source of food, fuel, and trading partnerships.[20] However, Chinese leaders dispute claims that they can significantly influence Kim's government. Although China has enforced UN economic sanctions against North Korean foreign currency sources, it rejects actions that could topple Kim's regime. Fearful of a possible refugee crisis and losing its barrier to South Korea and the US troops stationed there, Chinese leaders have no interest in supporting measures that may result in the dissolution of Kim's government.[21]

This study begins by discussing the limitations of Twitter and examining President Trump's unique Twitter style. It proceeds with an analysis of the president's Twitter discourse concerning the role of North Korea in US-Sino relations. Finally, this chapter concludes by examining the implications of President Trump's Twitter discourse and offering alternative actions that could help combat the potential negative consequences of this rhetoric.

Trump and Twitter: The Limitations of Social Media Platforms in Facilitating Political Discourse

Twitter has become an increasingly important tool for political leaders and political parties. As a result, scholars have engaged in a plethora of research examining Twitter's role in politics and political communication.[22] Researchers have examined whether and to what extent Twitter can be used to measure public opinion and predict election results.[23] Others have illustrated how Twitter use during conventions and debates evolves as these events unfold and whether they are accompanied by controversy.[24] John Parmelee and Shannon Bichard contend that political candidates, parties, and representatives use the platform to draw attention, galvanize activists, and circumvent the press.[25] Since 2008, Twitter has become increasingly important in US presidential campaigns. Presidential campaign officials use Twitter to indirectly and directly influence journalists.[26] The degree of autonomy granted to staffers and candidates to tweet on behalf of the campaign is an important factor in both engaging and influencing discourse both on and off the platform. Daniel Kreiss argues that digital campaign staffers with greater autonomy on Twitter have more flexibility in responding to and shaping emerging discourse and controversy.[27] Falling within this emerging critical literature on Twitter as a platform of political communication, I turn to the 2016 US presidential campaign and President Trump's subsequent first two years in office to examine how Trump has used Twitter to inject his "America First" rhetoric into the contested US–China relationship.

As the first US president to have a Twitter account, President Obama set expectations for presidential Twitter use. Obama's 2008 presidential campaign skillfully used Twitter and other social media platforms to engage young voters. Upon assuming the office of the presidency, Obama tweeted via the official account @POTUS. Through this account, President Obama and his staff kept followers apprised of important domestic and international developments, significant milestones of his presidency, and daily happenings in the White House. In the wake of Obama's 2011 Twitter Town Hall, more US politicians began using the platform "and the press took to using the tweets as hooks for stories."[28] Throughout the Obama years, Twitter served as an extension of Obama's signature rhetorical style, reaching broad audience while modeling prudence, civility, and a sense of hope.

As both a presidential candidate and a sitting US president, Trump refused to conform to the expectations of presidential Twitter activity forged by the Obama administration. Although Trump claimed he would give up Twitter after becoming president, he continued to tweet from his personal account @realDonaldTrump. Instead of having his staff manage the majority of the account's activity, President Trump has retained primary control over the account. While White House social media director Dan Scavino creates approximately "half of the president's tweets," Trump is responsible for the remainder of the account's activity.[29] Scavino has been collaborating with the president on his tweets since 2015. He checks the spelling and grammar of the messages in addition to incorporating specific examples and adding hashtags.[30] However, Trump is responsible for forging his own tweeting style, which includes using emotion-laced capitalization, grammar-challenged punctuation, and name-calling.[31]

President Trump's use of Twitter is unprecedented to say the least in terms of its highly personal nature. Trump has even tweeted about his communication style, stating "my use of social media is not Presidential—it's MODERN DAY Presidential."[32] In addition to issuing provocative tweets, Trump has personally used his account to bestow and retract favor by following, unfollowing, and retweeting accounts. The president uses Twitter to settle perceived scores, respond to personal slights, insult his opponents, challenge his critics, rally his supporters, and detract attention from events and issues unfavorable to himself and his presidency. Twitter affords Trump a means to respond to, and potentially shape, media coverage of his administration in real time. The platform allows the president "to manhandle the public's attention, constantly yanking the media spotlight back on himself whenever it starts to wander."[33] Despite the stark differences in content and style between Obama's and Trump's tweeting styles, both presidents have used Twitter to bypass "the so-called filter of the press."[34] Seemingly a reflection of the president himself, Trump's Twitter discourse is brash, unconventional, and unfiltered.

Although Twitter has enabled political leaders to broaden their reach, the platform has also been criticized for undermining the tenets of democratic civil discourse. While some have praised Twitter for being a potentially useful tool of social change, others have raised concerns about the platform's ability to perpetuate harassment, incivility, and misinformation.[35] As a range of scholars have noted, Twitter is characterized by simplicity, impulsivity, and incivility. The platform's design requires users to limit their tweets to brief statements, and even with Twitter's increase of the character limit from 140 to 280 characters in 2017, users are still restricted in terms of the length of their posts, making it difficult to imbue discussions of weighty matters like politics, race, and immigration with substance and depth.[36] In turn, Twitter's short character limit and ease of uploading tweets requires little effort from the platform's users. As a result, Twitter fails to encourage users to reflect on and consider the potential consequences of their tweets before posting them. "Tweeting is, in short, a highly impulsive activity, something that one can do easily," one critics notes, "even if one has nothing considered or important to say."[37] Moreover, Twitter encourages incivility by its informality and depersonalization of communication. Incorrect grammar and punctuation plague Twitter as users quickly create instantaneously shared messages. Twitter also depersonalizes communication, as it does not encourage users to "consider how their interactions will affect others."[38] Scholars have therefore found that frequent Twitter users gravitate toward aggressive and negative messages.[39] Twitter, in short, is a machine of grievances, the very opposite of considered political communication.

Donald Trump's tweets exemplify Twitter's negative characteristics. In a study of Trump's Twitter discourse from October 2015 to May 2016, Zachary Crockett found his tweets were overwhelmingly characterized by repetitive simple words.[40] For example, Trump heavily relies on monosyllabic words like "bad" and "sad."[41] His tweets are typically negative as he frequently disparages fellow politicians, corporations, foreign leaders, and private citizens.[42] The "failing *New York Times*," "crooked Hillary," and "uneducated Lebron James" are just a few of his targets.[43] Crockett also noted that Trump refuses to abide by commonly accepted rules of capitalization and grammar. Trump often tweets in all capital letters, capitalizing words that are not usually capitalized, and he uses multiple exclamation points.[44] By employing unconventional capitalization and punctuation style, Trump heightens the "emotional impact" of his negative messages.[45]

Trump did not alter his Twitter style after he was elected president. In an administration derided for issuing contradictory statements and policies, Trump's Twitter style has been remarkably consistent. Critics have warned the president's blustery, impulsive tweets can have significant negative implications for US domestic and foreign policy. For example, critics have derided Trump for emboldening white nationalists and racists through his racially charged tweets.[46] Others claim the president's Twitter habit is a monumental liability for US foreign policy and warn of the potential devastating consequences of Trump's tweets targeting foreign nations and their leaders.[47] As Krishnadev Calamur explains, when a president engages in "spontaneous interactions," "the greater the chances for the dreaded gaffe, which is why the president's Twitter feed has been known to cause heartburn among U.S. national-security professionals."[48] In October 2017, Trump tweeted that then secretary of state Rex Tillerson was "wasting his time trying to negotiate with Little Rocket Man" and advised, "Save your energy Rex, we'll do what has to be done."[49] The president's "public dismissal of diplomacy with North Korea, and of his secretary of state, Rex Tillerson, further raised fears he intended to go to war."[50] More recently, critics have lambasted Trump for tweeting that Iranian President Rouhani should "NEVER, EVER THREATEN THE UNITED STATES AGAIN OR YOU WILL SUFFER CONSEQUENCES THE LIKES OF WHICH FEW THROUGHOUT HISTORY HAVE EVER SUFFERED BEFORE."[51] Such derisive and unpredictable discourse risks escalating tensions, inciting violence, and derailing diplomatic efforts to resolve disputes between the United States and foreign nations.

A Rogue Nation and a Menacing Problem: President Trump's Portrayal of North Korea

Throughout his presidential campaign and during the first year and a half of his presidency, Trump described North Korea as a dangerous "problem" that could only be solved through extreme measures. Responding to reports in December 2017 that China allowed oil shipments to reach North Korea, thereby violating U.N. sanctions, President Trump tweeted "there will never be a friendly solution to the North Korea problem if this continues to happen."[52] According to the president, North Korea was not a sovereign nation but a problem in need of a solution. It is important to note that casting North Korea as a problem is not a new phenomenon in US presidential discourse. Since the establishment of the People's Democratic Republic of Korea in 1948, US presidents have struggled to address the challenges posed by North Korea. Many presidents have depicted North Korea in negative terms. President Bush's declaration that North Korea was part of an "Axis of Evil" during his 2002 State of the Union address is perhaps the most well-known example. Describing North Korea as evil was "purposely chosen to rule out any diplomatic effort, famously summarized by Dick Cheney: 'You do not negotiate with evil. You destroy evil.'"[53] In this regard, Trump's rhetoric about North Korea reprises longstanding Cold War themes and images.

Nonetheless, Trump's negative depictions of North Korea diverge from his predecessors in terms of their extreme nature. Trump repeatedly used ad hominem attacks in his Twitter discourse to target North Korea and Kim Jong Un. Ad hominem is an argumentative fallacy in which a speaker attacks a person's character instead of her or his argumentative position. For instance, Trump labeled North Korea as a "rogue nation" and described Kim as a "madman."[54] Most notably, the president repeatedly denigrated Kim by referring to him as "rocket man." In September 2017, Trump tweeted "I spoke with President Moon of South Korea last night. Asked him how Rocket Man is doing. Long gas lines forming in North Korea. Too bad!"[55] The president's use of negative tone and ad hominem attacks in his tweets concerning North Korea and Kim share similarities with his rhetorical attacks on perceived domestic foes. When confronted with criticism or lack of support from a domestic actor, such as fellow politicians, celebrities, and even private citizens, Trump often crafts negative tweets that include ad hominem attacks to criticize opponents. By using such negative discourse, the president casts challengers' criticism as unfounded, challenges their credibility, and questions their intelligence. In so doing, Trump positions himself as superior to his critics through his willingness to "hit back hard." Scholars have cited such discourse as evidence of Trump's reliance on "toxic masculinity." For example, William Liu explains how toxic masculinity encompasses the "idea that men have to be the alpha male in all situations and that they're not supposed to be emotional or affectionate."[56] According to Liu, "Some men express anger and rage because those are the only normalized forms of emotions for them."57 Trump's performance of masculinity is problematic as it normalizes toxic masculinity and "gives voice to not only misogyny and sexism but also racism."[58]

Along with his troubling reliance on ad hominem attacks, Trump is also a frequent user of the rhetorical fallacy of argumentum ad baculum, wherein a speaker uses threats of force to coerce someone to accept her or his position. During the early part of his presidency, Trump repeatedly used ad baculum arguments to threaten North Korea's existence and the survival of Kim's regime. In his Twitter tirades, the president regularly used negative, declarative statements to imbue his claims and threats with a sense of certainty. For example, Trump declared, "The U.S. has been talking to North Korea, and paying them extortion money, for 25 years.

Talking is not the answer."[59] The president's threats against North Korea varied in their specificity as some were more pointed than others. However, they shared the commonality of threatening the use of military force against North Korea. In September 2017, the president threatened, "They [North Korea] won't be around much longer."[60] In a statement to reporters at his Bedminster golf club after news broke that North Korea had developed the capability to affix nuclear warheads to missiles, Trump declared North Korea should not threaten the United States, warning if they fail to stop their provocations, "They will be met with fire and the fury like the world has never seen."[61] The president combined an ad hominem attack against North Korea's leader with a vague ad baculum threat in September 2017 when he tweeted "Kim Jong Un of North Korea, who is obviously a madman who doesn't mind starving or killing his people, will be tested like never before."[62] Through his use of ad hominem and ad baculum fallacies, Trump amplifies and extends previous presidents' negative characterizations of North Korea to dangerous extremes.

In addition to heightening Trump's toxic masculinity, such discourse also portrays the president as an "uncontrollable leader." Jennifer Mercieca has argued that Trump has used argumentative fallacies to cultivate a persona of an "uncontrollable leader."[63] This persona "rejects restraints: he speaks of not being constrained by his party, media, other candidates, political correctness, facts—anything, really."[64] Demagogues often use argumentative fallacies such as ad hominem and ad baculum. Categorizing Trump as a demagogue, Mercieca explains he is "a leader who capitalizes on popular prejudices, makes false claims and promises, and uses arguments based on emotion rather than reason."[65]

Trump's uncontrollable leadership is evidenced by his unpredictable foreign policy. Nikki Haley, US ambassador to the United Nations, credited President Trump's unpredictability with pressuring China to support "tougher" sanctions on North Korea. Haley said she would tell foreign leaders, "I can't promise you that President Trump won't use the military," and "I can't promise that there won't be more forceful actions, so why can't we do this and see if we can start to cut the revenue in North Korea?"[66] CNN reporter Laura Koran noted the parallels between Trump's unpredictable approach and the "'mad man theory' developed by Henry Kissinger and Richard Nixon in the 1970s, with then-President Nixon portraying himself as unstable to confuse U.S. adversaries."[67] Trump's use of argumentative fallacies conveys he is unwilling to be controlled or constrained by precedent, protocol, or political correctness. While this persona may resonate with the president's base, it has generated contradictory consequences, as "America's adversaries seem far less destabilized by Trump than do America's allies."[68]

Deflecting Responsibility for the North Korean "Problem": Trump's Portrayal of China

While Trump portrayed North Korea as a dangerous menace, he claimed one nation had the power to solve this problem. During his presidential campaign and the early part of his presidency, Trump claimed China could "easily solve North Korea" but selfishly chose not to accomplish this.[69] The president repeatedly asserted China had complete control over its unpredictable neighbor. In April 2017, Trump tweeted that "China is very much the economic lifeline to North Korea so, while nothing is easy, if they want to solve the North Korean problem, they will."[70] According to the president, China was the only reason North Korea continued to survive. US presidents have long claimed China can and should do more to address the North Korea "problem." Past administrations have tried to press China to exert economic and political pressure on North Korea. As reporter Robin Wright explains, "Since the 1953 truce in the Korean War, long and tortuous negotiations—on any issue—have not produced a single enduring agreement."[71] According to President Trump, the North Korean problem persists due to both China's reluctance to act and previous US presidents' failed policies. In July 2017, Trump tweeted he was "very disappointed in China."[72] "Our foolish past leaders have allowed them to make hundreds of billions of dollars a year in trade, yet . . . they do NOTHING for us with North Korea, just talk. We will no longer allow this to continue."[73] According to Trump, part of previous presidents' failings involved making bad "deals" with China. The president claimed China owed the United States to solve the North Korea problem because of the unfair benefits it reaped through its trade practices. This discourse parallels Trump's penchant for scapegoating domestic opponents. The president often "uses negative other-presentation to shift blame to the previous administration and the mainstream media, while presenting himself positively."[74] In the case of the North Korean "problem," Trump places the blame on China and past US presidents. By characterizing China as able but unwilling to solve the North Korea problem, Trump portrays China as an untrustworthy adversary. Claiming China has done "nothing" to meaningfully address North Korea's provocations, Trump reduces the complexity of US-Sino relations. Instead of acknowledging that North Korea is one issue in an array of subjects that links the United States and China, the president obscures the importance and mutually beneficial nature of the relationship. By so doing, Trump promotes a one-dimensional and transactional view in which he assumes China can and should do his bidding.

Trump also tried to exacerbate the fracture between North Korea and China in order to persuade Chinese leaders to take a tougher approach to North Korea. The president claimed North Korea was "a great threat and embarrassment to China."[75] Kim's repeated missile tests were causing China to lose face. However, Trump's strategy of emphasizing how North Korea has disrespected China can appear hypocritical given his past abrasive rhetoric toward China and Chinese leaders. During the 2016 US presidential campaign, he accused China of raping the United States due to its currency manipulation and unfair trading practices. At a campaign rally in Indiana, Trump thundered that the United States "can't continue to allow China to rape our country, and that's what they're doing. It's the greatest theft in the history of the world."[76] The president tried to use Chinese leaders' growing impatience with North Korea's provocations to his advantage. Some of North Korea's provocations did appear timed to embarrass China and Chinese.[77] However, Trump's penchant for using abusive, vulgar rhetoric weakens the credibility of his allegations against North Korea.

Trump's claim that China enjoys total control over North Korea is rife with contradictions. For if China had absolute control over its unruly neighbor, it would be unlikely North Korea would undertake what Trump himself deemed "disrespectful" actions. It is true that China could decimate North Korea economically given that China accounts for over ninety percent of the country's trade, yet Trump overlooks the significant constraints China faces in its dealings with North Korea. Most importantly, Chinese leaders are wary of taking action that could jeopardize Kim's regime, as a collapse would trigger a refugee crisis spilling over into China's borders.[78] Even if China were to economically destroy the Kim regime, such action does not ensure North Korea will denuclearize, as North Korea views nuclear weapons as fundamental to its survival.[79] For example, North Korean leaders have "described the diplomatic efforts to persuade Colonel Gadhafi to give up his arsenal of unconventional weapons as an invasion tactic."[80] They are also "convinced that the nuclear deterrence guarantees the survival of the regime in the eventuality of an internal revolt, as happened in Libya."[81] Although studies have found that sanctions can incite "small policy changes," they "cannot persuade a government to sign its own death warrant."[82] Trump also overlooks Chinese leaders' previous attempts to punish North Korea through instituting sanctions and limiting trade. These actions have often "backfired, with North Korea instead increasing its provocations, often timed to embarrass Beijing."[83] By dismissing the formidable constraints China faces in its relationship with North Korea, Trump grossly oversimplifies the complexity of the situation, thereby failing to move the nations' negotiations forward in meaningful ways.

Trump's Twitter Discourse Cools: The President's Tweets as an Emotional Barometer

Trump's fiery Twitter rhetoric concerning North Korea began to cool in conjunction with conciliatory gestures made by Kim's regime. North Korea began to take actions that appeared designed to reduce tensions on the Korean peninsula beginning in early 2018, when Kim went on a charm offensive leading up to the 2018 Winter Olympics in Pyeong Chang. In January 2018 Kim announced that North Korea might participate in the Winter Olympics. Twenty-two athletes would travel to Pyeong Chang to represent North Korea at the games. Kim's sister, Kim Yo Jong, attended the Olympics as a representative of her brother. As a result, she became the first member of Kim's family to visit South Korea since 1953. While visiting South Korea, she conveyed an invitation for South Korean president Moon Jae-in to visit North Korea. Then, during a meeting between South and North Korean officials in Pyongyang on March 7, 2018, a North Korean official expressed Kim's willingness to discuss the future of his nuclear weapons program with the United States. The official also conveyed that Kim was willing to halt missile and nuclear tests during dialogue with the United States. Two days later, Trump accepted Kim's invitation to meet. In late April 2018, North Korea announced it had halted long-range missile and nuclear tests. Officials also stated their intention to close the country's nuclear test site. Buoyed by these developments, Trump tweeted "big progress!" "This is very good news for North Korea and the World."[84] Then, in advance of Trump and Kim's meeting, North Korea released three American prisoners. At this point, it seemed the United States, China, and North Korea were enjoying a thaw in relations.

Trump's Twitter discourse can be understood as an emotional barometer for his views on North Korea and US–China relations. The substance and tone of his tweets show how supportive the president believes North Korea and China have been of his agenda. When Trump views North Korea's and China's actions and discourse unfavorably, he uses negative, declarative statements, inflammatory language, and argumentative fallacies to threaten his perceived opponents. In contrast, the president adorns his tweets with glowing adjectives praising Chinese and North Korean leaders as "helpful," "smart," and "gracious" when he views their rhetoric and actions as favorable.[85] For example, in a March 2018 tweet, Trump reported how President Xi expressed his appreciation that the United States "is working to solve the problem [North Korea] diplomatically rather than going with the ominous alternative." Trump concluded, "China continues to be helpful!"[86] Disparaging nicknames like "Rocket Man" were then replaced by proper names. Instead of negative declarative statements, the president relied on open-ended statements, such as the phrase "we'll see." For example, after receiving a positive message from Kim expressing his desire to hold the summit after Trump canceled the meeting, the president tweeted, "Very good news to receive the warm and productive statement from North Korea."[87] The president continued, "We will soon see where it will lead, hopefully to long and enduring prosperity and peace. Only time (and talent) will tell!"[88]

Trump uses the phrase "we'll see" to accomplish several different aims. The president has used the phrase to deflect from a question he does not want to answer, issue threats, and tease journalists.[89] Additionally, Trump may use the phrase "because he doesn't have an answer. It may be because he's not sure he understands the question or a host of other reasons."[90] According to David Cay Johnston, using "we'll see" places "him in a position of power and it destabilizes your thinking."[91] As political critic Kathleen Hall Jamieson explains, rather than communicating projections and being responsible for those projections, Trump is "opening the possibility that there are a range of possibilities not anticipated for which he does not want to be held accountable."[92] By using open-ended statements like "we'll see" in his tweets, Trump defers responsibility, avoids providing specific policy details, and lowers expectations for his decisions and actions.

Conclusion: The Rhetorical Implications of President Trump's Twitter Discourse

Trump's Twitter discourse concerning North Korea and China is problematic as it promotes an outdated Cold War mentality that casts North Korea as an evil, rogue state. It is true North Korea commits severe human rights abuses and its development of nuclear capabilities is troubling. However, depicting North Korea as evil dismisses the possibility of dialogue as it is impossible to reason with "evil" entities.[93] The president's claims that China has complete control over North Korea evoke Cold War narratives, reprising the old canard that the Soviet Union controlled Chinese Communists. China's participation in the Korean War appeared to support the theory that the People's Republic of China "was an activist member of the Soviet bloc, propagating a renegade ideology, exercising domestic tyranny, and launching external military aggression."[94] By declaring that China controls North Korea, Trump oversimplifies the complexity of the situation and ignores the constraints China faces in its relationship with North Korea. In so doing, the president precludes gaining deeper insight into and understanding of the nations' relationship.

Lastly, Trump fails to recognize the United States' role in creating the North Korean "problem." US political leaders have historically deflected attention from "America's Cold War in literally giving birth to that 'problem' in the first place."[95] By scapegoating foreign adversaries for US political, economic, and military problems, US leaders "protect Americans from understanding the glaring domestic policy failures underpinning their economic woes."[96] Placing the tensions plaguing Asia squarely on North Korea allows Trump, like presidents who preceded him, to ignore the United States' Cold War role in creating this "problem." As a result, such discourse deflects responsibility from the United States' Cold War actions. In short, Trump's Twitter discourse promotes a Cold War mentality that impedes understanding, deflects attention from the United States' Cold War role, oversimplifies North Korea and its relationship with China, and relies on inflammatory and fallacious rhetoric that escalates tensions and risks igniting conflict.

Interestingly, Trump credited his tough rhetoric for paving the way for the 2018 Singapore Summit. "I think without the rhetoric we wouldn't have been here," said Trump after the summit. The president disparaged previous administrations' "policy of silence," for refusing to respond when opponents "said something very bad and very threatening and horrible."[97] "That's not the answer," declared Trump.[98] While the president admitted he "hated to do it" and at times "felt foolish doing it," he resolutely asserted "we had no choice" to use such tough rhetoric.[99] Trump's linking of progress with North Korea to his blistering rhetoric is problematic as it evinces a superficial and dangerous approach to diplomacy. The president fails to consider alternative reasons for Kim's willingness to engage with Trump. North Korea has previously promised to "denuclearize" in exchange for aid and sanctions relief while simultaneously continuing to develop its nuclear weapons program.[100] For example, in 2008 North Korean officials destroyed a cooling tower that was part of the Yongbyon nuclear plant. However, it was later revealed several years later "that North Korea had been building a huge uranium-enrichment facility all the while, giving it another source of fissile material."[101] Multiple efforts to halt North Korea's nuclear weapons program have ended in failure. North Korea's charm offenses are typically short lived and often fail to translate into meaningful change in terms of its nuclear weapons program. Indeed, it is highly unlikely North Korea will ever agree to denuclearize, as Kim, like his predecessors, views nuclear weapons as indispensable to North Korea's survival.[102]

Still, the president's acrimonious rhetoric dissipated during the winter of 2017, as Chairman Kim bowed to economic and military pressure, deemed his nuclear program "complete," sent a delegation to the Winter Olympics, and invited Trump to meet with him.[103] President Trump credited his skill in developing a personal relationship with Kim for the historic Singapore Summit in 2018. He "began framing the diplomatic effort to denuclearize North Korea in far more personal, triumphalist terms, as something he alone could accomplish because of his dealmaking savvy and chemistry with Kim."[104] Establishing a diplomacy rooted on personal relationships, Trump has repeatedly touted his close relationship with Chairman Kim, revealing the leaders exchange warm letters.[105]

However, cracks in the façade of Kim and Trump's diplomatic friendship emerged as subsequent meetings in Vietnam and North Korea failed to produce substantive progress. Both North Korea and the United States accused each other of failing to uphold the agreements reached at the June 2018 summit. Less than a month after the summit, North Korea criticized US officials for making "gangster-like" demands in their subsequent negotiations.[106] North Korean officials also failed to attend a meeting concerning the repatriation of American remains from the Korean War with US counterparts at a Korean border village. In August 2018, North Korea's Foreign Ministry issued a statement deriding the United States for "inciting international sanctions and pressure against [North Korea]," even after the country had repatriated US service members' remains and implemented "such practical denuclearization steps as discontinuing nuclear test and ICBM testfire."[107] US national security adviser John Bolton expressed frustration over the lack of progress, stating "We're waiting for the North Koreans to begin the process of denuclearization, which they committed to in Singapore and which they've not yet done."[108] Additionally, tensions escalated as North Korea launched a series of short-range ballistic missiles in 2019 and Trump once again warned of possible US military action and disparaged Kim as "Rocket Man" in his tweets.[109] In December 2019, the North Korean UN ambassador revealed he was not optimistic about the future of the nations' relationship, announcing "denuclearization is off the negotiating table with the United States and lengthy talks with Washington" were "not needed."[110] Reports alleging North Korea is constructing intercontinental ballistic missiles have heightened concerns that the negotiations are following a familiar trajectory of agreements, deception, and ultimately, failure.[111]

While Trump's Twitter-driven diplomacy toward North Korea must be appraised as a complete failure, his Twitter discourse has broader implications for the future of US–China relations. For example, the president's strategy of rebuking his critics on Twitter appears to be gaining a foothold among Chinese officials who are using the platform to counter US criticism of China. Often tweeting pointed messages in English, Chinese officials are thought to be following Chinese foreign minister Wang Yi's recommendation that they embrace "a fighting spirit."[112] For example, Chinese foreign ministry official Lijian Zhao has been a vocal critic of the United States, tweeting "racial discrimination, gun violence, violent law enforcement are chronic diseases deeply rooted in U.S. society."[113] Other Chinese officials have followed suit, ironically using a platform that is banned in China to lambaste critics of their nation. This approach "suggests at the very least that Communist Party leaders believe they must do more to control the narrative about their country—and that Twitter is a critical battleground."[114] Although it is unclear whether Chinese officials' Twitter usage was mainly spurred by the US president's predilection for the platform, their tweets share many commonalities with Trump's Twitter discourse. For example, their tweets typically contain harsh language and sharp criticism.[115] Twitter has become an important tool for both the expression and circulation of transnational rhetoric regarding US–China relations.

Twitter has also become a means for Chinese people to critique China's leadership and the nation's censorship methods. Although Twitter is banned in China, Chinese citizens use technology such as VPNs to traverse the Great Firewall and participate on the platform. Some Chinese Twitter users use the medium not only to flout Chinese censorship but to criticize it. A 2019 study of Chinese Twitter users' tweets concerning internet censorship found that the discourse centered on the themes of "sharing technical knowledge, expressing political opinions, and disseminating alternative news items."[116] Anti-CCP dissidents and activists have also turned to Twitter to help expand the reach of President Trump's tweets. For instance, Jeff Ding and two other volunteers created the account @Trump_Chinese to "spread Trump's messages in the Chinese-speaking world" by translating the president's tweets into Chinese.[117] Critics of the Chinese government and supporters of Trump, the volunteers see the account as a "service" to "Chinese people around the globe, especially mainland Chinese who use VPNs to climb over the Great Firewall."[118] Established in September 2018, the account has amassed over 150,000 followers.[119] While Ding and the other volunteers try to accurately translate the president's tweets, they do take some liberties. Instead of using the word "China" when translating Trump's tweets that are critical of the nation, they substitute the word for "the Chinese Communist Party" to distinguish between China's government and its people.[120] For some Mainland and overseas Chinese people, Twitter is a useful tool for criticizing the CCP and challenging Chinese censorship. It will be interesting to see whether and to what extent this activism on the platform continues and evolves as President Trump battles for a second term.

The important work of diplomacy is often fraught with complications, tensions, and high risks. Diplomacy requires thoughtful statements, informed policy, and careful cultivation of relationships. There is perhaps no better testament to President Trump's inability to undertake the critical work of diplomacy than his Twitter feed. Twitter's inherent limitations, coupled with the president's use of the platform to propagate rash, negative statements illustrate the medium's risks as a diplomatic tool. While Trump's cultivation of an uncontrollable persona marked by toxic masculinity may appeal to members of his base as he denigrates foreign leaders and proclaims "America First," it sows confusion among US allies and risks destabilizing alliances and igniting conflict. Instead of launching Twitter tirades, the president would be well served to devote his energy to acquiring the skills needed to engage in the complicated dealings of diplomacy. Devoting more time to foreign policy briefings prepared by experts would be a productive step.[121] Rather than firing off his musings on foreign policy in hasty tweets, the president, in collaboration with his advisers, should craft thoughtful, nuanced statements.

However, it seems unlikely Trump will relinquish his Twitter account or adopt a more professional tweeting style given his predilection for the social media platform. Instead of just disseminating Trump's tweets in their news stories, journalists should deconstruct the president's tweets in order to reveal the inaccuracies of his claims and the problematic implications of his messages.[122] Additionally, Twitter in the age of Trump demands increased information literacy from members of the public. Citizens must cultivate "a new kind of Twitter literacy" in order to effectively interpret messages and assess their potential implications.[123] In this sense, I hope my attempt to decipher Trump's Twitter-driven discourse about North Korea contributes to the larger project of making sense of how social media impacts US–China relations.

NOTES

1. Tom Phillips, "Trump Praises China and Blames U.S. for Trade Deficit," *The Guardian,* November 9, 2017, https://www.theguardian.com/world/2017/nov/09/donald-trump-china-act-faster-north-korea-threat.

2. Phillips, "Trump Praises China and Blames U.S. for Trade Deficit."

3. Donald Trump (@realDonaldTrump), "President Xi of China has stated that he is upping the sanctions against #NoKo . . .," Twitter, November 11, 2017, 3:32 p.m., https://twitter.com/realDonaldTrump/status/929492038231429120.

4. Donald Trump (@realDonaldTrump), "Caught RED HANDED . . .," Twitter, December 28, 2017, 8:24 a.m., https://twitter.com/realDonaldTrump/status/946416486054285314.

5. Tom O'Connor, "China Tells Trump 'This Is Not How a U.S. President Should Behave' after North Korea Tweet," *Newsweek,* December 29, 2017, http://www.newsweek.com/china-tells-trump-not-how-us-president-should-behave-north-korea-tweet-764757.

6. O'Connor, "China Tells Trump 'This Is Not How a U.S. President Should Behave' after North Korea Tweet."

7. O'Connor, "China Tells Trump 'This Is Not How a U.S. President Should Behave' after North Korea Tweet."

8. O'Connor, "China Tells Trump 'This Is Not How a U.S. President Should Behave' after North Korea Tweet."

9. Stephen Lucas, "The Stylistic Artistry of the Declaration of Independence," in *Readings in Rhetorical Criticism,* 2nd ed., ed. Carl Burgchardt (State College: Strata, 2000), 564.

10. Eleanor Albert, "The China–North Korea Relationship," Council on Foreign Relations, March 28, 2018, https://www.cfr.org/backgrounder/china-north-korea-relationship.

11. O'Connor, "China Tells Trump 'This Is Not How a U.S. President Should Behave' after North Korea Tweet."

12. O'Connor, "China Tells Trump 'This Is Not How a U.S. President Should Behave' after North Korea Tweet."

13. Camila Domonoske, "Why Is North Korea Threatening Guam?," NPR, August 9, 2017, https://www.npr.org/sections/thetwo-way/2017/08/09/542384201/why-is-north-korea-threatening-guam.

14. O'Connor, "China Tells Trump 'This Is Not How a U.S. President Should Behave' after

North Korea Tweet."

15. Alex Lockie, "North Korea Again Threatens Nuclear Strike near Guam, Mocks Trump's 'Fire and Fury' Threat," *Business Insider*, August 9, 2017, http://www.businessinsider.com/north-korea-guam-threat-missile-strike-2017-8.

16. Donald Trump (@realDonaldTrump), "Just heard Foreign Minister of North Korea speak at U.N. . . .," Twitter, September 23, 2017, 8:08 p.m., https://twitter.com/realDonaldTrump/status/911789314169823232.

17. Elise Hu, "President Trump's Biggest Foreign Policy Headache for 2018," NPR, December 29, 2017, https://www.npr.org/sections/parallels/2017/12/29/571138442/president-trumps-biggest-foreign-policy-headache-for-2018.

18. Craig Osth, "Enabled by China, North Korea Is Still a Bully with Impunity," The Hill, January 26, 2018, http://thehill.com/opinion/international/370904-enabled-by-china-north-korea-is-still-a-bully-with-impunity.

19. Osth, "Enabled by China, North Korea Is Still a Bully with Impunity."

20. Associated Press, "China Sending Envoy to North Korea Following Trump Visit," *Politico*, November 15, 2017, https://www.politico.com/story/2017/11/15/china-envoy-north-korea-following-trump-visit-244920.

21. Associated Press, "China Sending Envoy to North Korea Following Trump Visit."

22. Andreas Jungherr, "Twitter Use in Election Campaigns: A Comprehensive Literature Review," *Journal of Information Technology & Politics* 12, no. 1 (2016): 72–91.

23. Joseph DiGrazia, Karissa McKelvey, Johan Bollen, and Fabio Rojas, "More Tweets, More Votes: Social Media as a Quantitative Indicator of Political Behavior," *PloS one* 8, no. 11 (2013): e79449; and Karissa McKelvey, Joseph DiGrazia, and Fabio Rojas, "Twitter Publics: How Online Political Communities Signaled Electoral Outcomes in the 2010 U.S. House Election," *Information, Communication & Society* 17, no. 4 (2014): 436–50.

24. Jungherr, "Twitter Use in Election Campaigns"; and Daniel Kreiss, Laura Meadows, and John Remensperger, "Political Performance, Boundary Spaces, and Active Spectatorship: Media Production at the 2012 Democratic National Convention," *Journalism* 16, no. 5 (2015): 577–95.

25. John Parmelee and Shannon Bichard, *Politics and the Twitter Revolution: How Tweets Influence the Relationship between Political Leaders and the Public* (Lanham, MD: Lexington, 2012).

26. Daniel Kreiss, "Seizing the Moment: The Presidential Campaigns' Use of Twitter during the 2012 Electoral Cycle," *New Media & Society* 18, no. 8 (2014): 1473–90.

27. Kreiss, "Seizing the Moment."

28. Nicholas Carr, "Why Trump Tweets (and Why We Listen)," Politico, January 26,

2018, https://www.politico.com/magazine/story/2018/01/26/donald-trump-twitter-addiction-216530.

29. Terry Gross, "Who Is Mystery Man behind @realDonaldTrump? (Besides the President),"
NPR, April 19, 2018, https://www.npr.org/2018/04/19/603904858/who-is-the-mystery-man-behind-realdonaldtrump-besides-the-president.

30. Gross, "Who is Mystery Man Behind @realDonaldTrump? (Besides the President)."

31. Gross, "Who is Mystery Man Behind @realDonaldTrump? (Besides the President)."

32. Donald Trump (@realDonaldTrump), "My use of social media is not Presidential
. . ." Twitter, July 1, 2017, 6:41 p.m., https://twitter.com/realdonaldtrump/status/881281755017355264?lang=en.

33. Carr, "Why Trump Tweets (and Why We Listen)."

34. Tamara Keith, "Commander-In-Tweet: Trump's Social Media Use and Presidential Media Avoidance," NPR, November 18, 2016, https://www.npr.org/2016/11/18/502306687/commander-in-tweet-trumps-social-media-use-and-presidential-media-avoidance.

35. Mohammed El-Nawawy and Sahar Khamis, *Egyptian Revolution 2.0: Political Blogging, Civic Engagement, and Citizen Journalism* (New York: Springer, 2016); and Brian Ott, "The Age of Twitter: Donald J. Trump and the Politics of Debasement," *Critical Studies in Media Communication* 34, no. 1 (2017): 59–68.

36. Ott, "The Age of Twitter," 60.

37. Ott, "The Age of Twitter," 61.

38. Amelia Tait, "The Strange Case of Marina Joyce and Internet Hysteria," *The Guardian*, August 4, 2016, https://www.theguardian.com/technology/2016/aug/04/marina-joyce-internethysteria-witch-hunts-cyberspace?CMP = oth_b-aplnews_d-1.

39. Michael Thelwall, Kevan Buckley, and Georgios Paltoglou, "Sentiment in Twitter Events," *Journal of the American Society for Information Science and Technology* 62, no. 2 (2011): 415.

40. Zachary Crockett, "What I Learned Analyzing 7 Months of Donald Trump's Tweets," Vox, May 16, 2016, http://www.vox.com/2016/5/16/11603854/donald-trump-twitter.

41. Crockett, "What I Learned Analyzing 7 Months of Donald Trump's Tweets."

42. Jasmine Lee and Kevin Quealy, "The 487 People, Places and Things Donald Trump Has Insulted on Twitter: A Complete List," *New York Times*, July 10, 2018, https://www.nytimes.com/interactive/2016/01/28/upshot/donald-trump-twitter-insults.html.

43. Lee and Quealy, "The 487 People, Places and Things Donald Trump Has Insulted on Twitter."

44. Crockett, "What I Learned Analyzing 7 Months of Donald Trump's Tweets."

45. Ott, "The Age of Twitter," 64.

46. Ben Kharakh and Dan Primack, "Donald Trump's Social Media Ties to White Supremacists," *Fortune*, March 22, 2016, http://fortune.com/donald-trump-white-supremacist-genocide/.

47. Krishnadev Calamur, "The International Incidents Sparked by Trump's Twitter Feed in 2017," *The Atlantic*, December 19, 2017, https://www.theatlantic.com/international/archive/2017/12/trump-tweets-foreign-policy/547892/.

48. Calamur, "The International Incidents Sparked by Trump's Twitter Feed in 2017."

49. Donald Trump (@realDonaldTrump), "I told Rex Tillerson . . .," Twitter, October 1, 2017, 7:30 a.m., https://twitter.com/realDonaldTrump/status/914497877543735296?ref_src=twsrc%5Etfw%7Ctwcamp%5Etweetembed%7Ctwterm%5E914497877543735296&ref_url=https%3A%2F%2Fwww.theatlantic.com%2Finternational%2Farchive%2F2017%2F12%2Ftrump-tweets-foreign-policy%2F547892%2F.

50. Calamur, "The International Incidents Sparked by Trump's Twitter Feed in 2017."

51. Alex Ward, "Trump's Catastrophic Foreign Policy Weekend, Explained," Vox, July 23, 2018, https://www.vox.com/2018/7/23/17602360/trump-iran-tweet-north-korea-russia-war; and Donald Trump (@realDonaldTrump), "To Iranian President Rouhani," Twitter, July 22, 2018, 8:24 p.m., https://twitter.com/realDonaldTrump/status/1021234525626609666.

52. Donald Trump (@realDonaldTrump), "Caught RED HANDED . . .," Twitter, December 28, 2017, 8:24 a.m., https://twitter.com/realDonaldTrump/status/946416486054285314.

53. Loretta Napoleoni, *North Korea: The Country We Love to Hate* (Crawley: University of Western Australia Publishing, 2018), 148.

54. Donald Trump (@realDonaldTrump), "North Korea is a rogue nation . . .," Twitter, September 3, 2017, 4:39 a.m., https://twitter.com/realdonaldtrump/status/904307898213433344?lang=en; and Donald Trump (@realDonaldTrump), "Kim Jong Un of North Korea, who is obviously a madman . . .," Twitter, September 22, 2017, 3:28 a.m., https://twitter.com/realdonaldtrump/status/911175246853664768?lang=en.

55. Donald Trump (@realDonaldTrump), "I spoke with President Moon of South Korea last night. . . .," Twitter, September 17, 2017, 4:53 a.m., https://twitter.com/realDonaldTrump/status/909384837018112000?ref_src=twsrc%5Etfw%7Ctwcamp%5Etweetembed%7Ctwterm%5E909384837018112000&ref_url=https%3A%2F%2Fwww.vox.com%2Fworld%2F2018%2F7%2F6%2F17540184%2Ftrump-north-korea-kim-elton-john-pompeo.

56. William Ming Liu, "Why Trump's Toxic Masculinity Is Bad for Other Men," *Time*, April 14, 2016, http://time.com/4273865/donald-trump-toxic-masculinity/.

57. Liu, "Why Trump's Toxic Masculinity is Bad for Other Men."

58. Liu, "Why Trump's Toxic Masculinity is Bad for Other Men."

59. Donald Trump (@realDonaldTrump), "The U.S. has been talking to North Korea . . .," Twitter, August 30, 2017, 5:47 a.m., https://twitter.com/realdonaldtrump/status/902875515534626817?lang=en.

60. Donald Trump (@realDonaldTrump), "Just heard Foreign Minister of North Korea speak at U.N. . . .," Twitter, September 23, 8:08 a.m., https://twitter.com/realdonaldtrump/status/911789314169823232?lang=en.

61. Noah Bierman, "Trump Warns North Korea of 'Fire and Fury,'" *L.A. Times*, August 8, 2017, http://www.latimes.com/politics/washington/la-na-essential-washington-updates-trump-warns-north-korea-of-fire-and-1502220642-htmlstory.html#nt=card.

62. Donald Trump (@realDonaldTrump), "Kim Jong Un of North Korea, who is obviously a madman . . .," Twitter, September 22, 2017, 3:28 a.m., https://twitter.com/realdonaldtrump/status/911175246853664768?lang=en.

63. Jennifer Mercieca, "The Rhetorical Brilliance of Trump the Demagogue," The Conversation, December 11, 2015, https://theconversation.com/the-rhetorical-brilliance-of-trump-the-demagogue-51984.

64. Mercieca, "The Rhetorical Brilliance of Trump the Demagogue."

65. Mercieca, "The Rhetorical Brilliance of Trump the Demagogue."

66. Laura Koran, "Nikki Haley Says She Used Trump's Unpredictability to Win North Korea Sanctions," CNN, May 22, 2018, https://www.cnn.com/2018/05/22/politics/nikki-haley-north-korea-china-sanctions-trump/index.html.

67. Koran, "Nikki Haley Says She Used Trump's Unpredictability to Win North Korea Sanctions."

68. Jeffrey Goldberg, "A Senior White House Official Defines the Trump Doctrine: 'We're America, Bitch,'" *The Atlantic,* June 11, 2018, https://www.theatlantic.com/politics/archive/2018/06/a-senior-white-house-official-defines-the-trump-doctrine-were-america-bitch/562511/.

69. Donald Trump (@realDonaldTrump), "they do NOTHING for us . . .," Twitter, July 29, 2018, 4:35 p.m., https://twitter.com/realdonaldtrump/status/891442016294494209?lang=en.

70. Donald Trump (@realDonaldTrump), "China is very much the economic lifeline to North Korea . . .," Twitter, April 21, 2017, 6:04 a.m., https://twitter.com/realdonaldtrump/status/855406847200768000?lang=en.

71. Robin Wright, "In a Testy Letter, Trump Cancels the North Korea Summit," *New Yorker*, May 23, 2018, https://www.newyorker.com/news/news-desk/the-new-iffiness-of-trumps-north-korea-diplomacy.

72. Donald Trump (@realDonaldTrump), "I'm very disappointed in China . . .," Twitter, July 29, 2017, 4:29 p.m., https://twitter.com/realDonaldTrump/status/891440474132795392?ref_

src=twsrc%5Etfw%7Ctwcamp%5Etweetembed%7Ctwterm%5E891440474132795392&ref_
url=https%3A%2F%2Fwww.theguardian.
com%2Fus-news%2F2017%2Fjul%2F30%2Fdonald-trump-says-china-does-nothing-to-
thwart-north-koreas-nuclear-quest.

73. Donald Trump (@realDonaldTrump), "I'm very disappointed in China . . .," Twitter, July 29,
2017, 4:29 p.m., https://twitter.com/realDonaldTrump/status/891440474132795392?ref_
src=twsrc%5Etfw%7Ctwcamp%5Etweetembed%7Ctwterm%5E891440474132795392&ref_
url=https%3A%2F%2Fwww.theguardian.
com%2Fus-news%2F2017%2Fjul%2F30%2Fdonald-trump-says-china-does-nothing-to-
thwart-north-koreas-nuclear-quest.

74. Ramona Kreis, "The 'Tweet Politics' of President Trump," *Journal of Language and Politics*
16, no, 4 (2017): 614.

75. Donald Trump (@realDonaldTrump), "North Korea is a rogue nation . . .,"
Twitter, September 3, 2017, 4:39 a.m., https://twitter.com/realdonaldtrump/
status/904307898213433344?lang=en.

76. Associated Press, "Trump Accuses China of 'Raping' U.S.," *New York Times*, May 2, 2016,
https://www.nytimes.com/video/us/100000004378852/trump-accuses-china-of-
raping-us.html.

77. Max Fisher, "Bad News, World: China Can't Solve the North Korea Problem," *New York
Times*, September 6, 2017, https://www.nytimes.com/2017/09/06/world/asia/china-
north-korea-nuclear-problem.html.

78. Adam Mount, "How China Sees North Korea," *The Atlantic*, August 29, 2017, https://www.
theatlantic.com/international/archive/2017/08/china-military-strength-north-korea-
crisis/538344/.

79. Loretta Napoleoni, *North Korea: The Country We Love to Hate* (Crawley: University of
Western Australia Publishing, 2018), 153.

80. Napoleoni, *North Korea*, 154.

81. Napoleoni, *North Korea*, 154.

82. Fisher, "Bad News, World: China Can't Solve the North Korea Problem."

83. Fisher, "Bad News, World: China Can't Solve the North Korea Problem."

84. Donald Trump (@realDonaldTrump), "North Korea has agreed to suspend all Nuclear
Tests . . ., Twitter, April 20, 2018, 3:50 p.m., https://twitter.com/realdonaldtrump/
status/987463564305797126?lang=en.

85. Donald Trump (@realDonaldTrump), "Chinese President XI JINPING and I spoke at
length . . .," Twitter, March 10, 2018, 8:15 a.m., https://twitter.com/realdonaldtrump/
status/972506194978983937?lang=en; Donald Trump (@realDonaldTrump), "North

Korea has announced that they will dismantle Nuclear Test Site . . .," Twitter, May 12, 2018, 2:08 p.m., https://twitter.com/realdonaldtrump/status/995410516129538048?lang=en.

86. Donald Trump (@realDonaldTrump), "Chinese President XI JINPING and I spoke at length . . .," Twitter, March 10, 2018, 8:15 a.m., https://twitter.com/realdonaldtrump/status/972506194978983937?lang=en.

87. Donald Trump (@realDonaldTrump), "Very good news to receive the warm and productive statement from North Korea . . .," Twitter, May 25, 2018, 5:14 a.m., https://twitter.com/realdonaldtrump/status/999986971660423170?lang=en.

88. Donald Trump (@realDonaldTrump), "Very good news to receive the warm and productive statement from North Korea . . .," Twitter, May 25, 2018, 5:14 a.m., https://twitter.com/realdonaldtrump/status/999986971660423170?lang=en.

89. See Tamara Keith, "Trump Teases, Threatens and Dodges with 'We'll See What Happens,'" NPR, October 21, 2017, https://www.npr.org/2017/10/21/559011234/trump-teases-threatens-and-dodges-with-we-ll-see-what-happens; and Katie Rogers, "'We'll See,' Trump Says on North Korea. And Iran. And Nafta. And So On," *New York Times*, May 2, 2018, https://www.nytimes.com/2018/05/02/us/politics/trump-well-see-what-happens.html.

90. David Cay Johnston qtd. in Keith, "Trump Teases, Threatens and Dodges with 'We'll See What Happens.'"

91. Johnston qtd. in Keith, "Trump Teases, Threatens and Dodges with 'We'll See What Happens.'"

92. Kathleen Hall Jamieson qtd. in Rogers, "'We'll See,' Trump Says on North Korea. And Iran. And Nafta. And So On."

93. Napoleoni, *North Korea*, 148.

94. Evelyn Goh, *Constructing the U.S. Rapprochement with China, 1961–1974: From 'Red Menace' to 'Tacit Ally'* (Cambridge: Cambridge University Press, 2004), 19.

95. Jodi Kim, *Ends of Empire: Asian American Critique and the Cold War* (Minneapolis: University of Minnesota Press, 2010), 240.

96. John Kuo Wei Tchen and Dylan Yeats, eds., *Yellow Peril!: An Archive of Anti-Asian Fear* (New York: Verso, 2014), 229.

97. Associated Press, "Trump Says Tough Rhetoric Led to North Korea Summit," *NewsHour*, PBS, June 12, 2018, https://www.pbs.org/newshour/politics/trump-says-tough-rhetoric-led-to-north-korea-summit.

98. Associated Press, "Trump Says Tough Rhetoric Led to North Korea Summit."

99. Associated Press, "Trump Says Tough Rhetoric Led to North Korea Summit."

100. Part of the complexity of these dealings is that the United States, China, and North Korea are each deploying a different definition of what it means to "denuclearize," hence

shrouding the deliberations in confusion.

101. Anna Fifield, "North Korea Declares Its Nuclear Test Site Disabled Hours before Trump Cancels Summit," *Washington Post*, May 24, 2018, https://www.washingtonpost.com/world/north-korea-expected-to-close-nuclear-test-site-despite-squabbles/2018/05/24/37968082-5f0e-11e8-8c93-8cf33c21da8d_story.html?noredirect=on&utm_term=.25b6bfb829c9.

102. Napoleoni, *North Korea*, 153.

103. Uri Friedman, "Inside the Collapse of Trump's North Korea Policy," *The Atlantic*, December 19, 2019, https://www.theatlantic.com/politics/archive/2019/12/donald-trump-kim-jong-un-north-korea-diplomacy-denuclearization/603748/.

104. Friedman, "Inside the Collapse of Trump's North Korea Policy."

105. Donald Trump (@realDonaldTrump), "A very nice note from Chairman Kim of North Korea . . .," Twitter, July 12, 2018, 12:32 p.m., https://twitter.com/realDonaldTrump/status/1017446575474335744.

106. Gardiner Harris and Choe Sang-Hun, "North Korea Criticizes 'Gangster-Like' U.S. Attitude after Talks with Mike Pompeo," *New York Times*, July 7, 2018, https://www.nytimes.com/2018/07/07/world/asia/mike-pompeo-north-korea-pyongyang.html.

107. James Griffiths, Richard Roth, and Will Ripley, "North Korea: U.S. Not Adhering to Its Side of the Bargain since Trump–Kim Summit," CNN, August 9, 2018, https://www.cnn.com/2018/08/09/politics/north-korea-un-negotiations-denuclearization-intl/index.html.

108. Griffiths, Roth, and Ripley, "North Korea: U.S. Not Adhering to Its Side of the Bargain since Trump–Kim Summit."

109. Josh Smith, "North Korea Revives 'Dotard' Label in Warning to Trump over 'Rocket Man' Remarks," Reuters, December 5, 2019, https://www.reuters.com/.

110. Michelle Nichols and David Brunnstrom, "North Korea's U.N. Envoy Says Denuclearization off Negotiating Table with United States," Reuters, December 7, 2019, https://www.reuters.com/.

111. Sophie Tatum, "WaPo: New Indicators Show North Korea Potentially Working on Missiles," CNN, July 31, 2018, https://www.cnn.com/2018/07/30/politics/north-korea-missiles/index.html.

112. "China Demands 'Fighting Spirit' from Diplomats as Trade War, Hong Kong Protests Simmer," Reuters, December 4, 2019, https://www.reuters.com/article/us-china-diplomacy/china-demands-fighting-spirit-from-diplomats-as-trade-war-hong-kong-protests-simmer-idUSKBN1Y80R8.

113. Lijian Zhao (@zlj517), "3. Racial discrimination, gun violence, and violent law enforcement . . .," Twitter, November 30, 2019, 7:45 p.m., https://twitter.com/zlj517/

status/1200938841311309825?s=20.

114. Nahal Toosi, "In Response to Trump, China Gets Mean," Politico, December 8, 2019, https://www.politico.com/news/2019/12/08/china-trump-twitter-077767.

115. Toosi, "In Response to Trump, China Gets Mean."

116. Shiwen Wu and Bo Mai, "Talking About and Beyond Censorship: Mapping Topic Clusters in the Chinese Twitter Sphere," *International Journal of Communication* 13 (2019): 5072.

117. Zhaoyin Feng, "'Why I Translate All of Trump's Tweets into Chinese,'" BBC, August 9, 2019, https://www.bbc.com/news/world-us-canada-49092612.

118. Feng, "'Why I Translate All of Trump's Tweets Into Chinese.'"

119. @Trump_Chinese, Twitter Account, https://twitter.com/trump_chinese?lang=en (accessed January 24, 2020).

120. Feng, "'Why I Translate All of Trump's Tweets into Chinese.'"

121. Stephen Collinson, "Trump's Improvisation Faces Decades of North Korean Preparation," CNN, June 11, 2018, https://www.cnn.com/2018/06/10/politics/donald-trump-kim-jong-un-summit/index.html.

122. George Lakoff, "A Taxonomy of Trump Tweets," *On the Media*, WYNC, January 13, 2017, http://www.wnyc.org/story/ taxonomy-trump-tweets/.

123. Damian Rivers and Andrew Ross, "Discursive Deflection: Accusation of 'Fake News' and the Spread of Mis- and Disinformation in the Tweets of President Trump," *Social Media +Society* (2018): 10.

PART II

State Media

Convergence Culture and Professionalism Practices in the Short-Form News Videos of the *Beijing News*

Fengjiao Yang and Xiao Li

Online short-form news video has been growing fast in China, where video consumption has tended to take place in mobile environments and fragments of time. According to Trustdata (a mobile internet big-data monitoring platform in China), active daily users of short-form video applications reached 160 million by the end of 2017.[1] Short-form videos are usually measured in seconds and are mainly shot and edited on mobile smartphones, and they can be shared instantly and docked seamlessly with social media platforms.[2] Compared to traditional television programs, short-form videos differ not only in length and channel but also in production pattern. An ordinary person with a smartphone can produce, post, and repost short-form videos easily in the era of the mobile internet. As for content, some researchers have concluded that short-form videos are brief, concrete, vivid, amusing, easy to spread virally, and they can cater to mobile consumers' habits of fast viewing.[3] Given these conditions, the prosperity of short-form videos is "inspired by social sharing on mobile applications."[4] Moreover, more and more traditional news organizations regard short-form videos as a strategy for responding to technological transformation, as they post short-form news videos on their websites, video mobile applications, and social media platforms. This transformation has deepened the convergence of professional journalists and video consumers, as well as the convergence of traditional news organizations and video platform companies.

Within the Chinese context, there is great demand for substantial sources of news videos, meaning user-generated content (UGC) has become indispensable.[5] This can be explained in several ways: First, the number of journalists working in traditional news organizations is limited, and it is hard for them to obtain breaking news videos all over the world. And second, these videos are taken from the perspective of ordinary people, and the style of them is closer to the tastes of video consumers. The widespread use of smartphones makes it possible for "grassroots" individuals or groups to shoot and post short-form videos. However, traditional news organizations need to cooperate with video websites and social platforms, which have access to large numbers of users. These websites and platforms also need high-quality news videos to enrich their content, so some traditional news organizations and platform companies cooperate by setting up joint venture companies. Within this convergence of users, websites, news organization, social media platforms, and new communication technologies, one question keeps arising: What does this convergence and the arrival of short-form news videos mean for standards of professionalism? And, thinking more broadly, what do our evolving norms of professionalism mean, when filtered through these new forms of convergence, for the quality of communication in contemporary China?

To answer these question, we chose the *Beijing News* as our research site. The *Beijing News* was co-founded by *Nanfang Daily* and *Guangming Daily* in November 2001. As a pilot of institutional innovation, it was the first non-national newspaper authorized to operate as a trans-provincial newspaper. It started exploring omni-media reporting in 2012 and strengthened its cooperation with IT companies in 2015 in order to combine its advantage of original content production with the IT companies' advantages of technology, channel, and capital.[6] Then, in September 2016, the *Beijing News* and Tencent co-founded a joint venture called Beijing FengQiYunYang Communication Technology Company and started a news video program called WeVideo, aiming to "become the biggest and most influential brand of news video on mobile applications."[7] "WeVideo" was named by Yuechun Wang, the former chief editor of the *Beijing News*. In her opinion, "We" means convergence; sure enough, the *Beijing News* has the ability to produce quality news, while Tencent owns powerful distribution channels and internet technologies, making for a unique convergence of production capabilities, news resources, and mixed markets.[8]

According to Tencent's introduction on its homepage, the company was founded in November 1998 and has since grown into a competitive internet value-added service provider. Its core services include providing social platforms and digital content, such as Instant Messenger QQ, mobile social platforms Weixin and WeChat (the international version of Weixin), the portal website QQ.com, and Tencent News. Weixin is one of the most popular social applications in China. According to the 2018 Weixin data report released by Tencent, the average number of active Weixin users per month exceeds one billion, making it among the world's largest providers of social media and online customer services.[9]

Thus, the unique operation model of WeVideo is that the *Beijing News* provides content and Tencent provides financial assistance, distribution channels, and technical support. More concretely, the copyrights of videos produced by WeVideo are bought by Tencent exclusively, and the short-form news videos of WeVideo are published predominantly on Tencent's platforms, including the Tencent video website, Tencent News, Kuaibao (a digital media distributing platform using artificial intelligence), and the Tencent News plug-in on Weixin. Tencent can also provide precise user data analysis to help WeVideo capture the user's viewing habits. In fact, Tencent coordinators give tips for spotlighting both user trends and possible new stories to WeVideo via an online working group. This means that Tencent is not just a passive recipient of already-made content, but is actively involved on the creative side of short-form news video production. Still, WeVideo largely relies on UGC, a tendency of the short-form videos field. When we interviewed Yuanwen Peng, the deputy general manager of WeVideo in charge of content production, he said that most news clues came from social media, especially Sina Weibo,[10] the Chinese equivalent of Twitter. In most cases, the clues may be little more than a photo or short video with news value. Once interested, journalists of WeVideo will try to contact the person who posts the photo or video to check the facts and get their approval to use the materials.

In addition, WeVideo has recruited a camera crew of "Pai Ke," meaning people who shoot films. They are ordinary citizens who are interested in shooting videos and have not received professional training. They provide news clues for journalists when they find something interesting or important. Furthermore, when there are big events breaking in distant places, journalists will ask local Pai Ke to produce news videos before journalists can get there. More and more, Pai Ke participate in the production of short-form news videos, deepening the convergence of professionally generated content (PGC) and UGC. Another group called "correspondents," who are also not trained journalists, also provide video materials when needed. All of these unprofessional providers enlarge and diversify the available sources of news videos, and save time and production costs for news organizations. As a result, fact-checking and verification have become more important for the news organization. A new position called "office journalist" has emerged, referring to the job of fact-checking and interviewing via the phone, internet, and social media from the office. This differs once more from journalists in the past, who needed to be on the scene before they could report the news. This transformation in how "news" gets produced means UGC comes in from the field, and is then fact-checked by professionals in traditional news offices in Beijing, who then release the UGC via Tencent's platforms, to the public. The model is clearly working, for just one year after its establishment, WeVideo released more than 5,000 short-form news videos and Tencent reported more than 3 billion clicks on its platforms. By September 2017, WeVideo was releasing an average of thirty short-form news videos daily, with an average daily view count of 20 million.[11] This amounts to a massive shift in how "news" is produced in China, and raises the question of what this transformation means for standards of professionalism.

Previous Research on Short-Form News Videos and Convergence Culture

Numerous studies have been conducted on short-form news videos in China since 2014, growing fast after 2016 as the industry of mobile short-form videos entered into a period of rapid growth. The number of related research articles in 2017 rose to 295 from 57 the year before, according to data from CNKI (China National Knowledge Infrastructure). It is difficult to give a comprehensive overview of the articles about this subject, but there is a relatively clear research map.

First, most research focuses on how news organizations produce and distribute competitive short-form news videos. Since short-form news videos emerged earlier in Western countries, there are some articles focusing on studying Western models and discussing how Chinese news organizations respond to this new technology and form. "Simplified news narrative, powerful video, new distributing model, recognizable brand" are discussed as necessary for Chinese media to develop short-form news videos successfully.[12] There are also many case studies on how successful short-form video platforms, such as Pear Video, produce and distribute news and information,[13] and how traditional newspapers, such as *Paper Video* and *Green Pepper Video*, have adapted to the short-form news video format.[14]

Second, there is some research focusing on the changes of audio-visual languages brought about by mobile internet communication. According to one empirical study, many audio-visual language elements that were considered to be attractive or indicative of journalistic professionalism in the television news era—such as panning shots and sound effects—did not have positive effects on audiences' actual preferences.[15]

Third, some studies discussed the importance of UGC in the production model of short-form news videos and analyzed how news organizations and platforms recruit and train non-professional video makers. The concept of UGC has been defined according to three criteria. One is user contribution. UGC is different from interactive activities, as "simply receiving or forwarding content and similar activities don't qualify."[16] Furthermore, UGC means creative work: "Merely copying a portion of a television show and posting it onto an online video website wouldn't be considered UGC."[17] The second criterion is that in order to promote information sharing and discussion, UGC must be accessible to the public or a group.[18] And third, UGC is "creation outside of professional routines and practices."[19] The importance of UGC is based on the advantages of collective intelligence. The form and content of UGC have developed alongside constantly updating technology, yet the essence of UGC remains consistent.

Departing from the three perspectives mentioned above, this article presents extensive research on how traditional news organizations perform journalistic professionalism as UGC and commercial platforms are converging. The key issue of this research is different from most research on media convergence in China, which pays more attention to technological convergence, distributing platforms convergence, and adjustment of communication strategy.

According to Henry Jenkins's theory of convergence culture, convergence should not be understood primarily as a technological change, such as a communication device integrated with multiple services: "Instead, convergence respects a cultural shift as consumers are encouraged to seek out new information and make connections among dispersed media content."[20] From this perspective, media convergence means much deeper change for people's perceptions and behaviors in the era of network communication, as well as changes for the production patterns of news organizations. In his opinion, convergence culture means elimination of boundaries between old and new media, and it is a kind of culture "where grassroots and corporate media intersect, where the power of the media producer and the power of the media consumer interact."[21] Traditional media have to adapt to the entire industry of convergence and user participation.

The relationship between the adoption of UGC in news production and journalistic professionalism has been an important topic during these years. On the one hand, UGC not only can shorten the time of reporting breaking news but also reflects the news and facts from diverse perspectives, "adding a view from the bottom of society to the top."[22] This is also considered a shift of discursive power, "realizing agenda-setting by citizens themselves through individual and diverse expressions and thereby influencing the agendas of established media outlets."[23] On the other hand, some critics say UGC cannot be compared with the work of professionally trained journalists, and it will result in the decline of reporting quality.[24] These debates show contradictory attitudes toward the influence on journalistic professionalism brought by UGC.

The Concept of Journalistic Professionalism in China

To investigate how journalistic professionalism is influenced by the convergence of traditional media, UGC, and video platform companies, it is necessary to clarify the concept and meaning of journalistic professionalism in China, especially in the era of new information technology.

Journalistic professionalism first appeared as a concept in the West at the end of the nineteenth century, and journalistic professionalism theory became popular in America in the 1960s.[25] The principles are as follows: Journalism provides service for public interest; journalists are observers and reporters, not propagandists or agitators of any interest group; journalists are gatekeepers of information flow; journalists judge facts based on the rationality of empirical science, and obey facts rather than political or economic power; and they are guided by professional norms based on principles mentioned above, accepting the self-discipline of their professional community and not of other powers or authority.[26] Journalistic professionalism is the most important criterion for journalism, and its core ideas are objectivity and independence.[27]

Journalistic professionalism theory was introduced to China in the 1990s. Based on the unique media institution in China, there are differing opinions about it. Considering that the function of Chinese media is the "mouthpiece" of the Party and government, some scholars argued that "journalistic professionalism in China has a limited scope of application, and has not been applied systematically or broadly."[28] From this viewpoint, journalistic professionalism's stance on skill level can be applied to Chinese journalism—such as the requirement of accuracy and objectivity in information gathering, writing, and editing.

Although some scholars believe journalistic professionalism in China is limited, there are still many scholars who argue for its importance. Ye Lu and Zhongdang Pan analyzed the reform of journalism in China since the 1980s, including the rejection of fake news, the emphasis on facts, the advocation for media ethics and public opinion supervision via the press, and the separation of news gathering and managing. They put forward that the reform "has touched on a lot of ideas of journalistic professionalism," and that "journalistic professionalism has contributed to the reconstruction of the roles of media and journalists."[29] Zhenzhi Guo also insisted that journalistic professionalism and media ethics had positive meanings and normative values in China, saying that "it can promote Chinese journalism and help the relationship between government and media to develop benevolently."[30]

Most literature has discussed journalistic professionalism in China within a propaganda-versus-journalism frame. It is acknowledged that Chinese media are under supervision from the Communist Party of China and the government, for example, through the licensing system. However, studies have not investigated the positive impact on journalistic professionalism caused by the structural changes in the media industry since the 1990s. Many popular newspapers, magazines, TV channels, and radio programs rose up following the market-oriented economic transformation. The municipal newspaper is one such kind of organization. Different from a party organ such as *People's Daily*, municipal newspapers rely on retail and advertising, not state-subsidy. Although they need to consider "social impact" and emphasize constructive voices, which are required by the party and government, their coverage topics contain breaking news, political activities, financial information, entertainment industry news, and investigative reports, which are not confined to propagandist content.

At the same time, a lot of municipal newspapers take journalistic professionalism as the standard to improve the quality of news reports. For example, the *Beijing News* is a municipal newspaper supervised by the Propaganda Department of CPC Committee of Beijing City since September 2011, but it differs from municipal party organs such as the *Beijing Daily* in that the topics of the *Beijing News* are more relevant to urban life. According to the introduction on its website, it "sticks to the principle of independent and objective reporting" and "aims to provide readers with accurate and readable reports."[31]

With the emergence of new media and UGC, there is another dispute about the impact of internet technology on journalistic professionalism. Some academics are concerned that journalistic professionalism has sunk into an unprecedented crisis, as anyone can spread information via the internet and the boundaries of journalism have become blurred. Especially in the new context of social media, the information worth sharing and forwarding seems to be more important. "This means news and journalistic professionalism are not necessities anymore."[32]

But more scholars argue that journalistic professionalism still has significance. Investigative skills, ethics, and commitment to serving the public interest are still needed for in-depth and investigative reporting. The development of "we media" and social media is "not [a] terminator of journalistic professionalism, but [an] inspirer." The concept of journalistic professionalism is still "an indispensable theoretical resource and principle for practice."[33] Furthermore, Zhongdang Pan and Ye Lu elaborate on the importance of journalism for a democratic mode of public life, and "journalistic professionalism is rooted in rational communicative actions that constitute the civic life." They argue that journalistic professionalism "continues to be a relevant normative framework for journalistic practices."[34]

Challenged by the reduction of the threshold for information distribution and the emergence of the "post-truth" phenomenon on social platforms, journalistic professionalism should be continued and extended. Especially when media are cooperating with UGC and platform companies, it is necessary to emphasize journalistic norms, such as fact-checking, objectivity, neutrality, and so on. In addition, some scholars have put forward the idea that professional journalists "should act as the practitioner[s] of journalistic professionalism" in convergence culture, produce news and reveal truth based on normalized practices, and advocate rational behavior in the process of news production and distribution on public forums "in order to make clear the key elements which can reflect democracy, rationality, and ethics in public discourse."[35]

Research Questions

In order to make up for some of the overlooked aspects of the research of journalistic professionalism in the convergence of traditional media, UGC, and commercial platforms, this study takes the *Beijing News*'s WeVideo as its research object and attempts to answer the following research questions:

Firstly, how does the *Beijing News* adopt UGC in news production? UGC adoption is an important tendency in journalism, such as CNN iReport and BBC UGC Hub. UGC can increase available resources and reflect consumer perspectives. It is necessary for news organizations to embrace UGC and take the advantage of collective intelligence in the age of media convergence.

Secondly, how does WeVideo perform professional journalism in convergence with UGC? As stated above, although supervised by the Propaganda Department of CPC Committee of Beijing City, the *Beijing News* is a municipal newspaper that differs from Party organs by sticking to objective reporting and emphasizing professional duty. In the past, journalists were responsible for the entire process of traditional news production. But when non-professionals are also involved in journalism production, it will be a challenge for news organizations to guarantee the accuracy of information.

Lastly, the third question is about the influence brought about by the cooperation between the *Beijing News* and Tencent. As a dominant platform with the most internet users in China, Tencent supports WeVideo with subsidy, channels, and technology. Considering the power of the platform and its market orientation, which is different from the goal of journalism, that is, of serving the public interest, we will analyze whether this alliance affects news production and recommendation and discuss how this cooperation influences news value and journalistic professionalism.

Data and Methods

The study used a web crawler to capture the information of short-form videos posted by WeVideo on the homepage of the *Beijing News* on the Tencent video website from September to December 2017.[36]

WeVideo was founded in September 2016, and, after a year of development, its daily output has increased to a stable level and its production patterns and styles are becoming steady. The content of this period can represent the overall content style of WeVideo to a certain extent and can be used as the object of a content analysis.

There were 2,396 videos captured in total, and 226 of them have more than 1 million clicks. From the perspective of editors who work for WeVideo, a video is regarded as "popular" when its click volume exceeds 1 million. In the newsroom, one million clicks is one of the standards for judging whether a news video is good or not. Journalists and editors who have produced a news video with more than 1 million clicks will receive a certain reward.

A high click volume results from the combination of content and distribution collaboration. "Clicks volume" is the main index to examine the effect of a news video: the higher the click volume, the better the effect. News videos with high clicks volume have their own characteristics that appeal to the audience. In addition, wide dissemination also depends on effective channels. The 226 videos with more than 1 million clicks reflect not only the content characteristics of WeVideo but also the audience's content preferences. Therefore, this study focused on videos with more than 1 million clicks.

The research methods applied in the study involve conducting a content analysis of the video samples, interviewing the deputy general manager of WeVideo, and reflecting on an internship in the WeVideo newsroom as participant observation. Because the goal of this study is to discuss how the *Beijing News* practices journalistic professionalism in short-form news videos in the age of convergence culture and how this convergence affects professional journalism, the first step is to use content analysis to verify whether WeVideo considers creators of UGC to be important collaborators during the production of short-form news videos. Specifically, we analyzed the providers of the 226 videos. The second step of this study is to analyze how WeVideo performs journalistic professionalism. To answer this question, we examine whether journalists and editors of WeVideo conduct fact-checking to verify user-generated materials and do additional interviewing to increase valuable information, which is another important practice of professional journalists. The third step is to analyze the titles, topics, and news value of the 226 video samples, aiming to understand the choices made by journalists during production. From this we can see whether and how convergence has influenced the development of journalistic professionalism.

Our interview with the deputy general manager and the data collected through participant observation show the impact of commercial platforms and UGC on journalists in the news production process, which can be difficult to observe from outside of the newsroom. As an intern-editor in WeVideo, one of the researchers was able to observe the process of journalists' seeking out story ideas through social media platforms and the chief editor's selection of these stories. This participatory observation gave the researcher a more intuitive understanding of the content preference of WeVideo and the reasons behind it. Furthermore, the researcher observed the communication and negotiation process between the news organization and the Tencent platform, showing how the relationship between publication and platform can shape news as well.

Result and Discussion

The Content Analysis

As indicated above, this study examines the popular videos posted by the *Beijing News* on the Tencent News website. The results of this study show that UGC has been an indispensable part of short-form news videos production, and the professional journalists and editors of WeVideo still emphasize fact-checking and news value, which are commonly accepted norms and basic requirements of journalistic professionalism. However, the adoption of user-generated content and the cooperation with commercial platforms affect the criteria of the content. WeVideo tends to report news with shocking visuals whether they are actually significant or not.

Material Source

Non-professional video makers enlarge and diversify the sources of news videos. By watching and analyzing the content of 226 videos, the researchers divided the sources of video materials into the following five types. It can be seen that UGC is the main source of WeVideo news videos. As figure 1 shows, videos made by WeVideo journalists account for only 10 percent of all videos, while UGC makes up a large proportion (76 percent) of WeVideo's daily news videos.

As can be seen in figure 1, the most common source of news materials is the internet (68 percent). Here, "internet" means journalists found story ideas and videos made by netizens and used the netizen-generated videos as the main material of news videos. Netizen-generated video is a common form of user-generated content.

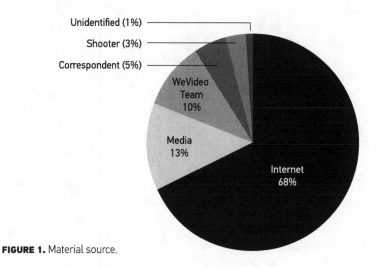

FIGURE 1. Material source.

In order to ensure the veracity of videos generated by netizens, journalists usually conduct a telephone interview with the person concerned, and administrative workers check the reality of the news and gather more information about it.

"Correspondents" and "shooters" are two other important material sources of UGC, which also require journalists to fact-check. However, they differ from netizens in that correspondents and shooters have made cooperative relationships with news organizations. "Correspondents" in this context mean the staff in some public institutions and departments (such as schools, hospitals, police, government, and so on) who engage in publicity work, not the people employed by a news organization to report on a particular subject or to send reports from a foreign country. The correspondents provide journalists with news stories and materials free of charge because they need to cooperate with news organizations to fulfill their work for their own institutions or departments. However, their cooperation with news organizations is not exclusive because they can provide materials and leads to multiple news organizations at the same time. When different journalists have access to the same news leads and materials, the professional ability of journalists will be a major factor that influences the quality of news reports.

"Shooters" refer to non-professional video makers all around the world (though mainly located in China's mainland) who are called Pai Ke (pronunciation) in China, recruited and instructed by the media. The relationship between shooters and news organizations is based on economics, which means that the latter need to pay the former if the leads or materials are used in a report. Shooters play an important role in WeVideo's news video production. Shooters can provide news leads to their partner journalists, which guarantees the production of WeVideo content to a certain extent. Additionally, when an emergency event occurs, journalists will contact local shooters and send them to the scene to take some videos and report the latest news, which provides evidence for the editor to judge whether it is necessary to dispatch a journalist to the scene for further interviews, or to use as a buffer report before the journalists arrive. The shooters across the country reduce the reaction time for WeVideo in the face of breaking news, thus improving the timeliness of news.

This cooperation between journalists and shooters represents a deeper convergence between UGC and PGC because it is not casual or occasional, but rather tends to be regular and stable. Shooters not only take part in content production but also affect the process of deciding the reporting plans of news organizations by proactively providing news information and materials. In our interview, Yuanwen Peng, the deputy general manager of WeVideo, affirmed the value of shooters.[37] But Peng also admitted that journalists cannot fully trust the information and materials provided by shooters because shooters have not received professional journalism education. As a result, the journalists still need to fact-check these materials.[38] No matter how important the information or videos provided by the shooters are, they are still only auxiliary agents in news production, and they cannot independently complete professional journalism work. Journalists still play a key role in news production.

Fact-Checking & Value-Added Information

Fact-checking is a commonly accepted norm and basic principle of journalistic professionalism. It is common for "office journalists" of WeVideo to spend a lot of time checking the facts of an event or a piece of video. By analyzing the content of 226 videos, we find that the most common way to verify facts and obtain value-added information is by conducting a telephone interview. Forty-four percent of news videos contain telephone interview recordings, and the interviewees include video shooters, persons concerned, witnesses, policemen, and administrative units.

During the telephone interview, for the reporters of WeVideo, verifying facts is the primary task and the key to ensuring the veracity of the news. Journalists often

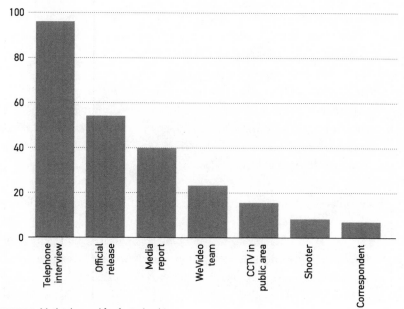

FIGURE 2. Methods used for fact-checking.

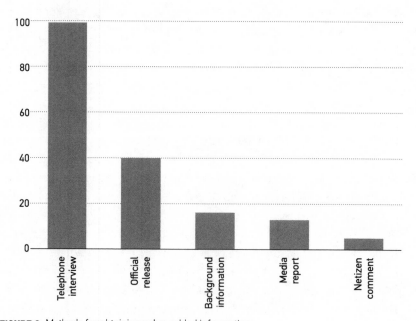

FIGURE 3. Methods for obtaining value-added information.

quote official information and other media reports in their news reports. These two sources of information are authoritative and can endorse the truthfulness of the news to a certain extent. "Truth" does appear to be a constant goal of journalistic professionalism in the convergence environment of the *Beijing News*.

Truth is an important part of media ethics and journalistic professionalism. In order to analyze how journalists and editors conform to media ethics and discuss the construction of journalistic professionalism, Professors Fei Wu and Feng Wu conducted a questionnaire survey of journalists and editors among major news organization in Zhejiang province.[39] The research found that the highest priority for the professional pursuit of editors is in the following order: accurate facts, objective reports, and fairness. This showed that the most important professional requirement of news media at that time was the truth of the news, which is also the law of news. Combined with these research results, it can be argued that in China truth is one of the principles to which news organizations have always attached great importance.

Value-added information is also one of the requirements of journalists for WeVideo who use UGC videos because a news video with insufficient information will not pass the editor's review. As UGC usually does not include all elements of a news story, journalists need to answer their "5 Ws" (When, Where, What, Who, Why) and "1 H" (How) questions through others means, such as background information gathered by interviews.

Furthermore, in the opinion of the editor, value-added information also reflects a journalist's professional ability to dig deeper. Since shooters and correspondents provide news leads and materials to different news organizations at the same time, the amount and quality of the information included in a final news story reflect the professional capabilities of different news organizations and journalists. For example, in a report titled "Chinese Tourists Were Shot in Cambodia,"[40] by carefully observing a news photo published by overseas media, the journalist found a phone number and used it to contact the owner of a local hotel in addition to interviewing the local police officer, embassy, and other administrative units. This effort achieved a breakthrough in finding interviewees in coverage of an international news story.

Topic

As shown in figure 4, there are eight kinds of common topics on WeVideo, and the most popular topics are correlated with "accident" (30.53 percent), "criminal" (24.78

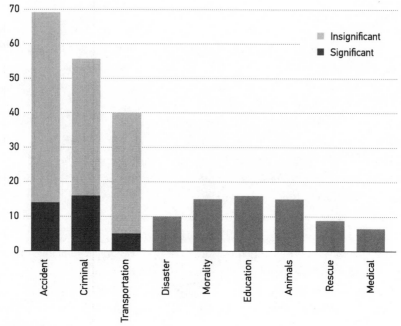

FIGURE 4. Topics.

percent) and "transportation" (17.70 percent) respectively. The topics analyzed above are not mutually exclusive, because a news video may belong to several topics. For example, a transportation accident news item titled "A Rolls-Royce Fell into a Huge Hole after a Road Surface Collapsed in Harbin" is about transportation and accidents.[41]

According to a journalist of the *Beijing News*, WeVideo tends to report visually shocking news and "dynamic" stories, that is, news with a lot of live footage. News with visually shocking footage, such as traffic accidents, is usually accompanied by different levels of casualties and economic losses, which are more of concern to the audience. And "dynamic" news with sufficient live footage can draw and maintain viewer's attention more easily. "Accident," "criminal," and "transportation" topics usually belong to these types.

UGC is one of the major resources of these short-form videos. The popularity of smartphones, dashboard cameras, and other short-video technologies make "recording life with video" a habit of many Chinese people. Taking *Kuai* as an example, it is one of the most popular short video applications in China, whose peak daily active users (DAU) exceeded 70 million in December 2017.[42] WeVideo journalists use *Kuai* to find news leads and frequently use the short videos from it as news materials.

It can be seen from figure 4 that significant news only accounted for a small proportion of the videos analyzed in this study. Perhaps it is because events with greater news value do not occur frequently, especially in the daily life of ordinary people. Besides, ordinary people have been excluded from some significant news scenes. However, these recordings of ordinary life made by ordinary people function as a kind of "agenda setting" for traditional news media.

Keywords in Title

The title of a news story has a great influence on the effect of news coverage, especially for short-form news videos. Titles become one of the key factors in audiences' deciding whether to watch, if not the primary factor. Differing from traditional news reports, news videos on some new media platforms only present titles (sometimes with covers). Therefore, compared to newspapers, headlines are more important for short video news in terms of attracting audiences. The keywords in the headline are the most important words that help the audience understand the news quickly and make the content more attractive. By analyzing the headlines, we found that there are ten categories of keywords that are most frequently used (see figure 5).

These headline keywords are independent but not exclusive. When we analyze a title from a different perspective, it contains different keywords. News of an accident titled as "A Chinese Google Female Engineer Lying Dead in California with Naked Body Floating in the Water and Unknown Dead Cause Yet" emphasizes female, sex, America, and thrilling.[43]

Figure 5 indicates that audiences are likely to be attracted by specific kinds of keywords. Take the keyword "money" as an example: a transportation accident news story titled "A Rolls-Royce Fell into a Huge Hole after a Road Surface Collapsed in Harbin" achieved a click volume of 6.091 million.[44] "A Rolls-Royce" are the keywords of this title, which indicates a great financial loss that is uncommon for ordinary people.

During participant observation, the researcher noticed that it is common for a journalist to modify a title five or more times. Journalists must try to guarantee that titles are accurate and neutral, but it is also important for them to make them

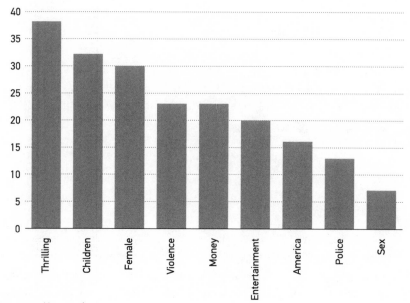

FIGURE 5. Key words.

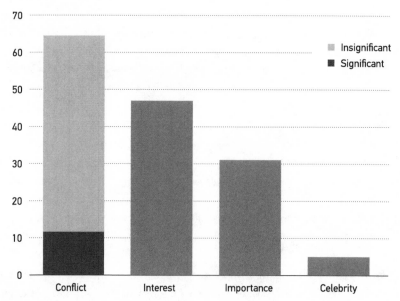

FIGURE 6. News value.

appealing. Even on new media platforms, professional journalists and editors still need to think carefully about titles to avoid producing "sensational headlines."

News Value

News value can be revealed directly from titles. As figure 6 illustrates, four main types of news value emerged from analyzing 226 titles.

The concept of "news value" was formed during the popular newspaper period in the United States in the 1830s. The elements of news value recognized by the American press are whether a story is timely, is unusual, contains conflict, has importance, has proximity to readers, is about a celebrity, and catches general interest.

The conclusions from the analysis of news value here are similar to the results of the keyword analysis: both accident- and crime-related events have the character of conflict, and users like conflict-related news most. This is because these kinds of news stories are critical to human life. And as mentioned before, video is a suitable form to report dynamic and conflict-related events because images of conflict tend to be more visually impactful and lively.

Interest and importance have been important news values since news reporting became an occupation. Furthermore, short-form videos are more lighthearted compared to traditional TV programs, and short-form videos are appropriate for presenting something funny because they are not as serious as traditional TV news. For example, a video titled "A Stupid Thief Had to Push a Motorbike for 30km in 8 Hours after Stole because He Couldn't Drive It" received 2.697 million views. It is neither important nor conflict-related, but the keywords "stupid thief" and the humorous background music make it amusing and attractive.[45]

Figure 6 shows that among the 226 short-form news videos that audiences are most interested in, only 31 (13.7 percent) are of importance. This suggests that when journalists in WeVideo judge the value of a piece of news, whether the event itself is important is not the main criterion for their judgment. The journalists are more concerned about whether the news footage is interesting or about conflict.

Through content analysis, it can be seen that news videos of WeVideo tend to be lightweight and soft, which is different from traditional news organizations in the topic selection and production of news. This is related to UGC's participation in content production and is also inseparable from the impact of the commercial platform.

The Negotiation between News Organizations and Platform

Website traffic represents the potential for attention, influence, and economic income. It is a more direct way to measure the effect of news videos than "circulation" and "audience rating." News organizations naturally expect content to be better disseminated, and there is also an urgent need of monetizing website traffic to provide continuous financial support for content production.

Some news organizations have established new ways of cooperation with commercial companies. Take WeVideo of *The Beijing News* as an example: WeVideo is an independent company established by the *Beijing News* and Tencent. As mentioned above, Tencent bought the exclusive copyrights to WeVideo content. This innovative approach for collaboration combines a professional news organization with an internet company that is professional in its distribution. As one of the mainstream media in Beijing, the *Beijing News* is responsible for content production, while Tencent is responsible for operation and distribution. The *Beijing News* can supply high-quality news coverage for Tencent and attracts more attention with the channel advantage of Tencent.

Tencent provides technical, channel, and financial support for WeVideo. As an internet company, it has advanced technologies such as artificial intelligence (AI) and machine learning (ML) to provide tools to support journalists as they deal with information overload, which helps the newsroom keep on top of breaking news. Some news agencies have been able to use these technologies in news production independently. For example, the Reuters news agency is building an AI tool to help journalists analyze big data sets and suggest story ideas. However, as a municipal news organization, the *Beijing News* has not been able to acquire such technology. Cooperation with Tencent makes up for this.

Through cooperation, the commercial platform has intervened in news production. One way this occurs is by providing story ideas to WeVideo. Randomly selecting twenty days in March 2019, the researcher found that in that time Tencent recommended seventy topics on domestic news, and fifty of them were found to have related coverage. Some topics may coincide with the choices of professional journalists, but not all of them do. In the course of observational research, it was found that when the editors thought some recommended topics had little news value but did not violate professional ethics, they would compromise in favor of the requirements of Tencent News. When certain events cannot be reported, the editor will reject Tencent's suggestion and give a reasonable explanation to convince them. Whether WeVideo fulfills these requirements actively or not, it can be seen from the results that WeVideo accepts Tencent's participation in news production.

The impact of the platform is also reflected in the layout position of news videos. For example, Tencent News is a sub-platform of Tencent, which collects and distributes the contents of different media to different positions. The layout position largely determines traffic. As far as determining distribution is concerned, the evaluation criteria of a commercial platform is based primarily on customers' interests and market orientation, while news organizations should fulfill the mission to serve the public interest. This difference may influence journalists' understanding of journalistic professionalism in a subtle way.

When news videos are placed on commercial platforms for distribution, traffic inevitably becomes one of the criteria for evaluating news and journalists. The preference of the platform greatly affects the traffic. The Weixin plugin is one of the most important platforms of Tencent for news distribution, where traffic can easily exceed 1 million viewers. The contents of WeVideo distributed on the Weixin plugin are similar to the popular news videos analyzed earlier: attracting viewers with conflict-filled and stimulating images, blurring the boundaries of news and entertainment. This content is very attractive to users, and this suggests that Tencent News seems to pay more attention to the ability of these videos to attract traffic.

At the 2018 China News Video Summit Forum, Aijun Wang, the general manager of WeVideo, published a speech on the developmental tendencies, characteristics, and issues of the mobile video industry. Wang said that news organizations in transformation must adhere to the public value of their content, which is the standard for measuring news content. News organizations should not only pursue website traffic flow and economic profits—rather, they must bear responsibility for serving the public interest and promoting the all-around development of human beings.[46]

Many traditional news organizations have built their own mobile applications, but these applications have far fewer users than large platforms. According to the "2018 Q1 China Mobile Internet Industry Development Analysis Report," the top twenty-five applications in China Mobile internet have the largest number of users. Each of them has more than 100 million active monthly users, but there are no professional news media applications among the top twenty-five.[47] Internet companies represented by Baidu, Alibaba, and Tencent are superior in terms of advanced technologies, strong capital, market insight, and flexible operation and have also gained great influence in the economic, social, cultural, and political fields.[48]

Not all the videos Tencent News prefers to recommend have the "public value" emphasized by the *Beijing News*. It should be acknowledged that even though WeVideo accepts Tencent News's suggestions on news topics, Tencent's preference of news does not always match WeVideo's criterion of news value. As a sub-platform of a commercial company, Tencent News does not need to adhere to journalistic professionalism as rigidly as a professional news organization.

Although the perception of news value by WeVideo is different from that of Tencent, traffic has nevertheless become an important factor in the newsroom. WeVideo selects and rewards "good reports" every month at the monthly summary meeting, and one of the criteria for selection is click volume. Many journalists are happy to see their news videos on the Weixin plugin of Tencent News, because this means that their videos are likely to get a lot of traffic and that the journalists will likely reap rewards for that. In this context, the traffic and subsequent rewards have reshaped journalists' perceptions of journalistic professionalism. This will make the news move further toward the domain of pop-culture kitsch and consumerism, diminishing the rational and critical spirit of news discourse that conforms to journalistic professionalism.[49]

It can be seen from the development of WeVideo that the alliance between news organizations and commercial platforms has made more room for the survival of journalists and journalistic professionalism. At the same time, the temptation of the market is also threatening journalistic professionalism.[50] The impact of both sides puts journalistic professionalism in a dynamic equilibrium.

The Journalists Still Insisting on Journalism

Engaging in journalism in China requires permission from the State Administration of Press, Publication, Radio, Film, and Television of the People's Republic of China. Not only do all newspapers, news agencies, TV stations, and other traditional news organizations and a small number of internet news organizations require administrative approval to be established,[51] but also the journalists working in these news organizations need to hold a press card issued by the General Administration of

Press and Publication.[52] The press card is a symbol of the identity of the journalist and the right to interview.

Working for a professional news organization means that journalists have the right to interview and have access to promising professional prospects. In fact, working in an authoritative news organization is itself an affirmation of a journalist's ability to work. Therefore, journalists' recognition of their identity includes emotional dependence on the organization—that is, loyalty to the organization.[53]

But when news organizations are unable to meet journalists' pursuit of journalistic professionalism or material needs, or more seriously, journalists feel that their identity is not respected, the relationship between journalists and news organizations become crippled. This can result in reporters migrating to other news organizations or even leaving the news industry. The commercial platform boom and the demand for content provide possibilities for journalists to leave news organizations and readily find work elsewhere. Other aspiring journalists can switch to other news organizations, looking for a balance between journalistic professional ideals and reality in an imperfect industrial environment.

During our observation at WeVideo, many reporters talked about the work experience of one WeVideo editor. In their words, the editor once worked in a newspaper in a city in southwest China, and his news reports were often obstructed by non-professional factors. The editor believed that working for a more authoritative and larger news organizations was a better way to continue his career, so he came to Beijing to look for another job. In the words of these journalists, the editor's professional ability and news ideals were the main reasons for his persistence today. Many journalists of WeVideo saw him as a role model for young journalists. This kind of recognition implied that at WeVideo, journalists believed that journalistic professionalism was of great significance to professional journalists.

It can be concluded that in a news organization that provides journalists with more freedom and reasonable returns, journalists will have more opportunities to become famous and to have higher professional competence and more loyalty to the organization.[54] In our interview with Yuanwen Peng, deputy general manager of WeVideo, he acknowledged that the cooperation with Tencent has provided great economic support for WeVideo. Peng was proud to say that the cooperation allows them to report without considering cost while at the same time providing reporters with munificent material rewards, which is the premise for them to conduct professional news reports.[55]

Conclusion

The rise of convergence culture in China—and in particular, the convergence of professionally generated content and user-generated content, and the cooperation between news organizations and commercial companies—has had great influence on the production of short-form news videos and the journalistic professionalism that guides news production. This study is dedicated to exploring how news organizations respond to the convergence environment and how journalists perform professionalism within it.

Users are playing an increasingly important role in the production of media content. The deputy general manager of WeVideo admitted in an interview that the production of short-form news videos is inseparable from the short videos taken by netizens.[56] They have advantages in terms of geographical location and perspective, and professional news organizations need to accept and use these advantages to optimize their content and adapt to the developments of the industry. But at the same time, the quality of the content produced by users is uneven, and the truth of them cannot be guaranteed, which brings difficulties for professional news production, such as spending a lot of time to gather information about and to ensure the truth of the content.

In the era of media convergence, practicing journalistic professionalism is not only a common requirement for news production, but also one of the coping strategies chosen by the news industry in the face of external pressure. In the post-truth era, the "reversal" of news events consumes the users' trust in media. No matter how the media environment changes, human society is tirelessly pursuing information and truth. Under this circumstance, only the news organizations that adhere to standards of journalistic professionalism can stand out and defend the dignity of news organizations by providing professional reports. Practicing journalistic professionalism is one of the best ways for news organizations to develop sustainably in any era.

The cooperation between commercial companies and professional news organizations has brought more complicated effects to news production. On the one hand, commercial companies, especially the internet giants, have contributed to the advancement of news production and distribution patterns with their capital and technology. From the viewpoint of Yuanwen Peng, the deputy general manager of WeVideo, the smooth development of WeVideo is inseparable from the business cooperation model with Tencent.[57] On the other hand, the participation of platforms also creates negative impact for professionalism. Commercial platforms are more concerned with whether their investments are generating satisfactory returns, while the *Beijing News* as a professional news organization still emphasizes its responsibility to society. This contradiction inevitably interferes with news production and distribution.

Traditional news organizations in China have to explore transformation strategies to develop. On January 1, 2017, the newspaper the *Beijing Times*, which has had a certain influence in Beijing for fifteen years, was forced to suspend business due to a serious financial deficit. The suspension of the *Beijing Times* seems to support the argument that "paper media is dead."[58] Encountering the problems of "channel failure," loss of users, and decline in influence, traditional news organizations have embarked on transformation, and a proper transformation model becomes critical for traditional news organizations to survive.[59]

In July 2018, the *Shanxi Evening News* and the short-video platform Pear Video started a similar cooperation.[60] Although Pear Video is one of the more famous short-video platforms in China, as an internet company Pear Video does not have the right to conduct news gathering and editing and must rely on professional news organizations to fill in the blanks of its news content. While the *Shanxi Evening News* provides professional news content for Pear Video, it can also find better distribution channels for its content via Pear Video. However, it remains to be seen whether this cooperation model can be successfully replicated.

Taking WeVideo of the *Beijing News* as a case study, we can see that in the convergence environment of the Chinese news industry, news organizations have encountered new opportunities and challenges. Since journalism has become a profession, shared standards of professionalism have been the most important norms that distinguish it from other professions. In the current circumstances of convergence, although journalistic professionalism has been challenged by some factors from inside and outside the industry, it still plays an important role in routine news production.

However, the results of content analysis and participant observation also show that in the context of convergence, the *Beijing News* has also experienced some problems in the production and distribution of news videos when practicing journalistic professionalism. These issues suggest that the involvement of UGC and digital platforms has brought new challenges to journalists, forcing them to redefine the criteria for choosing news.

NOTES

1. "Annual Report: 2017 China Mobile Internet Industry Development Analysis Report," Sohu, last modified January 25, 2018, http://www.sohu.com/a/218908131_204078.

2. Yu Zhao, Yongze Wang, and Xin Ma, "The Current Situation of Short-Form Videos' Distribution," *Radio & Television Information*, no. 53 (September 2015): 53–55.

3. Xiaohong Wang and Yaoti Ren, "New Features and New Problems among Short Video Production in China," *The Press*, no. 17 (September 2016): 72–75.

4. Chuanzhi Gao, "Traditional News Organization's Strategy for Developing Short-Form News Videos," *Chinese Journalist*, no. 07 (July 2017): 51–53.

5. Gao, "Traditional News," 51–53.

6. Chen Li, "The Beijing News: Overview of the Innovation of Urban Newspaper under the Background of Media Convergence," *Chinese Journalist*, no. 10 (October 2016): 27–29.

7. Ying Chen, "Digging for Gold in 'Golden Times' of News Videos: Interview with Yuanwen Peng, Deputy General Manager of WeVideo," *China Publishing & Media Journal*, February 19, 2019, p. 8, http://www.cnepaper.com/zgtssb/html/2019-02/19/content_8_2.htm.

8. "Born for the News, WeVideo Is One Year Old Today," *Weixin* Public Platform, accessed April 28, 2019, https://mp.weixin.qq.com/s/Z92LasGHzNXIwYdrDl9-4A.

9. "2018 *Weixin* Data Report," Tencent, last modified January 9, 2019, https://support.weixin.qq.com/cgi-bin/mmsupport-bin/getopendays.

10. Yuanwen Peng, personal interview, Beijing, May 29, 2018.

11. "Born for the News."

12. Jiang Chang and Xiaopei Wang, "The Production of Short-Form News Video: Western Model and Local Practice," *China Publishing Journal*, no. 16 (August 2017): 3–8.

13. Lanlan Dong, "Information Production Strategy for Short Video—Analysis Based on Popular Short Video Published on 'Pear Video,'" *Journalism Research Guide* 8, no. 2 (January 2017): 38–39.

14. Zhixian Pan, "How to Create a Tipping Point for Short Videos—Taking China Youth Daily as an Example," *News Front*, no. 18 (September 2019): 17–18.

15. Zixuan Zhang and Junjian Liang, "Inheriting and Reshaping: Research on the Features of News Report's Audio-visual Language in Mobile Communication," *Journalism Bimonthly*, no. 05 (October 2017): 52–60.

16. Teresa K. Naab and Annika Sehl, "Studies of User-Generated Content: A Systematic Review," *Journalism: Theory, Practice & Criticism* 18, no. 10 (2016): 1256–73, doi:10.1177/1464884916673557.

17. OECD, *Participative Web and User-Created Content: Web 2.0, Wikis and Social Networking*, (Paris: OECD Publishing, 2007), https://doi.org/10.1787/9789264037472-en.

18. Naab and Sehl, "Studies of User-Generated," 1256–73.

19. OECD, *Participative Web and User-Created Content.*

20. Jenkins Henry, *Convergence Culture: Where Old and New Media Collide* (New York University Press, 2006), 2–3.

21. Henry, *Convergence Culture*, 2.

22. Jia Wang, "Moderate Reform Based on the Framework of News Professionalism: A Realistic Picture of Introducing UGC into Foreign Traditional Media News Production," *Media*, no. 5 (May 2011): 68–70.

23. Weizhen Lei and Chunxiang Ouyang, "The Influence of Video Shooter on Citizen Journalism," *The Press*, no. 2 (February 2010): 77–78.

24. Jia Wang, "Moderate Reform Based on the Framework of News Professionalism," 68–70.

25. Fei Wu and Ye Tian, "Journalistic Professionalism 2.0: Reconstruction of Ideas," *Chinese Journal of Journalism & Communication* 37, no. 7 (July 2015): 6–25, doi:10.13495/j.cnki. cjjc.2015.07.001.

26. Ye Lu and Zhongdang Pan, "Imagining Professional Fame: Constructing Journalistic Professionalism during China's Social Transformation," *Journalism Research* 20, no. 71 (April 2002): 17–53.

27. Zhenzhi Guo, "Supervision by Public Opinion and Journalistic Professionalism in the West," *Chinese Journal of Journalism & Communication*, no. 5 (October 1999): 32–38, doi:10.13495/j.cnki.cjjc.1999.05.009.

28. Liangrong Li, "Contemporary Fate and Historical Mission of Journalistic Professionalism," *News and Writing*, no. 9 (September 2017): 36–37.

29. Lu and Pan, "Imaging Professional Fame," 17–53

30. Zhenzhi Guo, "Journalistic Professionalism and Media Ethics in Age of Public Participation: The Chinese Issues," *Chinese Journal of Journalism & Communication* 36, no. 6 (June 2014): 6–15, doi:10.13495/j.cnki.cjjc.2014.06.001.

31. "About Us," *Beijing News*, http://www.bjnews.com.cn/about.

32. Feixue Nanyuan and Yiqing Hu, "The Crisis of Journalist Professionalism in Age of 'Post-truth,'" *Youth Journalist Journal*, no. 16 (June 2017): 12–14, doi:10.15997/j.cnki. qnjz.2017.16.007.

33. Fei Wu, "Will New Media Bring Revolutionary Influence on Journalistic Professionalism? Public Journalism Movement and the Duty of Professional Journalist," *The Journalist Monthly*, no. 03 (March 2013): 11–19, doi:10.16057/j.cnki.31-1171/g2.2013.03.004.

34. Zhongdang Pan and Ye Lu, "Going Public: Journalistic Professionalism Revisited," *Chinese Journal of Journalism & Communication* 39, no. 10 (October 2017): 91–124, doi:10.13495/j. cnki.cjjc.2017.10.006.

35. Pan and Lu, "Going Public," 91–124.

36. "WeVideo Channel—Video List," Tencent Video, http://v.qq.com/vplus/wevideo/videos.

37. Peng, personal interview.

38. Peng, personal interview.

39. Fei Wu and Feng Wu, "Analysis of the Construction of Journalistic Professionalism," *Journal of Renmin University of China*, no. 6 (November 2004): 122–29.

40. Tencent VFE Team, "4 Chinese Tourists Were Shot in Cambodia," Tencent Video, last modified July 1, 2018, https://v.qq.com/x/cover/s6gfsljzr2oq6rl/p07284qj6dr.html.

41. Tencent VFE Team, "A Road of Harbin Emerges a Huge Hollow, A Rolls-Royce Fall in It," Tencent Video, last modified October 2, 2017, https://v.qq.com/x/cover/dlt5rwkfupwvsl0/z0556gzdtfy.html.

42. "Annual Report," Sohu.

43. Tencent VFE Team, "A Chinese Google Female Engineer Lying Dead in California with Naked Body Floating in the Water and Unknown Dead Cause Yet," Tencent, last modified January 19, 2016, https://v.qq.com/x/cover/8tlns0w5lm75quo/i05179obgpi.html.

44. Tencent VFE Team, "A Road of Harbin Emerges a Huge Hollow."

45. Tencent VFE Team, "A Stupid Thief Have to Push a Motorbike for 30km in 8 Hours after Stolen because He Can Not Drive It," Tencent Video, last modified September 14, 2017, https://v.qq.com/x/cover/3uiii4erwl9j48w/i0550arf4tz.html.

46. Xueliang Sha, Mengyao Wang, and Xiangrong Li, "WeVideo Will Cover All Coverage Areas," *Beijing News*, September 13, 2018, 8–9, http://epaper.bjnews.com.cn/html/2018-09/13/content_731837.htm?div=2.

47. Trustdata, "2017 China Mobile Internet."

48. Guoming Yu, "The Age of Intelligence Media: Market Opportunities and Operational Routes of Traditional Media," *Media*, no. 4 (February 2019): 14–15.

49. Lu and Pan, "Imagining Professional Fame," 17–53.

50. Lu and Pan, "Imagining Professional Fame," 17–53.

51. "Regulations on Internet News Information Services," Office of the Cyber Security and Information Committee of the CPC Central Committee, May 2, 2017, http://www.cac.gov.cn/2017-05/02/c_1120902760.htm.

52. *Press Card Management Method* (2010), http://www.gov.cn/gongbao/content/2010/content_1565495.htm.

53. Lu and Pan, "Imagining Professional Fame," 17–53.

54. Lu and Pan, "Imagining Professional Fame," 17–53.

55. Peng, personal interview.

56. Peng, personal interview.

57. Peng, personal interview.

58. Zuping Zhang, "Discussing the Suspension of the 'Beijing Times' from the Reform of the Supply Side of the Newspaper Industry," People.cn, last modified February 20, 2017, http://media.people.com.cn/n1/2017/0220/c410918-29093795.html.

59. Yu, "The Age of Intelligence Media," 14–15.

60. PearVideo, "Shanxi Evening News Signed a Strategic Cooperation Agreement with Pear Video," July 20, 2018, https://www.pearvideo.com/video_1393361.

The News as International Soft Power

An Analysis of the Posting Techniques of China's News Media
on Facebook and Twitter

Qingjiang (Q. J.) Yao

Social media in general, and Facebook and Twitter in particular, have opened new ways of distributing news, changed the media ecosystem, and established what amount to new public spheres.[1] Such platforms are now ubiquitous, with significantly higher usage among the young, female, and technically literate groups who consume most of their news online.[2] A 2015 Pew survey shows that 65 percent of adults (not just netizens) in the United States use social media, an almost tenfold increase from the decade before.[3] Because Facebook and Twitter are two of the most popular social media platforms in developed societies,[4] they are also recognized by news media as tools to attract news audiences and sources of real-time news updates.[5] In the United States, then, news consumption increasingly involves social media, and especially the tightly designed platforms (discussed in earlier chapters) that users flock to, ensuring that users receive not only news but also news that echoes their pre-existing beliefs, amounting to what scholars are now calling "filter bubbles."[6] News dissemination on social media turns into a frontier of journalism research.

China's mainstream news media, such as Xinhua News Agency, China Central Television (CCTV), *People's Daily*, and *China Daily*, have likewise maintained accounts on Facebook and Twitter, where they hope to tell stories of China, or global stories in China's perspective, to audiences outside China. Because both Facebook and Twitter are censored in China, the Chinese news media accounts on these platforms are explicitly meant to reach users *outside of China*—meaning Chinese-produced but internationally distributed news is becoming one of the primary ways China spreads its message globally. This effort is apparently successful, for by March 14, 2019, by the author's own counting, on Facebook, Xinhua News had 58,598,416 followers; CCTV had 48,069,053 followers; *People's Daily* had accrued 60,815,531 followers; and *China Daily* had won 69,249,515 followers. On Twitter, which provided only rough estimations, Xinhua News Agency had 12 million followers; CCTV had 70.3 million followers; *People's Daily* had 5.6 million followers; and *China Daily* had 3.5 million followers.[7] China's top news outlets therefore post on Facebook and Twitter in English, reaching as many as 236 million users on Facebook and roughly 91 million users on Twitter, amounting to a massive online attempt to enhance China's soft power. It is no stretch to argue, therefore, that the future of US–China relations will hinge in part on the kinds of stories American, Chinese, and international news consumers encounter on social media platforms.

Despite these rapid developments, news dissemination on social media is still not thoroughly understood—more research is urgently needed.[8] How news media from China disseminate news and engage audiences globally on Facebook and Twitter is a neglected area of study and therefore is not fully understood. This study begins the work of filling that void by exploring the techniques China's mainstream news media use to communicate internationally on Facebook and Twitter, and by addressing the effectiveness of those techniques in gaining audience engagement. In so doing, the study also contributes to a more nuanced understanding of international social media use that aims to begin the work of mapping how social media users learn to think about China, the United States, and their entwined relationship.

These are important questions, because research has shown that in the US 51 percent of social media users receive and share news stories through platforms, mainly driven by the desire to talk to others about what is happening in the world. In Canada, 40 percent of people receive news on social media; in the United Kingdom, Facebook is the most important driver of traffic to news sites.[9] Largely through social media, people's relationship to news is now portable and participatory.[10] Social media platforms, mainly Facebook and Twitter, create an opportunity for users to be exposed to more news, civic information, and more diverse viewpoints, although they may also become media silos that limit attitude-challenging information and cultivate more extreme stances.[11] In short, social media—for good and for ill—have become a main traffic source to news sites.[12] The Pew Research Center's Project for Excellence in Journalism, for instance, has found social media a powerful news-referring source, with Facebook normally being the second or the third most important driver of traffic to the top twenty-five popular news websites in the United States.[13] Twitter also enables users to post brief messages (initially limited to 140 characters and now 280) about their daily activities.[14] Twitter has become the most popular and ubiquitous microblogging service and has emerged as a powerful source of news and real-time information updates,[15] changing the way people learn about news in the world.[16] Especially during the presidency of a heavy Twitter user,[17] it is reasonable to expect news consumption on Twitter to increase even more.[18] In short, Facebook and Twitter have revolutionized how users choose their news, how they consume it, how they interact with it, and even what people consider "news" at all.

While individual Facebook accounts have a symmetrical informational model, in which users can view each other's status update, Facebook's business pages, used by media outlets, have an asymmetrical informational flow between the page owner and followers. All followers of the page see the news update instantly, but no follower's personal update enters into the feed of the news page. That is similar to the asymmetrical model adopted by Twitter, a function ideal for news dissemination.[19] However, unlike Facebook's business page, whose readers need to follow the page to read its posts, tweets are public and can be seen by followers and non-followers alike.[20] Studies have accordingly shown that Twitter is more effective than Facebook in reaching an audience, although Facebook is confirmed as the most popular social media site for news consumption.[21] How Chinese news media outlets strive to use these platforms to tell China's stories to the world is therefore crucially important.

In thinking about the ways Chinese news media are trying to reach out to international users via social media, we should note that the effectiveness of their communication on Facebook and Twitter is likely mediated by the cultural differences embedded in the textual, nonverbal, or emotional elements of their messages. For instance, studies have revealed that East Asian netizens prefer a vertical style of the smiling emoticon Ù_Ù, while Western netizens favor a horizontal style of :-),[22] which may be because people from different cultures gauge conversational partners' emotions by monitoring different parts of faces, such as eyes or the mouth.[23] National cultures, as William B. Gudykunst argues,[24] influence communication by drawing upon, appealing to, or sometimes violating longstanding cultural norms.[25] In the United States, for example, most scholars agree that typical news consumers encounter a steady diet of biased coverage of China, meaning Chinese news outlets working on Facebook and Twitter likely encounter negative stereotypes.[26] For example, classic works such as *Four Theories of the Press* and *Agents of Power* view Communist media systems as state-controlled organs and propaganda machines that enjoy no freedom and little credibility.[27] Likewise, in his analysis of China's efforts to develop soft power and cultural diplomacy by supporting the global expansion of its national media, Flew argues that those efforts demonstrate a lack of understanding of the cultural dimensions of power, which will inevitably result in a distributional bias and low audience engagement.[28] From this perspective, China's news media outlets are both shackled at home and crippled abroad, where they are tasked with trying to make an authoritarian regime palatable to international news consumers. On the other hand, one study has shown that China's news outlets are achieving soft power successes in Africa, where viewers appear to relate more powerfully to CCTV than CNN.[29] Particularly as Trump pushes his xenophobic "America First" strategy, it seems reasonable to assume that the playing field for Chinese media will open up.

Given these complicated international contexts, and considering how local and regional politics interface with international communication strategies, research about how China's news media use Facebook and Twitter is urgently needed, especially if we hope to work toward an international media ecosystem driven by understanding rather than recrimination. Making sense of this messaging requires, however, fine-tuned analysis of the technical affordances embedded in these platforms, and especially the mechanisms of audience engagement, so I turn below to a discussion of how liking, commenting, and sharing create an affective economy of user engagement.

Facebook and Twitter Engagements, Topics, and Posting Techniques

Unlike the traditional form of mass news communication, in social media–based news communication, audience engagement is immediately observable with the audiences' feedback.[30] This feedback and engagement enhance civic engagement and are valid ways to measure the effectiveness of China's mainstream news media's communication on Facebook and Twitter in this study.[31] That user participation takes the following forms, which each point to one of the research questions driving this chapter.

Engagements: Liking, Commenting/Replying, Sharing/Retweeting

A prominent feature of Facebook and Twitter is the rich and innovative opportunities they provide for user engagement and social collaboration. Facebook and Twitter's three types of responses contain three levels of engagements, commitment, and cognitive effort: *liking*, an affective feedback, indicates mainly consuming and agreement; *commenting*, a cognitive feedback, indicates contributing to a post; and *sharing*, a promotional feedback, amounts to user-generated distribution.[32] Liking is the lightest version of participatory journalism on Facebook and Twitter because it requires only one click, but commentating or sharing news stories takes more effort.[33] Commenting reveals an association between the news and the self, thus requiring more thinking; sharing constitutes a self-presentation and disclosure, thus requiring more cognitive evaluation of the value of the news and more calculation of perceived benefits, risk, privacy concerns, informational control, and sensitivity.[34] Some industry experts therefore weigh the three type of responses with this formula: roughly, a share weighs as much as two comments, and a comment weighs as much as seven likes.[35] Therefore, liking, commenting, and sharing on Facebook and Twitter are related to each other, but their relationships may be different from the relationships among the three often-studied levels in the hierarchy model of responses: cognitive, affective, and conative.[36] Considering these various forms of user engagement with news distributed on social media, the first research question of this study is: How are Chinese news media's likes, comments, and shares on Facebook and Twitter distributed and associated with each other? The results of this study, which are elaborated later, show that these media outlets earned more likes than shares and comments on Facebook and Twitter, but the number of likes, comments, and shares are substantially correlated.

News Topics and Social Media Engagements

Likes, comments, and shares on Facebook and Twitter are also found to be generated by different content features: likes are generated more by sensory and visual elements, comments are more likely generated by rational and interactive elements, and shares tend reflect sensory, visual, and rational elements.[37] News content is more likely to be shared when it is interesting, helpful, or emotionally arousing or of quality (understood as some combination of enjoyment, relevance, and reliability).[38] A study of ten UK newspapers, including the *Daily Mail, Daily Telegraph, Guardian, Independent,* and *Times,* shows that entertainment news stories (involving sex, show business, human interests, animals, or an unfolding drama) are shared most often on Facebook and Twitter, followed by surprise news stories (involving an element of surprise/contrast) and bad news (stories of conflicts/ tragedies).[39] Another study finds that comments on pieces of soft news are more often shared on Facebook and Twitter and that sensational or celebrity news is more likely to be viral on those platforms.[40] A third study examines how news stories of the *New York Times* and *Guardian* are shared on Facebook and Twitter and finds that news about arts, technology, or entertainment and opinion pieces were shared more frequently. Also, for the *New York Times,* national news stories are more often shared than international news stories, but for the *Guardian,* international news stories are more frequently shared than national news stories.[41] Given this context, the second research question, therefore, is: What type of news from China's news media is more likely to gain engagement on Facebook and Twitter? The results show that social/criminal news stories that feature a funny or criminal component and domestic stories that happened within China are more likely to be liked, commented on, or shared than news stories of other topics, international stories, or stories that happened in another country.

Posting Techniques

In studying effective communication on Facebook and Twitter, researchers have collected data to identify useful posting techniques. Some of those studies involve big data. For instance, social media platform expert Buzzsumo has analyzed over one billion Facebook posts from 30 million brands for that purpose.[42] Based on such research and industry experts' personal observations, techniques such as posting with photos, videos, tags/mentions, hashtags, URLs/links, exclamation marks, or question marks have been recommended to engage the audience on Facebook or Twitter.

Posting photos or videos has emerged in multiple studies as a technique that makes a difference in social media communication. Kim and Yang find that

Facebook posts of organizational news with a video increase shares, and those with a photo increase likes and shares but decrease comments.[43] Industry experts also recommend using photos or videos in Facebook posts or tweets for more engagements.[44] Buzzsumo identifies the use of images, as well as questions, as the most engaging technique.[45] An analysis of 360 days of posts from the Facebook pages of twenty Australian public health organizations also confirms that video posts attract the most engagement as measured by the number of likes, comments, and shares.[46]

Getting others' attention may turn that attention into engagement. On Facebook, posts can "tag" a follower of the account to give the follower, as well as others following that account, notice of the post. On Twitter, the similar function is called "mention" and is more powerful because even non-followers can be mentioned.[47] Facebook "tag" and Twitter "mention" are both signaled as "@," a key part of making social media "social,"[48] and are both recommended for engagement generation. Hashtags, signaled with a # symbol at the beginning of a keyword at both Facebook and Twitter, is also an often-recommended posting technique. It is a handle for the quick search of all posts with the same hashtag keyword on each SNS platform and provides an easy way for readers to find out a larger group with the same interest.[49] Using hashtags has increased rapidly,[50] but experts caution against using more than two hashtags on any given topic.[51] Some industry experts even find that Facebook posts with hashtags obtain less engagements than those without.[52] Providing URLs or emojis in the Facebook or Twitter posts, which is normally shortened by software such as Bit.ly, is.gd, TinyURL, or ow.ly,[53] is also a method recommended to attract audience engagement.[54] Buzzsumo's analysis shows that Facebook posts linked to an article with 1000–3000 words secure the most engagements;[55] empirical studies have also shown that tweets with links spark more comments and shares.[56] Emojis in the posts can be engaging because they graphically represent the emotions of the posters, fulfill important social functions in social media interaction, help the audience to interpret the nuanced meanings of the posts, and stimulate more conversations.[57]

Another two posting techniques recommended by researchers or experts (i.e., Hootsuite, HubSpot, Social Media Examiner, and Buzzsumo): Write snappy copy. Cooper suggests an ideal length of fewer than eighty characters for Facebook posts.[58] Buzzsumo even suggests fewer than fifty characters; the longer the post, the lower the engagement level.[59] Urban also suggests 100 characters for a tweet.[60] And ask questions (i.e., use question marks).[61] Buzzsumo identifies this as the most engaging method.[62] As these comments indicate, social media have developed a wide array of functions to enable users to participate in the spread of "news" and other communication, amounting to a dizzying range of choices, each with their own technical affordances. At the same time, social media scholars are beginning to understand which functions produce the most user engagement. The third research question of this study therefore asks: How do China's news media use the aforementioned posting techniques, and how effective are those techniques in gaining likes, comments, and shares on Facebook and Twitter? The data show that they use most of the techniques discussed above, and their most effective techniques are posting photos and videos and using exclamation marks.

Methodology

SAMPLE

The process of sampling and coding Chinese news media's Facebook and Twitter posts lasted from January 23 to March 1, 2019. On each day of coding, a random number between one and ten was generated to locate the first post for coding; then all other posts for the media outlets for that coding day were sampled with a sampling interval of three (no post was sampled twice). On Facebook and Twitter respectively, one hundred posts were sampled for each of the four news outlets: Xinhua News Agency, CCTV, *People's Daily*, and *China Daily*, totaling 800 posts.

VARIABLES AND CODING

The three response variables, the number of likes (including all emotional responses under the liking button on Facebook), comments, and shares for each post were recorded from Facebook and Twitter directly. Such data were count data (integers from zero to greater) that did not distribute normally. Variables of posting techniques were coded based on a number of factors, such as hidden text and the number of lines of text, exclamation marks, question marks, direct quotes, emojis, URLs, tags/mentions, hashtags, photos (including gif/infographics), and videos used in posts. The specific posting time in each post's timestamp was also recorded, and the time length of posting was calculated by subtracting the posting time from the coding time (recorded when sampling and coding; all times were recorded on the researcher's computer using central daylight time as the standard).

Story locus and topic were coded with content analysis technique. For story locus, the post was coded as domestic (= 1) if the story was just about Chinese people in China; international (= 2) if the story involved two countries or people from two countries, if the story maintained a global or international perspective, or if the location of the story could not be identified; and other country (= 3) if the story was about people from and in another country. For story topic, the post was coded as politics (= 1; the main idea was about political leaders, government, law, international relations, etc.); economics/business (= 2; the main idea was about commerce, industry, construction, production, trade, etc.); culture (= 3; the main idea was about tradition, religion, arts, music, performance, exhibition, festival, cuisine, entertainment, sports, etc.); social/criminal news (= 4; the main idea was about eye-catching or funny social events or crimes, etc.); or education/ science/environment (= 5; including stories about endangered species, medical advancements, etc.). Cohen's Kappa was calculated for the inter-coder reliabilities of those two variables at the beginning of the sampling and coding process in late January 2019. Two coders coded thirty-six posts independently, and the Kappa for story topic was 0.65; for story locus, 0.77. One coder then coded all the rest of the 800 posts. When the sampling and coding were done on March 1, 2019, that coder coded the first forty-five posts again, without referring to any of the existing codes, and calculated Kappa for intra-coder reliability. For story topic, the second calculation of the Kappa was 0.91; for story locus, 0.83. In the analysis, story topic and locus were recoded into dummy variables.

Since news organizations might have different budgets, resources, and posting histories and patterns (e.g., number of followers and frequency of posting), dummy variables for news organizations were also created and used in the analyses to control the organizational heterogeneity. SNS platform (Facebook or Twitter) was also entered in the analyses as a dummy variable.

Results

The first research question examines the distributions of likes, comments, and shares gained by China's news media on Facebook and Twitter and the associations among those three types of social media engagements. On average, altogether on Facebook and Twitter, each post of those news media gained about 1,026 likes, 71 shares, and 21 comments (see table 1). Considering the immense number of followers on Facebook and Twitter as we mentioned before, the data presented here suggest that the ability of news media from China to generate user engagement

TABLE 1. Correlations among Likes, Comments/Replies, and Shares/Retweets

	COMMENTS/REPLIES	SHARES/RETWEETS
Likes	0.754, < 0.001, 800	0.728, < 0.001, 800
Comments/Replies		0.710, < 0.001, 800

1. On average, each post of China's media gained more likes (M = 1025.83, Mdn = 164, Mode = 1200, Min = 5, Max = 36000) than shares/retweets (M = 70.77, Mdn = 21, Mode = 6, Min = 0, Max = 3880), which were more than comments/replies (M = 21.09, Mdn = 6.5, Mode = 2, Min = 0, Max = 1400) on Facebook and Twitter.
2. Entries are, in order, Spearman's ρ correlations (due to the nature of count data of the variables), *p*-values, and sample sizes.

among international social media users is very low. The ratios of likes to shares to comments were consistent for each media outlet's posts on each platform. Those results will be further interpreted in the "Discussion" section.

Since the number of Facebook and Twitter likes, comments, and shares were count data that did not fall in normal distributions, the nonparametric Spearman's ρ correlation analyses were used to test the associations among them, and substantial associations were indeed confirmed (see again table 1). The correlation between likes and comments was 0.754, between likes and shares, 0.728, and between comments and shares, 0.710, all substantial. The distributions of likes, comments, and shares that those Chinese news media gained overall, as well as on Facebook and Twitter respectively, demonstrated that likes were the easiest response for their audiences to make, followed by shares. Comments were the hardest to obtain among the three types of engagements. Comments and likes, however, were correlated more closely than comments and shares, judging by the values for ρ, but no statistical test was found to test the difference between them.

Since the three dependent variables (i.e., likes, comments, and shares) were not only count data but also over-dispersed with variances greater than means (see data in table 2),[63] three negative binomial regressions (a model fitting over-dispersed count data) were modeled to answer the second and third research questions (again see table 2 for the statistics).[64] Negative binomial regression was also chosen in a previous analysis of Facebook likes, comments, and shares for the same reason.[65]

The second research question tests what type of news stories from China's news media are more likely to gain engagements on Facebook and Twitter. The binomial models show that social/criminal news that was about eye-catching or funny social events or crimes gained more likes, comments, and shares than political news, economics/business news, cultural news, or education/science/environment news. Compared with other types of news stories, social/criminal news stories were 102

TABLE 2. Negative Binomial Regressions of Likes, Comments/Replies, and Shares/Retweets

VARIABLES	LIKES		COMMENTS/REPLIES		SHARES/RETWEETS	
	B	EXP(B)	B	EXP(B)	B	EXP(B)
Intercept	4.264***	71.1	1.817***	6.15	2.804***	16.5
Hidden text (= 1)	−0.002	0.998	0.276	1.32	−0.07	0.93
Lines of text	0.029	1.03	−0.014	0.98	−0.012	0.99
Exclamation marks	0.513***	1.67	0.078	1.08	0.478***	1.61
Question marks	0.113	1.12	0.287	1.33	0.004	1.004
Direct quotes	−0.131	0.877	−0.118	0.889	−0.015	0.985
Emojis	−0.017	0.983	0.072	1.08	0.013	1.013
URLs	−0.138*	0.871	−0.179*	0.84	−0.226**	0.798
Tag/mentions	−0.640*	0.527	−0.546	0.58	−0.606	0.545
Hashtags	−0.059	0.942	−0.205***	0.814	0.025	1.03
Photos	0.138***	1.15	0.002	0.998	0.102***	1.107
Videos	0.625***	1.87	0.034	1.04	0.809***	2.246
Facebook (=1)	2.38***	10.84	1.302***	3.68	0.799***	2.22
Publishing time length	0.001	1.00	0.002***	1.002	<0.001	1.000
Xinhua News (=1)	−0.56***	0.57	0.055	1.06	0.047	0.954
CCTV	−1.87***	0.154	−1.04***	0.35	−1.03***	0.36
People's Daily	0.364***	1.44	0.602***	1.83	0.865***	2.38
Political news	0.100	1.11	0.429**	1.54	0.035	1.036
Economic news	−0.088	0.916	−0.257	0.773	−0.108	0.898
Cultural/criminal news	0.028	1.03	−0.169	0.845	−0.165	0.848
Social news	0.704***	2.02	0.615***	1.85	0.712***	2.04
Domestic news	0.521***	1.68	0.289*	1.34	0.316**	1.37
International news	0.156	1.17	−0.109	0.897	0.022	1.02
(Negative binomial)	0.735		0.983		0.883	
Model Info	Deviance (885.97/775) = 1.14. Omnibus χ^2(22, n = 800) = 1235.97, p < 0.001		Deviance (882.94/775) = 1.14. Omnibus χ^2(22, n = 800) = 542.18, p < 0.001		Deviance (884.99/775) = 1.14. Omnibus χ^2(22, n = 800) = 703.81, p < 0.001	

1. Out of 800 posts by China's media on Facebook and Twitter, 619 used photos/images (M = 1.94, Mdn = 1, Mode = 1, Min = 0, Max = 18); 183 used a video; 3 used tags/mentions (ranging from 1 to 5); 366 used hashtags (M = 0.68, Mdn = 0, Mode = 0, Min = 0, Max = 5); 279 used URLs/links (M = 0.39, Mdn = 0, Mode = 0, Min = 0, Max = 7); 122 used emojis (M = 0.11, Mdn = 0, Mode = 0, Min = 0, Max = 11); 32 used question marks (M = 0.05, Mdn = 0, Mode = 0, Min = 0, Max = 2); 61 used exclamation marks (M = 0.09, Mdn = 0, Mode = 0, Min = 0, Max = 3); 49 used direct quotes (M = 0.07, Mdn = 0, Mode = 0, Min = 0, Max = 5); Hidden texts appeared in 18 posts (M = 21.09, Mdn = 3, Mode = 2, Min = 0, Max = 37).

2. Entries are coefficient (B) and the Incidence Rate Ratio (Exp (B), with a baseline of 1 to determine the increase or decrease of the incidence rate ratio) of the three negative binomial regression models of likes, comments/replies, and shares/retweets. All three are count data and over-dispersed because their variances were greater than means (likes: M = 1025.83, SD = 2502.18, S^2 = 6260888.9; comments/replies: M = 21.09, SD = 61.75, S^2 = 3812.65; shares/retweets: M = 70.77, SD = 241.6, S^2 = 58370.49).

3. *** stands for p < 0.001, ** for < 0.01, * for < 0.05.

percent more likely to be liked, 85 percent more likely to be commented on, and 104 percent more likely to be shared, while political news stories were only 54 percent more likely to gain a comment. In terms of story locus, domestic news stories about Chinese people in China were 68 percent more likely to be liked, 34 percent more likely to be commented on, and 37 percent more likely to be shared or retweeted. Those news media from China also fared better on Facebook than on Twitter, with their stories 984 percent more likely to gain a like, 268 percent more likely to gain a comment, and 122 percent more likely to be shared, perhaps because they had more followers on the former. Among them, the most engaging was the *People's Daily*, whose stories were 44 percent more likely to have likes, 83 percent more likely to receive a comment, and 138 percent more likely to be shared.

The third research question examines the effectiveness of the posting techniques that were recommended by previous studies and industrial observations for China's news media to elicit audience engagements on the US SNS platforms Facebook and Twitter. All posting techniques recommended in the literature were used by those news media. Specifically, out of 800 posts, 619 used photos/images; 183 used a video; 3 used tags/mentions (between 1 to 5 tags or mentions); 366 used hashtags; 279 used URLs/links; 122 used emojis; 32 used question marks; 61 used exclamation marks; and 49 used direct quotes. Hidden texts accessible by clicking "see more" appeared in 18 of those posts.

Adding a photo to a post, as expected, gained about 15 percent more likes, judging from the exponent of the coefficient, i.e., the Incidence Rate Ratio (IRR, represented as Exp(B) in table 2.) and about 11 percent more shares, but made no difference in comments. Adding a video had even stronger positive effects, gaining about 87 percent more likes and about 125 percent more shares but again not more comments. Using an exclamation mark increased likes by 67 percent and shares by 61 percent, but using a URL/link decreased all types of responses: likes, by 13 percent; comments, by 16 percent; and shares, by 20 percent. Using a tag/mention decreased likes for about 47 percent, but had no influence on other types of responses. Using a hashtag also decreased comments for about 19 percent.

Discussion

Through analyzing 800 posts randomly collected from their Facebook and Twitter pages, this study examines the posting techniques that four mainstream news media from China (China Xinhua News Agency, CCTV, *People's Daily*, and *China Daily*) use to communicate with their audiences outside of China on two of the most popular US SNS platforms, Facebook and Twitter, and the effectiveness of those techniques in terms of gaining audience engagement (as measured by the number of likes, comments, and shares). The study identifies effective techniques for those news media to communicate cross-culturally and internationally on the two major American social networking platforms and enters an emerging but rarely studied area of intercultural communication research.[66] It may also shed light on the understanding of the effectiveness of SNS or intercultural communications in general.

The first thing noticeable in the findings is the distribution patterns of the three types of SNS responses (i.e., likes, comments, and shares) and their associations with each other. Liking, believed to be at the affective level,[67] is the most common type of engagement on Chinese news media's Facebook and Twitter pages.[68] Commenting is considered as a cognitive response to the Facebook or Twitter messages but ends up being the most difficult type of engagement for Chinese news media to secure (see results for the first research question),[69] judging from its frequency. Sharing is made more often than commenting but less than liking. So the engagement to China's news posts on Facebook and Twitter shows an affective-conative-cognitive hierarchy; this differs from the traditional cognitive-affective-conative hierarchy of responses that holds audience responses move from knowledge to attitude and then to behaviors as well as the widely believed formula about responses to SNS messages that a share roughly equals two comments and a comment roughly equals seven likes in efforts of information processing.[70] Further studies are needed to understand if this affective-conative-cognitive hierarchy is unique to consuming China's news on Facebook and Twitter or universal to all cross-cultural and international news consumption on SNS platforms. One possible reason for the frequency of commenting to be the lowest among the three types of responses could be that, when people share a Facebook post or tweet, they often also add some comments,[71] which are not shown on the news media's Facebook or Twitter pages and therefore cannot be included in the analysis in this study. That phenomenon, however, is universal to all Facebook and Twitter communications and not unique in the consumption of Facebook posts and tweets of news media from China.

The affective-conative-cognitive pattern of likes, shares, and comments identified in this study also provokes us to dwell on the nature of the information processing of SNS messages in general. That pattern is different than the hierarchy of responses in the literature of media effects, which normally follows a cognitive-affective-conative order.[72] Substantial correlations among those three types of response to an SNS message, however, are confirmed with the data in this study, and commenting appears to be associated more closely with liking than with sharing, which is actually consistent with findings of the traditional cognitive-affective-conative hierarchy. The nature of, and the relationships among, those steps of information processing on SNS platforms, as well as their relationships with traditional responses to media contents, need further research.

Unlike the *New York Times* or the *Guardian*, whose news stories about art, technology, and entertainment or opinion pieces are most often shared on Facebook and Twitter, social/criminal stories from news media in China gain the most engagement on the two social media platforms, indicating a cultural difference. The popularity of social/criminal news on Facebook and Twitter may also deviate from the intention of the news media in China, which is to communicate political or economic information from China's perspective or spread information about Chinese culture to counter stereotypes about China in developed societies, defend China's interests abroad, and perhaps maintain its national esteem.[73] The criminal components in this type of news could cast a negative light on China's society, especially given that Facebook and Twitters users are more likely to engage with such stories. The popularity of these stories about China indicates that Facebook and Twitter users are using these media outlets to understand things in China, especially happenings not covered by news media outside China.

Also noticeable in the results of this study is the confirmation of the effectiveness of posting techniques like using a video, photos, or exclamation marks. The most effective posting technique for China's news media is using a video,[74] which is seen in about 23 percent of analyzed posts. Video posts have almost double the likes and more than double the shares/retweets than non-video posts. The effectiveness of photos in harvesting likes and shares is also confirmed.[75] More than 77 percent of posts by China's news media use photos, sometimes up to eighteen, with most posts using only one photo. Each photo can increase the post's chance of gaining a like by 15 percent and a share by about 11 percent, showing the advantage of visual communication in crossing cultural or stereotypical hurdles. It is surprising to see that an exclamation mark,[76] which is used in about 8 percent of the posts by China's news media (numbers of the exclamation marks ranging from one to five), also increases the chance of gaining a like or share by more than 50 percent.

This may be due to the lighter mood or the sense of curiosity generated by the exclamation mark.

It is also surprising to see that some of the techniques recommended by previous studies or industry experts have no, or even negative, effects in engagement generation. The conspicuous one is the use of links/URLs,[77] which appears in about 35 percent of the posts. Link/URLs decrease the propensity for the posts to acquire likes, comments, and shares, possibly because the posts with more links/URLs are daily briefs of news that may be of less interest to the audience or because those links/URLs may take the readers away from those posts before they respond with a like, comment, or share. Using a tag/mention,[78] which few posts by China's news media do, decreases the chance of harvesting a like by about 47 percent, maybe because the nature of tagging/mention makes readers feel that they are not the only party in the conversation. Using hashtags,[79] which are seen in about 46 percent of posts by the four Chinese news media producers (ranging in number from one to seven in those posts), decreases the chance for the audience to make a comment by about 19 percent with each hashtag, confirming the observation of some previous studies.[80] The underlying psychological mechanism or cultural difference of such phenomena is unclear and needs further studies to reveal.

As a pilot exploration of Chinese news media's posting techniques on the US social media sites Facebook and Twitter and the effectiveness of those techniques, this study has limitations that should be kept in mind when interpreting its results. The sample of posts, although it was randomly collected on each day of sampling and coding and was sizable enough to keep the sampling error reasonably small, still concentrates on a period of about forty days, largely during the lunar Spring Festival time range. The representativeness of the sample can be enhanced in future research by collecting posts from a longer time period. Also, it is not certain that all responses to those posts of China's news media on Facebook and Twitter are genuine. Concern has been raised about those media's purchasing of likes, comments, or shares from "click farms," although such concern has not been confirmed in a reporter's investigation.[81] If fake engagement exists, the analyses of the effectiveness of the posting techniques could certainly have been biased. That bias, however, cannot be easily corrected in any research on SNS engagement. Also, although this study measures the effectiveness of Chinese news media's posts on Facebook and Twitter with the quantity of likes, comments, shares, specific meanings that are attributed by the audiences of those media to those behaviors beyond regular social media responses still need further exploration to unveil.

Although the focus of this study is on the effectiveness of China's news media on US-based social media platforms in engaging the global audience and therefore potentially providing some balance to the stereotypical coverage of China in global media discourse, the study might also make people wonder how effective the global news media's communication is inside China, whether through traditional media outlets or social media. Such communication is currently restricted in China.[82] Such restriction, although it might have helped to maintain the social stability in China, could also distort Chinese people's perception of China and the world beyond it, cultivate barriers to cross-cultural communications and international collaborations,[83] and therefore hinder Chinese people from becoming mature citizens of the world. How to relax the control of the media system while maintaining social tolerance and harmony is, however, the topic for another study.

Another issue related to this study, although not directly, is the new development of news weaponization between China and the United States. Amid the outbreak of the pandemic COVID-19, on February 3, 2020, the *Wall Street Journal* published an article titled "China is the Real Sick Man of Asia."[84] Using that insulting term, which echoes China's "century of humiliation," resulted in an uproar in the Chinese community globally, a protest within the *Journal* itself, and the Chinese government's revoking the press passes of three journalists in the *Journal*'s Beijing bureau. These actions were then mirrored by the US Department of State's designating five major Chinese news media outlets, including the four in this study, as foreign missions.[85] Both actions, on behalf of China and then America, were clearly acts of political retaliation.[86] These weaponized designations are even more complicated when considered within the current US government's unfavorable attitude toward mainstream media and the challenge to define "journalist" within the US legal system, as shown in the "shield law" debate.[87] In response, the Chinese government revoked press credentials of journalists working for the *New York Times*, *Washington Post*, and *Wall Street Journal* in Beijing, and told the publishers of those news outlets, who issued an open letter appealing the revocation, to address the issue to the US government.[88] This latest Sino-US struggle over news organizations and journalists does not change the analysis of this study, yet it indicates deepening Sino-US tensions, thus justifying the urgent need for bilateral understanding—which can be achieved through the communication phenomenon studied in this chapter.

NOTES

1. Eli Skogerbo and Arne H. Krumsvik, "Newspapers, Facebook and Twitter: Intermedial Agenda-Setting in Local Election Campaigns," *Journalism Practices* 9, no. 3 (2015): 350–66, https://doi.org/10.1080/17512786.2014.950471.

2. Kelly Quinn, "Why We Share: A Uses and Gratifications Approach to Privacy Regulation in Social Media Use," *Journal of Broadcasting and Electronic Media* 60, no. 1 (2016): 61–86, https://doi.org/10.1080/08838151.2015.1127245; Brain E. Weeks and R. Lance Holbert, "Predicting Dissemination of News Content in Social Media: A Focus on Reception, Friending, and Partisanship," *Journalism and Mass Communication Quarterly* 90, no. 2 (2013): 212–32, https://doi.org/10.1177/1077699013482906.

3. Andrew Perrin, "Social Networking Usage: 2005–2015," Pew Research Center Web, October 8, 2015, http://www.pewinternet.org/2015/10/08/2015/Social-Networking-Usage-2005-2015/.

4. Sanne Hille and Piet Bakker, "I Like News: Searching for the 'Holy Grail' of Social Media; The Use of Facebook by Dutch News Media and Their Audiences," *European Journal of Communication* 28, no. 6 (2013): 663–80, https://doi.org/10.1177/0267323113497435. Clark F. Greer and Douglas A. Ferguson, "Using Twitter for Promotion and Branding: A Content Analysis of Local Television Twitter Sites," *Journal of Broadcasting and Electronic Media* 55, no. 2 (2011): 198–214, https://doi.org/10.1080/08838151.2011.570824.

5. Sounman Hong, "Online News on Twitter: Newspapers' Social Media Adoption and Their Online Readership," *Information Economics and Policy* 24 (2012): 69–74, https://doi.org/10.1016/j.infoecopol.2012.01.004. Katrin Weller, Bruns, Axel Bruns, Jean Burgess, Merja Mahrt, and Cornelius Puschmann, "Twitter and Society: An Introduction," in *Twitter and Society*, ed. Katrin Weller, Axel Bruns, Jean Burgess, Merja Mahrt, and Cornelius Puschmann (New York: Peter Lang, 2014), xxix–xxxviii.

6. Mario Haim, Andreas Graefe, and Hans-Bernd Brosius, "Burst of the Filter Bubble?: Effects of Personalization on the Diversity of Google News," *Digital Journalism* 6, no. 3 (2018): 330–43, https://doi.org/10.1080/21670811.2017.1338145.

7. Alexa Olesen, "Where Did Chinese State Media Get All Those Facebook Followers?" *Foreign Policy*, March 14, 2015, https://foreignpolicy.com/2015/07/07/china-facebook-peoples-daily-media-soft-power/.

8. Weeks and Holbert, "Predicting Dissemination of News Content in Social Media."

9. Hille and Bakker, "I Like News."

10. Hong, "Online News on Twitter."

11. Eytan Bakshy, Solomon Messing, and Lada Adamic, "Exposure to Ideologically Diverse News and Opinions on Facebook," *Science* 348 (2015): 1130–32, https://doi.org/10.1126/

science.aaa1160.

12. Weeks and Holbert, "Predicting Dissemination of News Content in Social Media."

13. Kenny Olmstead, Amy Mitchell, and Tom Rosenstiel, "Navigating News Online: Where People Go, How They Get There and What Lures Them Away," Pew Research Center, May 9, 2011, http://www.pewresearch.org/wp-content/uploads/sites/8/legacy/NIELSEN-STUDY-Copy.pdf.

14. Greer and Ferguson, "Using Twitter for Promotion and Branding."

15. Paul D. Skalski, Kimberly Neuendorf, and Julie A. Cajigas, "Content Analysis in the Interactive Media Age," in *The Content Analysis Guidebook*, ed. Kimberly A. Neuendorf, 2nd ed (Thousand Oaks, CA: Sage Publications, 2017), 201-403. Weller, Bruns, Burgess, Mahrt, and Puschmann, "Twitter and Society."

16. Scot Hacker and Ashwin Seshagiri, "Tutorial: Twitter for Journalists: Become a Master of Community Engagement with KDMC's Complete Guide to the Art of Microblogging," UC Berkeley Advanced Media Institute Website, published 2014, https://multimedia.journalism.berkeley.edu/tutorials/twitter/.

17. Jayeon Lee and Young-shin Lim, "Gendered Campaign Tweets: The Cases of Hillary Clinton and Donald Trump," *Public Relations Review* 42, no. 5 (2016): 849–55, https://doi.org/10.1016/j.pubrev.2016.07.004.

18. Mathew Ingram, "Here Is Why Donald Trump Says He Loves Twitter and Plans to Keep Tweeting," *Fortune*, January 17, 2017, http://fortune.com/2017/01/17/trump-loves-twitter/.

19. Hong, "Online News on Twitter."

20. Hacker and Seshagiri, "Tutorial: Twitter for Journalists."

21. Skogerbo and Krumsvik, "Newspapers, Facebook and Twitter."

22. Masaki Yuki, William W. Maddux, and Takahiko Masuda, "Are the Windows to the Soul the Same in the East and West? Cultural Differences in Using the Eyes and Mouth as Cues to Recognize Emotions in Japan and the United States," *Journal of Experimental Social Psychology* 43, no. 2 (2007): 303–11, https://doi.org/10.1016/j.jesp.2006.02.004.

23. Jaram Park, Young Min Baek, and Meeyoung Cha, "Cross-Cultural Comparison of Nonverbal Cues in Emoticons on Twitter: Evidence from Big Data Analysis," *Journal of Communication* 64 (2014): 333–54, https://doi.org/10.1111/jcom.12086.

24. William B Gudykunst, "Cultural Variability in Communication: An Introduction," *Human Communication Research* 24, no. 4 (1997): 327–48, https://doi.org/10.1177/009365097024004001.

25. Park, Baek, and Cha, "Cross-Cultural Comparison of Nonverbal Cues in Emoticons on Twitter."

26. Michelle Murray Yang, *American Political Discourse on China* (New York: Routledge, 2017).

27. Fred S. Siebert, Theodore Peterson, and Wilbur Schramm, *Four Theories of the Press: The Authoritarian, Libertarian, Social Responsibility and Soviet Communist Concepts of What the Press Should Be and Do* (Champaign, IL: University of Illinois Press, 1984). J. Herbert Altschull, *Agents of Power: The Role of the News Media in Human Affairs* (New York: Longman, 1984). Hugo de Burgh, *China's Media in the Emerging World Order* (Buckingham, UK: University of Buckingham Press, 2017). Zhaoxi Liu, *Metro Newspaper Journalists in China: The Aspiration-Frustration-Reconciliation Framework* (New York: Routledge, 2017). Ran Wei, Ven-Hwei Lo, Katherine Yi-Ning Chen, Edson Tandoc, and Guoliang Zhang, "Press Systems, Freedom of the Press and Credibility: A Comparative Analysis of Mobile News in Four Asian Cities," *Journalism Studies* (2019), https://doi.org/1 0.1080/1461670X.2019.1691937.

28. Terry Flew, "Entertainment Media, Cultural Power, and Post-Globalization: The Case of China's International Media Expansion and the Discourse of Soft Power," *Global Media and China* 1, no. 4 (2016): 278–94, https://doi.org/10.1177/2059436416662037.

29. Herman Wasserman and Dani Madrid-Morales, "How Influential are Chinese Media in Africa?: An Audience Analysis in Kenya and South Africa," *International Journal of Communication* 12 (2018): 2222, http://ijoc.org.

30. Cheonsoo Kim and Sung-Un Yang, "Like, Comment, and Share on Facebook: How Each Behavior Differs from the Other," *Public Relations Review* 43 (2017): 441–49, https://doi.org/10.1016/j.pubrev.2017.02.006.

31. Bakshy, Messing, and Adamic, "Exposure to Ideologically Diverse News and Opinions on Facebook"; Christine Greenhow and Jianghang Li, "Like, Comment, Share: Collaboration and Civic Engagement within Social Networking Sites," in *Emerging Technologies for the Classroom: Explorations in the Learning Sciences, Instructional Systems and Performance Technologies*, ed. C. Mouza and N. Lavigne (New York: Springer, 2013), 127–41.

32. Kim and Yang, "Like, Comment, and Share on Facebook."

33. Hille and Bakker, "I Like News."

34. Kim and Yang, "Like, Comment, and Share on Facebook." Mehrdad Koohikamali and Anna Sidorova, "Informational Re-sharing on Social Networking Sites in the Age of Fake News," *Informing Science* 20 (2017): 215–35; Quinn, "Why We Share."

35. Kim and Yang, "Like, Comment, and Share on Facebook."

36. Qingjiang Yao, Praphul Joshi, Chiung-Fang Chang, Chelsea McDonalds, James Tran, William Wheeler, and Shiyue Hou, "Advocating a New Approach to Governing Water, Energy, and Food Security: Testing the Effects of Message Inoculation and Conclusion Explicitness in the Case of the WEF Nexus," *Journal of International Crisis and Risk Communication Research* 1, no. 1 (2018): 111–34, https://doi.org/10.30658/jicrcr.1.1.6.

37. Kim and Yang, "Like, Comment, and Share on Facebook."

38. Weeks and Holbert, "Predicting Dissemination of News Content in Social Media." Koohikamali and Sidorova, "Informational Re-sharing on Social Networking Sites in the Age of Fake News."

39. Tony Harcup and Deirdre O'Neil, "What Is News? News Values Revisited (Again)," *Journalism Studies* 18, no. 12 (2017): 1470–88, https://doi.org/10.1080/14616 70X.2016.1150193.

40. Bente Kalsnes and Anders Olof Larsson, "Understanding News Sharing across Social Media: Detailing Distribution on Facebook and Twitter," *Journalism Studies* 19, no. 11 (2018): 1669–88, https://doi.org/10.1080/1461670X.2017.1297686.

41. Marco Toledo Bastos, "Shares, Pins, and Tweets: News Readership from Daily Papers to Social Media," *Journalism Studies* 16, no. 3 (2015): 305–325, https://doi.org/10.1080/14616 70X.2014.891857.

42. Steve Rayson, "How to Improve Facebook Engagement: Insights from 1Bn Posts," Buzzsumo Web, February 7, 2016, https://buzzsumo.com/blog/how-to-improve-facebook-engagement-insights-from-1bn-posts/.

43. Kim and Yang, "Like, Comment, and Share on Facebook."

44. Dara Fontein, "18 Practical Twitter Tips for Beginners," *Hootsuite Blog*, December 17, 2015, https://blog.hootsuite.com/twitter-tips-for-beginners/; Rayson, "How to Improve Facebook Engagement"; Amanda Zantal-Wiener, "14 Essential Tips for an Engaging Facebook Business Page," *HubSpot Blog*, May 16, 2018, https://blog.hubspot.com/marketing/how-to-create-facebook-business-page-ht. Liz Alton, "7 Tips for Creating Engaging Content Every Day," Twitter Business, May 24, 2017, https://business.twitter.com/en/blog/7-tips-creating-engaging-content-every-day.html; Derek Cromwell, "26 Tips for Better Facebook Page Engagement," Social Media Examiner, October 3, 2016, https://www.socialmediaexaminer.com/26-tips-for-better-facebook-page-engagement/; Diana Urban, "50 Tweetable Twitter Tips You Wish You Knew Years Ago," *HubSpot Blog*, April 21, 2014, https://blog.hubspot.com/marketing/twitter-tips-list.

45. Rayson, "How to Improve Facebook Engagement."

46. James Kite, Bridget C. Foley, Anne C. Grunseit, and Becky Freeman, "Please Like Me: Facebook and Public Health Communication," *PLOS One* 11, no. 9 (2016), https://doi.org/10.1371/journal.pone.0162765.

47. Hacker and Seshagiri, "Tutorial: Twitter for Journalists."

48. Fontein, "18 Practical Twitter Tips for Beginners."

49. Fontein, "18 Practical Twitter Tips for Beginners"; Hacker and Seshagiri, "Tutorial: Twitter for Journalists."

50. Skogerbo and Krumsvik, "Newspapers, Facebook and Twitter."

51. Alton, "7 Tips for Creating Engaging Content Every Day"; Hacker and Seshagiri, "Tutorial: Twitter for Journalists"; Urban, "50 Tweetable Twitter Tips You Wish You Knew Years Ago."

52. Cromwell, "26 Tips for Better Facebook Page Engagement"; Rayson, "How to Improve Facebook Engagement."

53. Hacker and Seshagiri, "Tutorial: Twitter for Journalists."

54. Alton, "7 Tips for Creating Engaging Content Every Day."

55. Rayson, "How to Improve Facebook Engagement."

56. Skogerbo and Krumsvik, "Newspapers, Facebook and Twitter."

57. Park, Baek, and Cha, "Cross-Cultural Comparison of Nonverbal Cues in Emoticons on Twitter"; Urban, "50 Tweetable Twitter Tips You Wish You Knew Years Ago."

58. Paige Cooper, "21 Facebook Tricks and Tips Everyone Should Know in 2018," *Hootsuite Blog*, August 13, 2018, https://blog.hootsuite.com/facebook-tricks/.

59. Rayson, "How to Improve Facebook Engagement."

60. Urban, "50 Tweetable Twitter Tips You Wish You Knew Years Ago."

61. Alton, "7 Tips for Creating Engaging Content Every Day"; Cooper, "21 Facebook Tricks and Tips Everyone Should Know in 2018"; Cromwell, "26 Tips for Better Facebook Page Engagement."

62. Rayson, "How to Improve Facebook Engagement."

63. Kim and Yang, "Like, Comment, and Share on Facebook."

64. A. Colin Cameron and Pravin K. Trivedi, *Regression Analysis of Count Data*, 2nd ed. (New York: Cambridge University Press, 2013).

65. Kite, Foley, Grunseit, and Freeman, "Please Like Me."

66. Doreen Wu and Chaoyun Li, "Sociolinguistic Approaches for Intercultural News Media Studies," *Intercultural Communication Studies* 25, no. 2 (2016): 14–31, https://web.uri.edu/iaics/files/Wei-FENG-Doreen-D.-WU.pdf.

67. Kim and Yang, "Like, Comment, and Share on Facebook."

68. Hille and Bakker, "I Like News."

69. Kim and Yang, "Like, Comment, and Share on Facebook."

70. Kim and Yang, "Like, Comment, and Share on Facebook."

71. Weeks and Holbert, "Predicting Dissemination of News Content in Social Media."

72. Yao et al., "Advocating a New Approach to Governing Water, Energy, and Food Security."

73. Burgh, *China's Media*.

74. Alton, "7 Tips for Creating Engaging Content Every Day"; Cromwell, "26 Tips for Better Facebook Page Engagement"; Fontein, "18 Practical Twitter Tips for Beginners"; Rayson, "How to Improve Facebook Engagement"; Urban, "50 Tweetable Twitter Tips You Wish

You Knew Years Ago"; Zantal-Wiener, "14 Essential Tips for an Engaging Facebook Business Page."

75. Kim and Yang, "Like, Comment, and Share on Facebook"; Rayson, "How to Improve Facebook Engagement."

76. Alton, "7 Tips for Creating Engaging Content Every Day"; Cooper, "21 Facebook Tricks and Tips Everyone Should Know in 2018"; Cromwell, "26 Tips for Better Facebook Page Engagement"; Rayson, "How to Improve Facebook Engagement."

77. Alton, "7 Tips for Creating Engaging Content Every Day"; Hacker and Seshagiri, "Tutorial: Twitter for Journalists"; Park, Baek, and Cha, "Cross-Cultural Comparison of Nonverbal Cues in Emoticons on Twitter"; Skogerbo and Krumsvik, "Newspapers, Facebook and Twitter"; Urban, "50 Tweetable Twitter Tips You Wish You Knew Years Ago."

78. Fontein, "18 Practical Twitter Tips for Beginners"; Hacker and Seshagiri, "Tutorial: Twitter for Journalists."

79. Fontein, "18 Practical Twitter Tips for Beginners"; Hacker and Seshagiri, "Tutorial: Twitter for Journalists"; Skogerbo and Krumsvik, "Newspapers, Facebook and Twitter."

80. Cromwell, "26 Tips for Better Facebook Page Engagement"; Rayson, "How to Improve Facebook Engagement."

81. Olesen, "Where Did Chinese State Media Get All Those Facebook Followers?"

82. Olesen, "Where Did Chinese State Media Get All Those Facebook Followers?"

83. Paul Mozur, "China Spreads Propaganda to U.S. on Facebook, a Platform It Bans at Home," *New York Times*, November 8, 2017, https://www.nytimes.com/2017/11/08/technology/china-facebook.html; Bang Xiao, "'I Don't Know Facebook or Twitter': China's Great Firewall Generation Z Cut Off from the West," Australian Broadcasting Corporation, November 9, 2018, https://www.abc.net.au/news/2018-11-10/chinas-great-firewall-generation-who-dont-know-facebook/10479098.

84. Walter R. Mead, "China Is the Real Sick Man of Asia," *Wall Street Journal*, February 3, 2020, https://www.wsj.com/articles/china-is-the-real-sick-man-of-asia-11580773677.

85. Marc Tracey, "Inside the Wall Street Journal, Tensions Rise Over 'Sick Man' China Headline," *The New York Times*, February 22, 2020, https://www.nytimes.com/2020/02/22/business/media/wall-street-journal-sick-man-china-headline.html.

86. Lara Jakes and Steven Lee Myers, "U.S. Designates China's Official Media as Operatives of the Communist State," *New York Times*, February 18, 2020, https://www.nytimes.com/2020/02/18/world/asia/china-media-trump.html.

87. Jonathan Peters, "Shield Laws and Journalist's Privilege: The Basics Every Reporter Should Know," *Columbia Journalism Review*, August 22, 2016, https://www.cjr.org/united_states_project/journalists_privilege_shield_law_primer.php.

88. Huaxia, ed., "Full Text of Chinese Foreign Ministry's Reply to Open Letter Co-signed by Publishers of Three U.S. Media Outlets," Xinhua, http://www.xinhuanet.com/english/2020-03/28/c_138925384.htm.

PART III

Engagement and Disengagement

Mediating Agents on WeChat

A Local Turn in the Personification of State–Society Intermediaries

Wei Wang

One influential paradigm in studying post-reform China is state-society relations.[1] Many studies in this paradigm focus on the mediating space between the state and society. Scholars have used different terms to conceptualize this space, such as "public sphere,"[2] "civil society,"[3] and "the third realm."[4] Despite differences in usage, these terms denote the importance of mediating agents, including various forms of associations, in negotiating state-society relations. Social media have retrofitted the intermediating space between state and society, meaning we now have a wide range of digital spaces where citizens, associations, government bureaus, and other stakeholders convene to discuss controversial issues.[5] For example, WeChat, an instant messaging service and social media platform (which is studied in several other chapters in this volume), is a popular digital space for communication in Chinese social life. Eric Harwit has argued that WeChat serves an atomizing function by turning people away from national or broader-level communication to local-level and small-group intimate interaction.[6] But even while recognizing the limits of WeChat-based interaction, Harwit also points to its potential for mobilizing local groups to solve issues facing local communities.[7] Building upon that hope, this chapter studies three popular mediating agents from the Anhui province to show how the strong personal ties and trust underpinning WeChat groups can be marshaled to encourage civic participation rooted in a sense of local pride.

The existing literature has not studied how new online agents mediate state-society relations. On WeChat, some individuals have a more noticeable presence than others; these high-profile users build a large following, primarily based on personal relations and mutual trust. Some of them regularly post government policies, social issues, and news pieces, even becoming so prominent that they are then invited to participate in government policy-making—these online figures therefore become what I am calling "mediating agents," for they bridge the gulf between everyday social media users and the government. Their social issue-orientation distinguishes them from regular "internet celebrities" (网红, or *wanghong*), who mobilize their online popularity without tackling politics or building localized personal networks. These non-political *wanghong* accumulate national or even international audiences, with whom they have almost no personal ties; the mediating agents I study here, in comparison, base their online popularity and power on their deep connections to local issues, and hence amount to a new form of online civic leaders. This chapter therefore asks: How shall we conceptualize the role of these digital intermediaries between state and society? Who are these people? How do they assume and then fulfill the intermediary role? How do local communities and local governments perceive them? How does the rise of digital mediating agents contribute to an updated understanding of state-society relations in the digital era? And does this process amount to a new form of online civic engagement for China?

By answering these questions, this chapter contributes to an understanding of state-society relations in digital China. I argue that WeChat, representing a specific kind of digital platform, facilitates the emergence of digital mediating agents who negotiate state-society relations by conveying government policies to local communities and, in turn, collecting local sentiments for conveyance back to the government. The emergence of these digital mediating agents reflects the personification of state-society intermediaries in a commercially driven digital era. To pursue this argument, this chapter reviews studies on state-society relations in contemporary China. Then, it discusses the concept of mediating agents on new media platforms. Then it turns to three Anhui-based mediating agents on WeChat, with my analysis based upon a series of interviews and figures and data collected online. I selected three counties (县 xian) where I interviewed the social issue-oriented internet celebrities with a large following, who regularly post about government policies, social issues, and news pieces, in some cases even rising to a level of prominence where they were invited to participate in government policy-making. I chose county-level internet celebrities due to the characteristics of counties in China, hence echoing Elizabeth Perry's call for local county-level studies on state-society relations.[8] Within this county-based analysis of online mediating agents, I focus my analysis on three issues: how the mediating agents worked to preserving local cultures and customs, how they participate in and sometimes lead local volunteer activities, and how they advocate for improving the county town's (县城 xiancheng) appearance. As we will see in these case studies, the online mediating agents were remarkably successful in using globe-straddling social media platforms to create a sense of local allegiance and commitment. Thus, while these figures acted as mediating agents between everyday Chinese citizens and the government, they also linked international technology with local concerns.

State-Society Relations and Mediating Spaces and Agents

Scholars have produced a vast amount of research on state-society relations in post-reform China.[9] As Perry states, the third-generation studies on Chinese politics "turned to models of state-society relations drawn from the European tradition."[10] Scholars are interested in how the Chinese state, representing a unique assemblage of apparatuses, practices state-building and exerts control over society and how social forces react to state-building. Going beyond the state-society dichotomy, scholars acknowledge that state and society interpenetrate, meaning they both contend and cooperate with each other. Many studies in this paradigm, however, neglect regional differences in Chinese society. As Perry points out, "a central feature of Chinese history is, of course, a rich tradition of both regionalism and bureaucratic differentiation that both pre- and post-dates Europe's 'modern' transition. Fascination with this variation has led a whole generation of China historians to produce an impressive corpus of local area studies."[11] Building upon this tradition of "local area studies" within China, this chapter highlights the contextual specificity of state-society interactions by drilling down to the level of Anhui province.

Within the state-society literature, "public sphere" and "civil society" are two key concepts often used to describe the mediating spaces between state and society. Craig Calhoun and others used these concepts to study the Tiananmen protest movements in 1989.[12] Gordon White, Jude Howell, and Xiaoyuan Shang examine a sphere composed of voluntary associations mediating between the state and social groups. They define this sphere as a civil society.[13] Similarly, Jessica Teets notices the two-way communication function of civil society in bridging local officials and social forces. Local officials have thus developed a "social management" system to take advantage of the supporting role of civil society. This "social management system" is defined as consultative authoritarianism.[14] Not satisfied with these two European terms, Philip Huang coined the term "third realm" to denote the space between the state and the society.[15] Guobin Yang and Craig Calhoun describe the appearance of a green public sphere of environmental discourse and debates, where nongovernmental organizations play a critical role in shaping new avenues for civic engagement, amounting to what Phaedra Pezzullo and Jingfang Liu call "green communication."[16] Ya-Wen Lei examines the rise of a contentious public sphere where vibrant political discussion and contention emerge, despite state control.[17] Likewise, Patrick Dodge's edited collection, *Communication and Convergence in the New China: International Perspectives on Politics, Platforms, and Participation*, offers a series of case studies in how online platforms offer complicated avenues for citizen engagement, state control, and corporate innovation, with all parties jockeying for power and influence.[18] Across this literature, scholars hold different views regarding whether or not an autonomous field of citizen action lies between the state and society, and they also debate the applicability of Western terms in describing "Chinese realities."[19] Despite these disagreements, the concepts of the public sphere, civil society, and the third realm reveal the importance of these civic agents in negotiating state-society relations.[20] Building upon this literature, I propose that new agents also arise as state-society intermediaries on digital platforms.

Indeed, the rise of the internet has retrofitted the intermediating spaces between state and society.[21] One notable change is the advent of social media as a space where citizens, associations, government bureaus, and other stakeholders convene to discuss controversial issues.[22] For instance, volunteer associations that intermediate between state and society have opened accounts on major social media platforms, expanding their reach and influence. Meanwhile, individuals, exemplified by the verified users on Weibo and other social networks, exert substantial influence, with some serving as opinion leaders.[23] Among the studies of Weibo's role in public debates, Adrian Rauchfleisch and Mike Schäfer notice Weibo's local dimensions.[24] They find different types of public spheres on Weibo, one of which is "local public spheres." As they put it, "open debates with a strong degree of criticism towards sub-national authorities is possible, as they may be utilized by the Chinese national government as opportunities to legitimize itself by intervening in subnational matters on behalf of its citizens."[25] These local public spheres can evolve into much larger discussions if influential accounts post the attention-grabbing issues that transcend local concerns to reach national audiences.

If Weibo is a space where local discussions surface, then WeChat is the platform that fully embraces local discussions. Since being launched by Tencent, WeChat has become a dominant tool in Chinese social life. As Harwit puts it, "WeChat's proclivity to channel Chinese on-line discourse into small, cohesive collections of like-minded individuals could lead to the mobilization of local communities for small-scale social action."[26] However, studies about how local and regional discussions form on WeChat are scant. This chapter attempts to fill in this gap by investigating how three "local" mediating agents ascended to a level of influence that enabled them to mediate state-society relations. In this way, this chapter adds new nuance to our understanding of China's evolving digital public spheres.

WeChat and Internet Celebrities

Graeme Turner sees a "demotic turn" in popular culture,[27] which refers to "the increasing visibility of the 'ordinary person' as they turn themselves into media content through celebrity culture, reality TV, DIY websites, talk radio, and the like."[28] Proliferating media forms and production capacities enable media conglomerates to increasingly involve "ordinary people" and turn them into celebrities. One of the most prevailing forms of the demotic turn is reality TV, which not only normalizes the labor logic and power structures of the socioeconomic organization of neoliberalism, but also conveys the cultural dimensions of neoliberal self-management technologies.[29] This "demotic turn" has accelerated via online platforms, which are now the seedbed for a new generation of "internet celebrities" or "wanghong" (also see the third chapter in this volume).[30] On YouTube, Weibo, Facebook, WeChat, and similar social networking sites, users are empowered to present themselves to the public. Some users accumulate spectacular fame and become internet celebrities. The social, cultural, and economic implications of the rise of these internet celebrities are profound. In China, internet celebrities spearhead cultural trends, claim discursive power, and serve as good salespersons in e-commerce. On Weibo, Taobao, and WeChat, these internet celebrities build large followings and exert influence on followers. As a form of branding practice, they tend to present a specific image or a set of images to followers. For example, if an internet celebrity aims to become a fashion icon, she or he would selectively post selfies of their taste in fashion.

As critics have noted, these internet celebrities adopt cultural codes such as autonomy, self-reliance, competition, and self-promotion.[31] They brand themselves through carefully selected packages of texts, photos, and videos, amounting to crafted personae, individualized forms of strategic communication. Different from regular internet celebrities, the internet celebrities who I interviewed have a special attachment to the local. They adopt a combination of personal branding techniques and locally based information dissemination to create the appearance of being unedited, original, authentic selves. Their primary communication strategy is presenting themselves as "down to earth" (接地气 jie diqi). Their usernames are nicknames, which become a personal brand with significant local-level influence.

To explore how these local internet celebrities mediate between the state and society, I chose three counties in Anhui province. In each of the three counties, I selected a popular internet celebrity who had a large number of followers and was influential among local residents. I found them based on my observations on WeChat and recommendations from local friends. Following the selection of these three celebrities, I began to produce an online ethnography. I browsed their posts and compiled those from the first and last three days of the month, stretching from March to August 2018. From my observations of these posts, I categorized them into different types; I then documented the comments on the posts and analyzed how these mediating agents interacted with their followers. In addition to this online ethnography, I also conducted offline interviews with the management teams for these accounts. I asked them about what motivated them to open such accounts, what strategies they used to attract and maintain followers, what posts they chose to publicize, and what their relationships with followers and local establishments were like. In this way, I too served as a mediating agent, bridging the space between physical people and their online personae, and then between these online figures and both their audiences and the local governments with whom they interacted.

I chose county-level internet celebrities because counties are located at the intersection of locality and the digital cultural sphere. Thinking broadly, platforms constitute the major players in the digital sphere today; WeChat in particular has become the springboard of everyday activities for the Chinese people. Counties are embedded in the national and even international digital landscapes of these globe-spanning platform economies, which means the ways local residents in counties appropriate new media tools can reflect media usage at large. At the same time, counties are the locus of specific local contexts. Compared with top-tier or second-tier cities, counties are situated in more local arenas and therefore reflect a higher level of contextual specificity than municipalities or bigger cities. People living in counties follow relatively traditional lifestyles and are more embedded in traditional social networks. Studies of different local areas thus help us to delve into intra-society comparisons and to study how international digital platforms are used at the local level. Therefore, my analysis emphasizes how locality and national-level platforms simultaneously impact state-society intermediaries. To organize my commentary, the following sections of analysis ask three questions: how the mediating agents worked to preserve local cultures and customs, how they participated in and sometimes led local volunteer activities, and how they advocated for improving the county town's (县城 xiancheng) appearance.

County-Level Internet Celebrities on WeChat

The three accounts that I selected all had a large number of followers. They either use nicknames or are well known by nicknames. In Ningfeng county,[32] Zhong is a local internet celebrity who is about forty years old, always friendly and gentle.[33] In this county with a population of approximately 300,000, his WeChat official account accumulated around 100,000 followers. In Qianyi county, Hai is part of the management team of a popular official account that had about 100,000 followers.[34] In Shangshu county,[35] Tan manages an official account with about 72,000 followers.[36] Besides official accounts, they also have a large number of friends on their personal WeChat accounts. Given the population figures for Ningfeng county, then, we can see that these mediating agents reached deeply and widely into the community.

The people behind the accounts have become bridges between the local government and local residents to different degrees. Zhong had relatively deep engagement with the local government. A well-known personality in the county, he was a member of the county-level Chinese People's Political Consultative Conference (中国人民政治协商会议 Zhongguo renmin zhengzhi xieshang huiyi, hereafter the PCC). The PCC is an advisory conference consisting of delegates with different political and organization affiliations. It also invites independent members to participate in policymaking. In the PCC, participants convene to discuss local issues and submit policy proposals to the government and legislatures. Contrary to some stereotypes of political life in China, the PCC amounts to a thriving form of local democracy and citizen engagement.

Zhong also maintained vibrant connections with local social organizations as well as semi-governmental organizations. He participated in government policy-making and posted government policies to his official account and friend circles. In comparison, Hai's team had project-based collaborations with the local government. This team also posted local news on their official and personal accounts. Although Tang actively devoted himself to charity work, he did not have any connections with local charitable organizations. Rather, his relationship with the local government was paradoxical, an observation on which I will elaborate in the following section.

Preserving Local Culture

The impressive clout of Zhong's WeChat official account originated with his posting of several songs in the local dialect. In Ningfeng county, besides the mainstream and working language of the local Mandarin,[37] various local dialects flourish. With the campaign to popularize Mandarin and the local Mandarin, the younger generation has not been motivated to learn local dialects, concerning some that the local dialects in Ningfeng county might become endangered. For those who still speak the local dialects, especially those who work outside Ningfeng county, the local dialects are loaded with nostalgic and cultural meanings. And so, around 2013, Zhong hit upon the idea that singing a popular song with a local dialect would be fun. He posted the song online with a nickname, and to his surprise, the song went viral. These songs sounded familiar, interesting, and funny, with a local dialect as the signature language. Zhong rode the momentum and reproduced several songs in this local dialect, one of which garnered more than 1 million views. These songs circulated his name through Ningfeng county and among Ningfeng people who work outside the county's hometown. His personal account on WeChat was inundated with friend requests. From then on, Zhong began to post interesting and relevant news pieces on his personal friend circles (the "Moments" function of WeChat, known as "Pengyou quan" [朋友圈] in Chinese). As his personal account reached WeChat's friend list limit (approximately 5,000 friends), he opened an official account with his nickname. Official accounts are public accounts with no follower limit. The posts of these accounts can be publicly viewed by any WeChat user. Zhong's online nickname (his username) is cute, full of humor, and easy to remember. This nickname became his label, indicating a grassroots identity.

Following the popularity of these songs in the local dialect, Zhong posted information closely relevant to local residents. A very important feature that he sought to blend into the posts was the sense that he is *jiediqi* (down to earth 接地气). The goal of incorporating this feature is to make his posts interesting and important for local residents so that these posts can grab and anchor followers. Besides preserving local dialects, Zhong showed a deep interest in preserving local culture, promoting local cultural elements among local residents, and attracting tourists to Ningfeng county. He visited "ancient villages" (古村落 gu cunluo) with local cultural characteristics and posted delicately written essays and well-photographed pictures on his WeChat account. He also actively connected with experts in the local culture. The county-level PCC therefore included him as a representative in the local culture preservation sector. His commitment to the local culture and his WeChat influence enabled him to become part of the county's establishment. This PCC membership paved the way for him to be further involved in local governance, so even while he was bathed in the aura of *jiediqi*, he was also becoming locally powerful as an influencer.

For example, in one of the townships in Ningfeng county, the county-level Propaganda Department, the PCC, the Culture and Tourism Department, and a few other bureaus established a township-level Institute for Conservation of Historic and Cultural Works. Zhong was selected as the chair. One of the local major media outlets published an essay titled, "Haha, X (Zhong's nickname) is now an official (哈哈, X当官了 Haha, X dangguan le)." This title is telling of the image of Zhong in the local area. Zhong was considered as a friend and a local celebrity representing grassroots interests and culture. His participation in local governance was perceived as a well-received story of how a grassroots celebrity could rise to be part of the local establishment.

Zhong's WeChat official account was an effective venue for him to communicate with his followers about PCC conference progress and his proposal. Zhong collected comments and ideas about how to develop local cultural tourism. He summarized the comments in his own proposal to the county-level PCC. As Zhong's WeChat official account grew in popularity, he established a company that focused on video production, seeking to incorporate his expertise to preserve local culture. He endeavored to produce documentaries on the local culture, including folk activities, lineage traditions, and gourmet stories. Part of his preparation for this series of documentaries was to communicate with local cultural preservation organizations and with governmental departments in charge of local cultural preservation. For the local cultural preservation department, Zhong's WeChat influence made him a good fit for the local establishment.

Similar motivation to preserve local culture drove Hai as well. Hai is one of the leaders of the management team of a popular official account in Qianyi county. One of his friends, Wang,[38] was a funny figure among their friend circle. Wang's way of behaving, talking, and making facial expressions always entertained his friends. Hai, Wang, and another friend of theirs felt it would be a good idea to share Wang's humor and fun with other people. They sought to collaborate with an existing local WeChat official account to brand Wang as a funny media figure. They also sensed a business opportunity: if they could attract enough users, they could use this official account as a media outlet to earn advertising revenue. Soon enough, the funny episodes they made of Wang became popular among locals, as the team had expected. At the time of my interview, their official account had about 100,000 followers. Besides posting videos, they also selected interesting news articles and useful business information. The content manager in their team, a young woman with work experience in Shanghai, told me that content management in counties was quite different from that in big cities like Shanghai. She said that the most effective posts for attracting local residents are highly relevant to their everyday life, such as local housing price fluctuations and supermarket discounts. Additionally, when selecting news pieces, she said it was important to select sensational ones to attract followers. As these comments indicate, even while Hai's online persona felt authentic and original, the team driving this online persona was thinking strategically—suggesting that *jiediqi* may be less an authentic reflection of an online personality than a carefully crafted product.

Tang is from Changshu county.[39] He used to be a migrant and would often suffer homesickness. When he was working away from his hometown, he followed some official accounts that primarily posted news pieces. Two years ago, he opened an official account after returning home from his work. At first, he posted news, just as the other influential official accounts in his county. However, he became unsatisfied with this way of operating the account as he perceived a lack of diversity in its content. With the goal of documenting rural life, Tang migrated to a new account titled with his nickname. He said, "my account is unique. I have never seen any accounts like mine. I want to document my rural life. People like me are interested in seeing my rural life. . . . I don't have any expertise. My account is plainly documenting my daily life." Thus presenting himself as a local and non-professional poster rooted in local concerns, Tang's account attracted many followers, including migrants from Changshu county. One of his goals was to "make them less homesick" (解他们一点乡愁 jie tamen yidian xiangchou). According to him, most county-level official accounts have content about food, news, and information about daily life, but Tang did not intend for his account to be instrumental (实用性 shiyongxing) for his followers. He has since attracted roughly 70,000 followers. He feels that the number of followers, views, and comments has remained relatively constant. With his official account becoming increasingly popular among local residents, Tang began to feel a responsibility to contribute to charity work and hoped to motivate his followers to help others as well. In this way, Tang became a champion of local causes, an "every man" speaking for and with the local people.

In these cases, the local dialect is a pedestal on which the legitimacy and popularity of these accounts develop. The local dialect, symbolizing local culture, differentiates these accounts from other nonlocal accounts that also provide a great deal of information. In particular, for those who work as migrants away from their hometown, the familiar dialect connects them to affairs in their hometown. One of the highlights of the comments that I collected from the posts on these three accounts was their praise for the local dialect. As one of the posts' comments says, "our local dialect retains many historical components, but our local people are losing our local dialect. It is great that your official account uses this local dialect to shoot videos." Some people who work outside the county also express their excitement in hearing the local dialect.

Besides the local dialect, the local-centered content generated by these accounts also elicited responses that can be categorized as an everyday form of civic participation. For example, Hai's team posted a self-made song titled "I Am from Qianyi County." They used cameras and drones to shoot the music video, which showed appealing scenes from the county. The post including this song received about 12,000 views and fifty-three comments selected by the official account manager. These comments spoke highly of the video, and in addition to praise, they also gave suggestions to Hai's team to film certain places that were more unconventional sightseeing spots. One comment suggested Hai's team shoot a street, a part of which was of low quality and repaved many times. On these accounts, the comment area became a space where local residents and migrants could express concerns and propose suggestions about their hometown. These interactions can be seen as an everyday form of civic participation, originating from an attachment to the hometown and reinforcing an identity with the local. These accounts became the spaces in which local identities could be preserved and even expanded, thus using globe-straddling digital platforms to facilitate local forms of civic engagement and cultural preservation.

Volunteer Activities

In yet another act of mediating different spheres of action, both Zhong and Tang have shifted from being online figures to leading local volunteer activities around grassroots causes. Indeed, with increasing fame among local residents, Zhong has become a popular collaborator and guest for local organizations, especially those involved in volunteer activities. The Local Compassion Volunteer Organization recruited Zhong as a member, and he used his official and personal accounts to broadcast activities organized by this group. Although registered as a social organization, it received governmental support when it organized local activities. Zhong was thus a good fit for them to bridge governmental and social support. In a similar vein, when Tang was a child, his parents went to work in cities as migrant workers. As a left-behind child, he knew that help was much needed in the countryside. After saving enough money, he devoted himself to helping poverty-stricken families in his home county and visited at least one family every week. At the end of each year, Tang posts an invitation on WeChat to ask followers to attend his annual charity gathering. At these gatherings, he asks for donations from followers while contributing his own donations to those in need. In both cases, Zhong and Tang have become the nodes in local charity networks. Zhong's influence as an internet celebrity meets the demands of local volunteer activities. His involvement, publicized on his influential WeChat accounts, serves as a role model for his followers. In addition, Zhong's commitment to charity work guarantees his steadfast collaboration with local volunteer organizations. In contrast with Zhong, Tang initiated his own project to help local poverty-stricken households. He conducted charity work every week and built a network, originating online and extending to offline, to help others. These cases demonstrate the critical role of local internet celebrities in local volunteer activities and indicate how online action can evolve into grassroots leadership.

Improving the County Town's Appearance

After making some popular episodes featuring Wang on WeChat, Hai's team took the opportunity to specialize in video production. On the one hand, they produced videos for business clients. Their clients included local businesses and some nationally or provincially famous brands that had trouble accessing the local market. Impressed by the communicative power of Hai's videos, these business clients hoped to replicate this success with entertaining advertisements. They believed that the humor in the videos could better convey the persuasive messages of advertisements. On the other hand, Hai's team made humorous episodes to entertain followers. For instance, one video they produced mocked a person who littered and was well received by their followers. It was soon noticed by the local Hygiene Department and County Town Appearance Department. Recognizing the influence of such a video and Hai's team, the local County Town Appearance Department contracted with Hai's team to produce more videos for raising environmental awareness among local residents. Their collaboration generated several videos aimed at educating local residents not to litter and to keep the environment clean. As Hai said, these videos with "positive energy" (正能量 zheng nengliang) often received unexpected praise. Hai's team therefore employed strategic communication combining business interests, personal aspects, and civic engagement, producing a truly interdisciplinary and multi-modal online persona that impacted local communities.

WeChat as a Digital Bridging Space

As scholars have noticed, the internet provides a digital space where citizens can interact with each other. On earlier internet forums, such as Bulletin Board Systems (BBS), netizens convened freely and expressed ideas as a mass-to-mass communication form. On more recent platforms such as Weibo, many-to-many communication has become the norm. One difference that has developed is the presence of verified users who act as opinion leaders. On WeChat, the most common way to communicate is to initiate person-to-person chats or group chats. Both occur between friends. This means that on WeChat, for most situations, a user needs to be friends with someone to initiate chats. The only mass communication venue is the space under the posts of official accounts where readers can leave and like comments and authors can comment back. For the three cases discussed here, I analyzed their posts including the content, comments, and views. In the comment section under WeChat official accounts' posts, viewers would leave comments for these official accounts in a style that resembled chatting with friends. Some people might know the internet celebrities in real life, but most of them probably did not have personal ties with them. Nevertheless, these internet celebrities often would be addressed as familiar friends. This personal style can also be found in other digital venues, such as livestreaming platforms where broadcasters address viewers as friends. But in the cases I examined here, the interaction unfolded with more local or same-origin characteristics. A sense of "we as a unified group" underpinned the discussion. When viewers commented on posts that were about their hometown and things that interested them, these comments conveyed a sense of "a local community" and a "community-oriented identity." I have selected a few examples below:

> "Great (again)! Ningfeng people are very talented, and the land is fabulous. Ningfeng has a long history. Thumb up and clap for Ningfeng!!"
> "(Ningfeng's) Fame is much known."
> "I want to go back to my hometown to develop my career."
> "Home is sweet. I left my hometown when I was a teenager, and I very much like your life. I am not able to go back to my hometown for a career."

In Tang's case, he would collect followers' comments. In particular, as he was well known for charity work, some of his followers would leave comments to ask for help. When Tang found these comments, he would go and help those people in need. Through face-to-face interaction, some of his followers became good friends and continued their interactions with him online. As he said,

> (For) those people who often comment (under my posts), I help them. If there is anything they need help with, I then help them. I donate money to elderly people who live alone. All these pieces of information come from my net friends. (When) they say there are elderly people who live alone in their villages, I would go. Then they are touched by this and would interact with me very often.

At the end of the year, he would send out an online invitation on WeChat to ask his followers to attend his annual charity convention. In this way, Tang translated his online friends into offline friends, who furthered their interactions online. This can partly explain why his "plain" documents of daily life on WeChat attract a large number of followers.

Indeed, the three accounts that I selected share a common feature: they were well known as nicknames, and these nicknames became WeChat usernames. In the online and offline worlds, their nicknames boosted their fame among local people. Using nicknames built a funny, familiar, friendly, and easy to remember image for them. In their interactions online, their followers interacted with them as close friends, even though they probably did not know each other offline. In the context of the local county, the strategy for each account to win followers is both similar to and different from nationwide internet celebrities. More importantly, they position themselves as "down to earth," with the goal of being friends with local people. Combining a personal-branding ethos with an attachment to the local context, they are local internet celebrities.

Conclusion: The Personification of State-Society Intermediaries

In the decades following reform and opening, many state-society intermediaries acquired credibility through official recognition or group affiliations. Conventional social actors are organizations or officially recognized social groups; GONGOs and NGOs, for example, are officially registered organizations. They research special issues, collect data, generate proposals, and implement projects. Similarly, although village-level administrations are not part of the government, they are officially recognized as legitimate local governance committees. In contrast, these individuals on WeChat occupy mediating positions because of their personas, profiles, and self-branding strategies rather than any existing group affiliations. They adopt a specific set of techniques to build a public image that is friendly, humorous, grassroots-oriented, and attached to the local community. I have characterized this phenomenon as *the personification of state-society intermediaries*, which is embodied in two dimensions. First, in the context of individualistic culture, social media enable the rise of internet celebrities who wield personal influence in social networks. In my cases, the internet celebrities trumpet local characteristics to assume the role of mediating agents between the state and society. Second, these individuals have transformed themselves into personal brands. Each personal brand assembles a public image, a specific set of branding techniques, and a range of ways to interact with different stakeholders. These internet celebrities are "down to earth," being part of the local community; they are perceived to be trustworthy friends who care about local affairs and whose nicknames are personal brands. In this way, they become personified state-society intermediaries on digital platforms.

Through my analysis of three digital mediating agents, this chapter furthers the understanding of state-society relations in contemporary China. Accompanying the move from societal-level discussion and contention to local-level and community-based interaction, I have analyzed the roles of three digital mediating agents by focusing on three issues: preserving local culture, participating and even leading volunteer activities, and advocating for improving the county town's appearance. The three cases I selected represent different ways of mediating between the state and the society. Zhong's case illustrated how local internet celebrities get deeply involved in the local governance. Hai's team had short-term collaboration with the local government. Tang was committed to local charity work.

The emergence of these digital mediating agents also reflects the personification of state-society intermediaries. In the decades following the reform, many state-society intermediaries have acquired credibility due to group affiliations or group membership. In contrast, the individuals on WeChat in my study occupy mediating positions because of their personas, profiles, and self-branding strategies. They have branded themselves as friendly grassroots celebrities with an attentiveness to local needs. They interact with followers from the same place in a "down to earth" manner. They are trustworthy friends who care about local affairs in the local community. The personification of state-society intermediaries speaks to the individualistic culture in the digital sphere, which blends grassroots sentiments with personal branding strategies.

NOTES

1. Elizabeth J. Perry, "Trends in the Study of Chinese Politics: State-Society Relations," *China Quarterly* 139 (1994): 704–713; Fengshi Wu, "Evolving State-Society Relations in China: Introduction," *China Review* 17, no. 2 (2017): 1–6.

2. Ya-Wen Lei, *The Contentious Public Sphere: Law, Media, and Authoritarian Rule in China* (Princeton, NJ: Princeton University Press, 2018); Qing Liu and Barrett McCormick. "The Media and the Public Sphere in Contemporary China," *boundary 2* 38, no. 1 (2011): 101–134; Christoph Steinhardt and Fengshi Wu, "In the Name of the Public: Environmental Protest and the Changing Landscape of Popular Contention in China,"

China Journal 75, no. 1 (2016): 61–82.

3. Anthony J. Spires, "Contingent Symbiosis and Civil Society in an Authoritarian State: Understanding the Survival of China's Grassroots NGOs," *American Journal of Sociology* 117, no. 1 (2011): 1–45; Jessica C. Teets, *Civil Society under Authoritarianism: The China Model* (New York: Cambridge University Press, 2014); Gordon White, Jude Howell, and Xiaoyuan Shang, *In Search of Civil Society: Market Reform and Social Change in Contemporary China* (Oxford, UK: Clarendon, 1996).

4. Philip C. C. Huang, "'Public Sphere'/'Civil Society' in China?: The Third Realm Between State and Society," *Modern China* 19, no. 2 (1993): 216–40.

5. Ya-Wen Lei and Daniel Xiaodan Zhou, "Contesting Legality in Authoritarian Contexts: Food Safety, Rule of Law and China's Networked Public Sphere," *Law & Society Review* 49, no. 3 (2015): 557–93; Guobin Yang, *The Power of the Internet in China: Citizen Activism Online* (New York: Columbia University Press, 2009).

6. Eric Harwit, "New Social Media Technologies and Community Mobilization in China: The Growth and Potential of WeChat" (paper presented at the Annual Conference of the Association for Asian Studies, Seattle, WA, April 2016); Eric Harwit, "WeChat: Social and Political Development of China's Dominant Messaging App," *Chinese Journal of Communication* 10, no. 3 (2017): 312–27.

7. Harwit, "New Social Media Technologies and Community Mobilization in China"; Harwit, "WeChat: Social and Political Development of China's Dominant Messaging App," 312–27.

8. Perry, "Trends in the Study of Chinese Politics," 704–13.

9. Examples: Kang Chen, "Administrative Decentralization and Changing State-Society Relations in China," *International Journal of Public Administration* 21, no.9 (1998): 1223–55; Perry, "Trends in the Study of Chinese Politics," 704–13; You Ji, *China's Enterprise Reform: Changing State/Society Relations after Mao* (New York: Routledge, 1998); Wu, "Evolving State-Society Relations in China," 1–6.

10. Perry, "Trends in the Study of Chinese Politics," 704.

11. Perry, "Trends in the Study of Chinese Politics," 709.

12. Craig Cahoun, "Tiananmen, Television and the Public Sphere: Internationalization of Culture and the Beijing Spring of 1989," *Public Culture* 2, no.1 (1989): 54–70. Craig Calhoun, *Neither Gods nor Emperors: Students and the Struggle for Democracy in China* (Berkeley: University of California Press, 1994). See also Lewis Friedland and Zhong Mengbai, *International Television Coverage of Beijing Spring 1989: A Comparative Approach* (Association for Education in Journalism and Mass Communication, 1996).

13. White, Howell, and Shang, *In Search of Civil Society.*

14. Teets, *Civil Society under Authoritarianism.*

15. Huang, "'Public Sphere'/'Civil Society' in China?"

16. Guobin Yang and Craig Calhoun, "Media, Civil Society, and the Rise of a Green Public Sphere in China," *China Information* 21, no. 2 (2007): 211–36; Jingfang Liu and Phaedra C. Pezzullo, eds., *Green Communication and China: On Crisis, Care, and Global Futures* (East Lansing: Michigan State University Press, 2020).

17. Lei, *The Contentious Public Sphere.*

18. Patrick Shaou-Whea Dodge, ed., *Communication and Convergence in the New China: International Perspectives on Politics, Platforms, and Participation* (East Lansing: Michigan State University Press, 2020).

19. Guobin Yang, "Civil Society in China: A Dynamic Field of Study," *Chinese Review International* 9, no.1 (2002): 1–16.

20. Timothy Hildebrandt, *Social Organizations and the Authoritarian State in China* (New York: Cambridge University Press, 2013); Spires, "Contingent Symbiosis and Civil Society in an Authoritarian State."

21. Peter Dahlgren, "The Internet, Public Spheres, and Political Communication: Dispersion and Deliberation," *Political Communication* 22, no. 2 (2005): 147–62.

22. Lei and Zhou, "Contesting Legality in Authoritarian Contexts," 557–93; Yang, *Power of the Internet in China.*

23. Joyce Y. M. Nip and King-wa Fu, "Challenging Official Propaganda? Public Opinion Leaders on Sina Weibo," *The China Quarterly* 225 (2016): 122–44.

24. Adrian Rauchfleisch and Mike S. Schäfer, "Multiple Public Spheres of Weibo: A Typology of Forms and Potentials of Online Public Spheres in China," *Information, Communication & Society* 18, no. 2 (2014): 1–17.

25. Rauchfleisch and Schäfer, "Multiple Public Spheres in China," 148.

26. Rauchfleisch and Schäfer, "Multiple Public Spheres in China," 148.

27. Graeme Turner, "The Mass Production of Celebrity: 'Celetoids', Reality TV and the 'Demotic Turn,'" *International Journal of Cultural Studies* 9, no. 2 (2006): 153–65.

28. Turner, "The Mass Production of Celebrity," 153.

29. Nick Couldry, "Reality TV, or the Secret Theater of Neoliberalism," *Review of Education, Pedagogy, and Cultural Studies* 30, no. 1 (2008): 3–13.

30. David Marshall, "The Promotion and Presentation of the Self: Celebrity as Marker of Presentational Media," *Celebrity Studies* 1, no. 1 (2010): 35–48; see chapter 3 in this volume, Junyi Lv and David Craig, "Firewalls and Walled Gardens: The Interplatformization of China's Wanghong Industry."

31. Mitchell Dean, *Governmentality: Power and Rule in Modern Society* (London: Sage Publications, 1999); Michel Foucault, *The Birth of Biopolitics: Lectures at the Collège de*

France, 1978–1979 (*Lectures at the College de France*) (New York: Palgrave Macmillan, 2008); Aihwa Ong, "Neoliberalism as a Mobile Technology," *Transactions of the Institute of British Geographers* 32 (2007), 3–8.

32. This is a pseudonym.
33. This is a pseudonym.
34. This is a pseudonym.
35. This is a pseudonym.
36. This is a pseudonym.
37. This is a pseudonym.
38. This is a pseudonym.
39. Both are pseudonyms.

Social Media Art Practices as Prefigurative Politics

Echoes from China

Zimu Zhang

Introduction

More than half a century has passed since Andy Warhol famously claimed that "in the future everybody will be world famous for fifteen minutes."[1] Living in Warhol's future, we can find a less restrained version: that the role of the artist can be taken on by "everyone" simply by creating a meme on social media or buying another artist's social media account.[2] In the digital and social media age, norms of both "art" and "artist" have changed profoundly. One field that reflects this change is the still evolving and ambiguous practice of social media art. In this chapter, I will examine social media art practices in current Chinese society and explore how they carry out "prefigurative politics" through the pursuit of societal subjects and self-organization. Carl Boggs coined the term to describe how the new left movements in the 1970s imagined different modes of political organizing and embodied social relations, centering on participatory democracy.[3] Boggs argued that such imaginative works "prefigure" a more desirable society by envisioning alternative living experiences and political forms. Entering the twenty-first century, Nancy S. Love and Mark Mattern collected and analyzed various art cases from worldwide activism movements, all rooted in the context of expanding global communication networks built via digital means, and concluded that art and popular culture carry great "prefigurative capacity."[4] Both during and beyond political movements, they argue, such "prefigurative capacities" can inspire people to create and sustain new aesthetics, which are integral to reimagining a better world. This was also analyzed in Fredric Jameson's classic Marxist writing on the ideological and utopian attributes of art.[5]

Before introducing specific cases in current Chinese society, I will first establish the research context at the intersection of art and communication through the "social turn" in contemporary art practices. I will then problematize the substance of the social in ubiquitous social media networks following Geert Lovink and look closer at the challenges posed to art and artists in the digital and social media age. As a tentative response to the questions raised, I will provide fresh source material from Chinese social media art practices such as the *Residents* project and the projects of Theatre 44, to map the dynamics and valuable experiences of social media art practices in contemporary China. I argue that through socially engaged methods and decentralized self-organization, social media art practices, which are consciously confronting and experimenting with digital media, are carrying out prefigurative politics in Chinese society. This chapter thus speaks to and hopefully expands upon an emerging critical literature on art, communication, and engagement in contemporary China.

According to art critic Claire Bishop, a "social turn" has taken place in contemporary art since the early 1990s.[6] Through a variety of methods, artists began to use "social situations to produce dematerialized, anti-market, politically engaged projects that carry on the modernist call to blur art and life."[7] One of the leading figures of this art movement is Grant H. Kester, who proposed the "dialogical aesthetic" when examining the emergence of socially engaged art practices from 1990 to the early 2000s.[8] According to Kester, a dialogical aesthetic no longer positions the artist as the major locus of creativity and expression, but as "one defined in terms of openness, of listening and a willingness to accept dependence and intersubjective vulnerability."[9] The artwork occurs in the conversation between artist and the collaborator, thus creating social-political relations in "a performative, process-based approach" instead of a traditional object-making one, such as painting or sculpture.[10] Among the art projects Kester discussed, one of their core values was interpersonal communication. For example, in the *Zurich Boat Project*, art collective Wochenklausur invited a mix of politicians, journalists, sex workers, and activists to have a dialogue in a boat floating on the Zurich lake as an intervention on drug policy. This led to the creation of a boarding house to shelter drug-addicted sex workers. Kester remarked, "Conversation becomes an integral part of the work itself. It is re-framed as an active, generative process that can help us speak and imagine beyond the limits of fixed identities and official discourse."[11]

For the Chinese contemporary art scene, socially engaged art is still a novel and underdeveloped phenomenon. However, Wang Meiqin argues that the social turn of Chinese contemporary art should not be regarded as a new phrase of art discourse within the global milieu; rather, it should be seen as rekindling "the historical legacy of Chinese artists as socially charged intellectuals" during the Maoist era as well as the "Modern Woodcut Movement and the street theatre during the Republican era."[12] Zheng Bo proposes understanding the "pursuit of publicness" as a motivating force for Chinese contemporary art development, wherein publicness also contains counter-publicness in its construction of counter-discourse against the status quo of Chinese authoritarian social politics.[13] A case he used to analyze this dialectical publicness was his own art project, *Karibu Islands*, in which he worked with queer communities in Beijing to discuss imagined or fantasy lives in islands where time flowed backwards. The participatory art project produced queer counter-discourse against the Chinese social public norms but was also constrained by social institutions.[14] Both Wang's theorization and Zheng's art practices revealed that the social turn in Chinese art development was in closer reciprocal discourse with national political ideology than that of the ethical and aesthetical reformation of the West.

While direct contact and interpersonal relationships have been emphasized in social and public art projects, another important but often overlooked aspect is technological mediation. In the 1930s Walter Benjamin argued for a missing aura of artwork in the mechanical reproduction age, but he embraced film as the new art medium of its epoch, where the technology of reproducibility itself became the art form.[15] Besides film's apparatus, Benjamin's reading also highlighted film's unique reception by its audience as a "regrouping of a perception," not only optical but also tactile.[16] In other words, we can say that film, as a new art form at the time, created a new communication discourse with its audience through its mediation of audiovisual content, which differed greatly from traditional artwork such as painting, music, and photography. With technological advancement, we have witnessed the birth of video art in the 1960s, internet art in the 1990s, and new media art in the 2000s. Each art form, while facilitated by a new apparatus, is also dealing with the renewed social life mediated by new technological infrastructure. Moreover, as Patrick Shaou-Whea Dodge has demonstrated, the interface of these new art forms, when coupled with emerging civil society spaces and evolving norms of deliberation and dissent on the internet, have produced a remarkably rich scene in China, where art, commerce, protest, and Warhol-like spoofs proliferate.[17]

The Digital and the Social

In his best-selling book, *Being Digital,* Nicholas Negroponte imagined digital life as "decentralizing, globalizing, harmonizing, and empowering."[18] However, seen from today's digital milieu, Negroponte's vision was rather utopian. While digital media is often contrasted with analog media and acquires the prefix of "new," many scholars, such as Wendy Hui Kyong Chun, Alexander Galloway, and Geert Lovink, have critically examined the control and hegemony of the infrastructure inherited from "old" media. One particular criticism is directed at the social, where social media gained momentum in every aspect of modern life. According to *Statista,* there will be 3.02 billion active monthly social media users worldwide by 2021, which is around one third of the earth's entire population.[19] Geert Lovink examined the social in today's Web 2.0 and Mobile 2.0 environment, describing it as actually a network to "connect persons to data object to persons"[20]—a departure from the traditional reference to society and potential forces of solidarity bringing individuals to communities. He reminds us that while social media is turning into a new type of ideology, the infrastructure it provides is highly centralized and top-down, and users—as prosumers—have no real choice but to comply with the capitalism of digital platforms. This argument has also been captured in Siva Vaidhyanthan's *Anti-Social Media,* which offers a blistering critique of how social media leads to alienation.[21]

If we take a closer look at our own smartphones, we will find that the ideology of social media is indeed like air permeating both the digital and physical spheres. Every app in our smartphones is integrating social functions to further engage our eyes and minds; even the ticket vending app suggests that you should obtain your friend's clicks and likes to increase your chances of winning high speed railway tickets.[22] To be social in this way means to give out personal data in exchange for "better" service, which in turn means less privacy and constant surveillance. A recent notorious example is a pair of incidents of rape and murder related to the Chinese ride-hailing app, Didi Chuxing. Both incidents happened through Didi's hitch service, which is a car-pooling service used to pair passengers and private car drivers on the same route with a cheaper cost. The social function between drivers and passengers was promoted as a "futuristic and sexy" scenario by the company.[23] Among its many safety risks and management flaws, one very disturbing function that might lead to the encouragement of sexual assault was a commenting and tagging system between drivers and passengers. The function allowed drivers and passengers to comment on each other and also review previous comments, but certain comments from the drivers were only visible to other drivers and hidden from the passengers themselves. According to media reports, these comments tended to have strong sexual undertones toward young female passengers with tags like "long legs" and "hot as hell."[24] Following the incidents and the resulting criticism of the ambiguous social sphere that the Didi app facilitated, Didi overhauled its services including suspending the hitch function and removing comments and tags.

However, the commenting feature was not the only thing responsible for these murders. We should further question Didi's ideology-driven logistics as an example of the sharing economy and platform capitalism, which extracts surplus value and alienates the social. Similar to Uber and Airbnb, Didi utilizes digital platforms to enroll users of different services (drivers and passengers) in a social economic network. The company/platform provides connection knots and also "actively curates connections and infrastructure," profiting as the "rentiers of the network."[25]

When we switch the lens to art, we may find the troubling relationship between the digital and social even more intriguing. In the age of Web 2.0, more artists and art institutions are using social media as an important platform for display and distribution. Emerging artists find that they have to develop social media personas in order to promote their artwork in the competitive art scene. On an institutional level, more museums and galleries no longer see social media as a mere marketing tool or promotion method to attract visitors; rather, digital and interactive media have become curatorial platforms. Furthermore, if you are an artist searching for an artist residency, you may find opportunities to do a web residency for an online exhibition or to take over the organizer's social media account for a period of time. In this phenomenon, the digital locale is considered as important as the physical one.

Since 2016, *Schloss*, a transdisciplinary online forum for artistic research, has initiated web residencies for international artists with a focus on web-based practices. The web residency offers three calls per year with various themes proposed by curators, and each call selects four groups of participants for a four-week web residency. For its ongoing operation, approximately 750 artists, coders, designers, technologists, and scientists have participated.[26] For the first call in 2017, curator Tatiana Bazzichelli proposed the theme of "Blowing the Whistle, Questioning Evidence," hence tackling the emergence of data surveillance and control. Four selected artists contributed their projects as technological toolkits and art interventions for dismantling the mechanism of power and control in digital networks. The practices included a device to obscure geolocation, a website to show how Facebook stores your data, a method for tracing an internet service tracker in a country that had it embargoed, and an essay with ten strategies for manipulating public opinion based on historical happenings and recent technological developments.[27] Seen through these projects, the online residency allows more experimental and participatory art projects, which are progressive and often open-sourced so as to facilitate dialogue with web visitors.

However, while digital and networked infrastructures are ubiquitous in daily life and art creation, Claire Bishop reminds us that there is still a "digital divide."[28] She sharply observes that when art practices entered the digital age, many artists applied new technology pervasively throughout their artwork, but few confronted the question of "what it means to think, see, and filter affect through the digital."[29] While Kester highlighted how dialogical art in physical relationships significantly reformed ways of rethinking power structures and discursive exchanges through art practices, he neglected the more ubiquitous dialogical exchange in social media, which grew in parallel with the growth of contemporary art through globalization. Some observers remain hopeful, however, as Lev Manovich has pointed to how social media provide a democratized platform for non-professional producers to generate creative content and publish or exchange their work immediately.[30] But Manovich also considers globalization to be a significant challenge for professional art production, and wonders "Is art after Web 2.0 still possible?"[31] Or, more radically, "Can telecommunication between users by itself be the subject of an aesthetic?"[32]

Social Media in China

According to the *South China Morning Post*, in July 2018, the Chinese tech company Tencent became the first Asian company to surpass a value of US$500 billion, following Apple, Alphabet (Google), Microsoft, Amazon, and Facebook.[33] With the largest and still growing number of social media users in the world, China's contemporary culture is significantly intertwined with telecommunication platforms, such as Weibo and WeChat. Since the use of social media has penetrated every aspect of cultural production, social interaction, and political discourse building, it has also become a site of control and governance. With multilevel firewalls blocking popular international internet companies such as Facebook, Twitter, and YouTube, Chinese social media have grown into a model of "Copy to China" (C2C). For example, YouTube's equivalent Chinese video-sharing platform can be Youku. Twitter's equivalent site can be Sina Weibo. With blocked media finding doubles in China, Chinese social media has strived to innovate and adapt to Chinese social demand swiftly. Guobin Yang has conducted research on both the rise and setback of Chinese online activism in relation to "digital civil society" amid the state's censorship and demobilization strategy.[34] Eric Harwit views the trend of users transitioning from Weibo to WeChat as a move from wider public discussion to smaller community communication. While WeChat may foster localized small-scale social action, it also tends to increase social atomization and, as a result, caters to the government's control policy.[35]

It may be debatable whether the prosperous social media scene has created a freer and more discursive public sphere compared to the official media environment, but its contributions to alternative news sourcing and public debate are clear. Larissa Hjorth, Natalie King, and Mami Kataoka suggested that social media use in the Asia-Pacific region had an "explicitly political manner" compared with the non-politicized Eurocentric approaches.[36] They used the notion of "intimate publics" to refer to how digital and social mobile media "render the intimate *public* and the public *intimate*."[37] Utilizing this concept of intimate publics, the contributing writers of the book each shed light on how the social media engagements of the personal is political, and how art connects the effective and the affective. This is the context that led to the 2017 Beijing Solidarity Action, in which activists moved from social media to street locations to aid evicted immigrants and those described by policy executors as the "low-end population."[38] During the action, strangers grouped up and collaborated through social media to make a participatory map of Beijing's evictions, which served both as a document for immediate utility and future archival evidence. Such movements prefigure one possible scenario that reconnects social spaces, where the boundaries and hierarchies within both online and physical communities resolve and merge into a collective quest for progressive social changes.

Social Media Art in China: Sites of Multiplicity and Creative Intervention

With social media's usage constantly expanding in scale and depth in mainland China, innovative and critically charged art projects have been emerging over the past few years. In this section I want to introduce and analyze two groups of practices that evolve and activate social media on different levels: in the first group, I analyze social media as a content platform creating communicative discourse; in the second, I analyze it as a place to experiment with new forms of production and with creating new sensations and aesthetics. As I have been involved in these projects myself as an art practitioner and researcher, I will also draw on my own experience for reflections and criticism.

The first group is a series of projects initiated by curators Man Yu and Zheng Hongbin, as well as artist Liu Weiwei. They have been the catalysts for several socially engaged group art projects that highlighted exchange and procedural artistic output in the current Chinese art scene. The usage of social media as the first and major platform for ongoing art projects is a consistent strategy in their practices. For example, in 2017, they initiated the project *Residents* (*Ju Min*/居民) in the Chinese Pearl River Delta region. It emphasized self-initiated social practices, taking place in the broad field of the social realm. While the project was always open to new participants, the curators invited a first batch of participants with varied backgrounds, including professional artists, activists, scholars, and students. The project chose social media as its major platform for its easy access, immediacy, and growing role in information and knowledge production in mainland China. For this reason, the artists and participants chose WeChat, one of the most popular Chinese social media platforms, as their primary platform.

As a guiding principle, the team sought to embody and emphasize the *xianchang* (social locale) and to address the production of social knowledge and efficacy. Self-organization and decentralization were also important parameters throughout. Unlike conventional art projects, there was no contracted art gallery or other form of art institution to physically host and promote the work. The self-described artists are potentially archetypes of sovereign individuals or a collective through self-organization, and they should utilize all production means available to problematize and present a core issue based on their research. For the first edition, more than thirty participants launched their own projects in Guangzhou, Shenzhen, Dongguan, and Hong Kong, among other places. The projects spanned a range of topics, including self-built houses in urban villages, obtaining living permits for migrant workers, identifying unclaimed dead bodies in Guangzhou city, collecting bizarre WiFi account names, and painting a wall in a city corner with different colors as chosen by children. Although many projects could be situated within the area of social investigations, they still carried performative attributes. For example, architecture lecturer Xu Zhiqiang, together with his students and colleagues, made a series of sketches of an urban village's self-built houses to examine how low-end construction could wrestle with capital and regulation to form new urban spatial tissue.[39] They printed the sketches onto shopping bags, which contained research questionnaires and listed the cost of a self-built urban village house on the back. Afterwards they distributed the designed shopping bags among residents in the urban village for free. When residents moved around the urban village with the bag, they were also advertising their own creative architecture model. In this way, the project merged art performance, social investigation, and urban planning, hence prefiguring a healthy and interdisciplinary social debate about the alternative future of urban housing in China.

Some projects took more provocative forms. For example, in the project *Face* (*lian*/脸), artist Ma Lijiao attempted to recruit volunteers among factory workers to receive minor plastic surgery for free. Through this participatory event, he wanted to expose and examine dynamics between mainstream aesthetics, class solidification, and the individual's choice of narratives. From its initial stage, the project generated critical reactions and stimulated debates among other project members concerning ethics, information transparency, and body and gender politics, especially regarding the artist's position, responsibility, and power. I was one of the participants who first raised questions to him in the online discussion. As reflective and also communicative discourse, Ma Lijiao took screenshots of the debates in the internal WeChat discussion group and published the stills on his project's WeChat account as an update. His original plan was to take a vote from a committee, formed of the surgery volunteers, to decide on the final surgery recipient. However, after only two people volunteered, one female and one male, the artist chose the female to receive the surgery based on his own evaluation. There are seven updates for this project on its WeChat page, each detailing a stage of progress. For the viewers, it is not difficult to trace the trajectory of the project and observe how the project changed as a result of conditional compromises. This marks one of the distinguishing features of *Residents*: By utilizing social media as public space and delivering frequent updates, the normally rather mysterious and insular process of an art project is revealed. By inviting viewers to participate in

FIGURE 1. Poster of *Feeling Attack 1*, 2017, Luwei HD Channel, Peng Wenbiao. Courtesy of the artist.

the project in this way, *Residents* moved past a static representation of art into a more evocative and iterative process wherein collaborators debated gender, beauty, class, and other social norms.

Another important feature of the *Residents* project is that social media has greatly influenced project language, visuality, and presentations of data. One example of this is the project *Feeling Attack* (*Qing Gan Zhui Ji*/情感追击) by Luwei HD Channel (*Lu Wei Gao Qing*/卤味高清). The project is a playful video series in the form of a popular love and reality television program in the 1980s. Under a surface of conflicts of love and trivial household affairs, the stories were actually embedded in the context of urban village transition and modeled after real relocation disputes.

By acting and reenacting the events with local artists and their circle of friends in a highly imitative yet revealing style, the series was received well and viewed widely. The body of work was also constructed with a dynamic hybridity of multimedia, such as video, GIFs, and digitally manipulated photos. It provided a fresh form and a new opportunity to present a social topic that was out of the spotlight of major media coverage.

However, if we look at both *Face* and *Feeling Attack* through a social media lens, we can see that neither project contained much embedded online discussion interacting with the progress. In addition, all of the content was made by the artists and updated in a rhythm of the artists' choosing, which was normally infrequent. The major content was also mostly text, combined with a linear video that hardly differed from how it would be viewed in a physical gallery space. Except for the short introduction and comments applied using the share function on WeChat Moments, there was also no immediate and simultaneous interaction between the artists, content, and audience via the social media platform. The use of social media in these projects mostly focused on using the medium as a content container rather than a content incubator.

A real social media moment was achieved by coincidence when the *Residents* project exhibition in Shenzhen was partially censored. Titled *Recruitment* (*Zai Zhao Mu*/再招募), the exhibition showcased the projects' ongoing process and aimed to inspire and encourage more people to take the initiative and become involved. The exhibition venue was located in OCT Harbour, one of the busiest shopping malls in Shenzhen, with the projects' display strategically distributed in two parts. One part was in the shopping mall corridors, where every project was summarized in one sentence and installed within transparent square boxes scattered in the mall space. Following the box-installations, visitors would arrive at the main art space where the other part of the display could be found. This contained more project archives, including text documents and audiovisuals. An incident occurred during the installation, before the exhibition's opening: the shopping mall decided to censor certain characters of some project slogans. The decision to self-censor came both from concern over sensitive social topics as well as from commercial concerns. These so-called commercially censored characters included death, "evilly," "poisonous snake," and "Old Wang next door" among others, which the shopping mall considered as a disturbance to "the joyful and harmonious" shopping atmosphere aimed at consumers.[40] But, rather than withdrawing the exhibition, the curators collected and covered up these censored words on the wall of the art

FIGURE 2. Censored project slogan of *Residents* at OCT Harbour shopping mall, Shenzhen, 2017, Man Yu. Courtesy of the curator.

FIGURE 3. Censored project slogan of *Residents* with on-screen writing, 2017, Zimu Zhang. Courtesy of the artist.

space while leaving the missing character slogan boxes as they were. Participating artists also began to circulate pictures of these incomplete slogans on social media, with onscreen handwriting to complete the censored slots. The censored display therefore transformed into another *xianchang* of social conditions and made the artists' responses visible as critical and playful art interventions through social media communication.

Overall, the *Residents* project offered an experimental field to augment art projects with social media. Valuable experiences could be drawn from aspects such as topic selection, design choices, and interactive discourses. Such experiences motivated artists and curators to keep working in the medium and perform more extensive tasks of constructing and deconstructing this platform. One particular example is Liu Weiwei's 2018 art project *Australia* (澳大利亚). He created a social media poll for his brother Liu Chao in order to help him determine whether to stay in China or migrate to Australia. According to the artist, after working in Singapore for several years as a technical worker and then returning to China, his brother had a difficult time adapting to Chinese domestic life. Because some of his co-workers in Singapore had since migrated to Australia, Liu Chao found it a tempting choice but faced many obstacles, such as finances, language, and opposition from his family. Liu Weiwei claimed that his brother could not choose between migrating to Australia and remaining in China and had an equal number of positive and negative reasons for both choices. Therefore, they decided to seek an answer from the social media public. The poll was set for a one-month duration and afterwards, as stated by the artist, "whatever the result, whatever would happen to the public vote procedure, Liu Chao would execute the final result."[41]

Two video campaigns were made addressing each choice. In both videos, Liu Chao, facing the camera, delivered a sincere speech outlining facts and intentions. The speech tone and gesture, explained by Liu Weiwei, was a result of Liu Chao watching many American politicians' campaigns and using them as a reference. After release, the project triggered controversial feedback and even accusations of manipulation. On the second day of the poll, Liu Weiwei discovered that the votes for staying in China had inexplicably increased by three hundred, but the total votes exceeded the overall number of views of the post—indicating the voting had been rigged. The vote-riggers themselves then spread a digital document titled *Statement from Liu Chao Fate Decision Office* through WeChat groups stating several reasons why they bought the votes. Imitating the style of a governmental statement and ironically applying official jargon, the document stated that their reasons were the patriotic goal of keeping Liu Chao as a technical worker for their homeland's construction, as well as their passion for Liu Weiwei's art project. Since there was no ban on rigging votes, they considered it a reasonable way to participate in the art project. Furthermore, the office stated that they would be very interested to see the Liu brothers' take on the final decision.

Liu Weiwei responded quickly with dismissive statements, criticizing the action as mirroring the prevalence of other corrupt behavior in different levels of Chinese social and political life, but he neither demanded its end nor dismissed the vote.[42] One day later, the option to migrate to Australia increased by a thousand votes, a change that was believed to be caused by the same vote riggers as before. At the end of the vote, the option to stay in China won over that of migrating to Australia with a vote of 2782 vs. 2632. As estimated by Liu, there were at least three more vote-rigging actions. In the latest update of the project, he stated he would investigate and justify the result, but he did not mention what he and his brother would do accordingly. On the surface, this project seemed to be a commentary on democracy: one vote per person to help someone make a life decision. But with the vote interventions and the subsequent debate, the project actually mirrored the social media environment the vote was set in, which seemed to be transparent, accessible, and democratic, but was in fact deeply dependent on rhetoric and invisible digital infrastructure. Of course, it also brought forward the question of the ethics of art. Liu Weiwei, in his own reflection, referred to the project as "Event Art," in that "it aims to create division instead of unity."[43] He also emphasized the communication process of his art project, that conceptual art should enter public debate with a gesture of resistance and action. Rumors spread that the people behind the "Fate Decision Office" who conducted the vote interventions were also an artists' group. In this way, the project and its various interventions became a performative process of commenting on the precarious nature of voting, a social media reality built on reconfigured communication.

Man Yu summarized these experiments with the belief that "art should not intervene with social movements, but be part of them."[44] From *Residents* to *Australia*, the artists brought societal topics into the social media field with a refined focus. But in their approach, the artists still inhabited the position of auteur in that they remained the core actors of the projects. Digitality and the essence of the social was confronted but not examined in depth.

Another group named Theatre 44 provided more intricate explorations of social media art projects. Theatre 44 emerged from a dynamic thinking community named

OnPractice (*Shi Jian Lun* /实践论), which often employed theatre and literature to "construct feasible situations."[45] Comparatively, Theatre 44 is a more rhizomatic network, with flowing and non-fixed members coming from different geographical corners, with diverse backgrounds and interests. It is a porous group, constantly in a state of flux. Through the way it is organized and mobilized, it intends to overthrow the inertia of power and dismantle the illusion of subjectivity.[46] Since 2016, Theatre 44 has launched four cycles of work, with themes including, but not limited to, archives, historicity, gender, and internet violence. I will choose two representative projects to further analyze their practices.

At the end of 2016, they initiated the first project under Theatre 44's frame with the concept of "Urban Nomads," which reestablished the fictive troubadour figure in the old Chinese metropolitan city: people wandering and reading poetry scripts at night on the streets of Guangzhou. In connection with the theme, various public research meet-ups were held about related text and audiovisual materials, from which the event attendants and their outputs were further integrated into the growing project. Among the three months of rolling project, two special "WeChat stickers battles" were held across both physical and virtual space. The battles mirrored the popular usage of WeChat stickers among WeChat users in their daily communication. Stickers (*Biaoqing*/表情) refer to a broad range of visual content, including Emoji, GIF, screenshots, and any other kinds of user-made hybrid images. As suggested from ethnography research by Gabriele de Seta, "Biaoqing are central protagonists of Chinese digital media ecologies in terms of both everyday use and public discourse."[47] Titled *Sticker Battle Arena* (*Dou Tu Lei Tai*/斗图擂台), a WeChat group was set up to host the event. "Battlers" could participate not only virtually through the open QR code but also physically by showing up to a meet-up location in Guangzhou at the announced time.

I attended the first battle in person on January 8, 2018. There were about ten people on location, with a total of around twenty in the battle group. A Theatre 44 member livestreamed the event via a popular streaming website named Douyu (斗鱼) from his phone; he also projected his mobile screen on the street wall using a portable projector. Custom battle rules were made: for example, only non-duplicate stickers were allowed, and self-made as well as original stickers would win bonus points. There were also recommended themes for the stickers such as "love and peace" and "institutional critique." A crucial moment occurred when a policeman came and tried to stop the event, accusing the group of being an illegal public assembly. While the policeman interrogated some of the "battlers," the other participants and the online attendants did not pause the battle. Instead, they started producing stickers imbued with police elements. Even though the battle was eventually physically relocated to an indoor barbecue restaurant, its online procedure was performed until the winner was chosen. While the stickers battle can be seen as another iteration on meme culture, which is often seen as nihilistic and parodic, it can also be seen as a subject that reflects rich data culture, hybrid visualities, and ambivalent, affective communication throughout its production and distribution. As scholar Limor Shifman has pointed out, internet memes can be seen as "socially constructed public discourses."[48] For Theatre 44's stickers battle, the cross-media setup and emergent participation conceived of an alternative form of broadcasting as well as a new way to archive a police encounter. The embodied action of making, posting, and communicating through symbols during a strained situation turned the battlers into a new form of community. Together, with their social media avatars, they created a performative public assembly. As one of the participants later commented in a public WeChat post, it was also a form of resistance, which was "mediated or filtered by cyberspace and may be transmitted into the organism of the empire through the stickers' revelry."[49] By prefiguring alternative social possibilities in China, this event/project merged online with physical creative interventions while creating spaces for new communities to emerge and form.

Theatre 44's latest project, under the theme *Man without Signal* (*Deng Xin Hao De Ren*/ 等信号的人) marked the group's endeavor in examining the internet's pervasiveness in daily life. The project's departure point was to experiment with the coexistence of laziness and creativity. "After all, is it possible to conduct work besides eating, drinking and having fun together?"[50] Therefore, curator Zhang Hanlu and artist Xinwei, two Theatre 44 members, proposed to experiment with using vlogs. Imitating popular vlog trends, the first Theatre 44 vlog was made during the casual gaming and chatting of a group of friends, but the conversation was loosely structured to include current social debates. While gaming, five friends (two men and three women) chatted about the differences between flirting and sexual harassment, which for them contained very different overtones. Mixing layered visuals, news screenshots, and meme symbols, the vlog engaged in dialogue with the ongoing Chinese #MeToo movement but avoided being sterile and preachy. With similar mentalities, three more vlogs were made on the topics of Alibaba's convergent online and offline grocery retail, the aesthetics and politics of displaying animals in the zoo, and what seemed like a travel journal through the Chinese city Yiwu—the world's largest wholesale market for daily commodities.

Besides vlog production, Theatre 44 started a documentary theatre to reenact the social tragedy of a nineteen-year-old girl from Qingyang, who jumped to her death after becoming the victim of a sexual assault by her high school teacher and failing to obtain justice from both the school and legal system. Adding to the tragedy was the fact that some bystanders jeered at her and urged her to jump, and her suicide was livestreamed and circulated through social media with a number of hostile comments. The incident provoked public outcry regarding the girl's mistreatment, the failure of social systems, and Chinese social media ethics. Theatre 44 decided to collect the incident's archives beyond journalism reports and paid particular attention to internet communication and social media violence. Members chose different roles and situations related to the incident and wrote scripts from collective discussion based on their findings. The writing process was conducted mostly online with the participants in different places. For the final performance at the Shanghai Ming Contemporary Museum, a livestreaming video was embedded as a narrative and performative strategy. The livestreaming video was operated by someone using a smartphone wandering around different actors as if they were an onlooker of the recreated incident. Subtitles and comments were also enabled from streaming audiences.

Through acknowledging the digital and social condition of situated post-modern life, Theatre 44 provides alternative and inspiring engagements with emergent participatory discourse. While it does not change the top-down social media infrastructure, it mobilizes a bottom-up user intervention. By often using limited museum exhibition funds to create long-term heterogeneous projects outside the "white box" exhibition space, it also consciously acts on the current ecology of the art systems and economy flow as well as with voluntary and interest-driven exchange labor systems. On the self-organization level, it has contributed meaningful attempts to carry out work with affective responsibility, voluntary division of labor, and interest-driven exchange as well as discursive collaborations. As remarked by the group's introduction, "it gives impetus to the act of uniting talent and thus allowing it to overflow."[51] "Talent" here should not be interpreted as extraordinary artistic proficiency, but rather a "gift" that individuals hold within, which they are willing to share and exchange in the dynamic of a collective project.

Conclusion: Social Media Art as Prefigurative Tactics in China and Beyond

As Marshall McLuhan pointed out in the 1960s regarding technological acceleration, "to prevent undue wreckage in society, the artist tends now to move from the ivory tower to the control tower of society."[52] However, our current era, in which advanced technological tools are extremely accessible but the gap of affective communication is ever larger, the role of the artist should arguably be more of a mediator and a connector, more symbolic and collective, rather than a fixed position within the industry. Seen through cases like *Residents*, *Australia*, and the Theatre 44 projects, the ethics and aesthetics of art are brought into the spotlight again with critical discourse and new treatments built upon digital social media, thus building a shared future with prefigurative tactics, including self-organizing, cross-platform cooperation, open frameworks, imagination, and the practice of "commoning."[53]

As Theatre 44 shows us, when everyday social media becomes an art medium, we can venture to overthrow the sterile dichotomy of form and content in order to generate new social relations that will not exclude the lazy, the fun, or the daily interactions and frictions. Such art practices are prefigurative, especially in terms of how they envision possible relationships between technology and the social. Apart from the popular scenario of a militarized, consumerist, apocalyptic, or utopian techno world, these prefigurative endeavors suggest alternative technological possibilities to embody an evolving subjectivity with social media art practices. The social element is often criticized as contributing to a rise of so-called "influence art" and, more explicitly as artist and writer Brad Troemel commented, "both shattering art's traditional relationship to capitalism as well as being the hyper-charged embodiment of it."[54] However, Theatre 44 demonstrates a preliminary but valuable attempt to redistribute labor and create an alternative gift economy within the dominant data economy.

Using these case analyses, I have not attempted to offer an overarching image of a novel art movement in China; rather, I hope to have presented some examples of how contemporary artists and activists are merging our digital social habitat with critical art interventions. While these cases can provide contextualized and irreducible multiplicities in China's postmodern society, they are also situated in the international art milieu and global communication networks. While my comments have focused on this process within China, it seems evident that such prefigurative collaborations between social media users, artists, and activists can also impact transnational cultural comprehension and action—for the networks of communication addressed herein transcend geographical borders, perhaps prefiguring a coming age of truly international citizenship.

NOTES

1. Jeff Guinn and Douglas Perry, *The Sixteenth Minute: Life in the Aftermath of Fame* (New York: Tarcher, 2005), 4.

2. Artist Darren Bader announced on his social media accounts that he would sell his Instagram and Twitter accounts as art, and that the auction winner would receive a certificate of the artwork as well as becoming the owner of the account. Sarah Cascone, "#Duchamp? Darren Bader Is Selling His Instagram and Twitter Handles as Readymade Art," Artnet News, April 3, 2018, https://news.artnet.com/art-world/darren-bader-selling-instagram-handle-1259240.

3. Carl Boggs, "Marxism, Prefigurative Communism, and the Problem of Workers' Control," *Radical America* 11, no. 6 (1977): 99–122.

4. Nancy S. Love and Mark Mattern, eds., *Doing Democracy: Activist Art and Cultural Politics* (New York: SUNY Press, 2013), 11.

5. Fredric Jameson, *The Political Unconscious: Narrative as a Socially Symbolic Act* (Ithaca, NY: Cornell University Press, 1981).

6. Claire Bishop, "The Social Turn: Collaboration and Its Discontents," *Artforum* 6, no. 44 (2005): 178, http://cam.usf.edu/CAM/exhibitions/2008_8_Torolab/Readings/The_Social_Turn_CBishop.pdf.

7. Bishop, "The Social Turn," 178.

8. Grant H. Kester, "Dialogical Aesthetics: A Critical Framework for Littoral Art," *Variant* 9, (1999): 1–8.

9. Grant H. Kester, *Conversation Pieces: Community and Communication in Modern Art* (Berkeley, CA: University of California Press, 2004), 110.

10. Kester, *Conversation Pieces*, 1.

11. Kester, *Conversation Pieces*, 8.

12. Meiqin Wang, "Place-Making for the People: Socially Engaged Art in Rural China," *China Information* 32, no. 2 (2018): 244–69.

13. Bo Zheng, *The Pursuit of Publicness: A Study of Four Chinese Contemporary Art Projects* (Rochester, NY: University of Rochester, 2012), 6.

14. Zheng, *The Pursuit of Publicness*, 168–203.

15. Walter Benjamin, *The Work of Art in the Age of Mechanical Reproduction* (London:

Penguin UK, 2008).

16. Rodolphe Gasché, "The Deepening of Apperception: On Walter Benjamin's Theory of Film," *Mosaic: An Interdisciplinary Critical Journal* 41, no. 4 (2008): 27–39.

17. Patrick Shaou-Whea Dodge, "Imagining Dissent: Contesting the Façade of Harmony through Art and the Internet in China," in *Imagining China: Rhetorics of Nationalism in the Age of Globalization*, ed. Stephen John Hartnett, Lisa B. Keränen, Donovan Conley (East Lansing: Michigan State University Press, 2017), 311–38.

18. Nicholas Negroponte, *Being Digital* (New York: Vintage, 1996), 239.

19. "Number of Social Media Users Worldwide from 2010 to 2021 (in Billions)," *Statista*, accessed November 11, 2018, https://www.statista.com/statistics/278414/number-of-worldwide-social-network-users/.

20. Geert Lovink, "What is the Social in Social Media," *E-Flux* 40, no. 12 (December 2012), https://www.e-flux.com/journal/40/60272/what-is-the-social-in-social-media/.

21. Siva Vaidhyanathan, *Antisocial Media: How Facebook Disconnects Us and Undermines Democracy* (Oxford University Press, 2018).

22. "Railway Departments with Ticket Snatching Software: Restrictive Measures," January 28, 2019, https://jqknews.com/news/132811Railway_Departments_with_Ticket_Snatching_Software_Restrictive_Measures_Implemented.html.

23. Xiaoci Deng, "Didi under Fire for Sex Assault, Murder Cases," *Global Times*, October 8, 2018, http://www.globaltimes.cn/content/1117466.shtml.

24. Wee Sui-Lee, "Didi Suspends Carpooling Service in China after 2nd Passenger Is Killed," *New York Times*, October 26, 2018, https://www.nytimes.com/2018/08/26/business/didi-chuxing-murder-rape-women.html.

25. Rachel O'Dwyer, "Money Talks: The Enclosure of Mobile Payments," *MoneyLabReader: An Intervention in Digital Economy* (Amsterdam: Institute of Network Cultures, 2015), 234.

26. More information about the web residency can be found at Schlosspost: https://schloss-post.com/overview/web-residencies/.

27. More information about the selected residencies can be found at Schlosspost: https://schloss-post.com/category/web-residents/blowing-the-whistle/.

28. Claire Bishop,"Digital Divide," *Artforum International* 51, no. 1 (2012): 434–41.

29. Bishop, "Digital Divide."

30. Lev Manovich, "The Practice of Everyday (Media) Life: From Mass Consumption to Mass Cultural Production?" *Critical Inquiry* 35, no. 2 (2009): 319–31.

31. Manovich, "The Practice of Everyday (Media) Life," 329.

32. Lev Manovich, *The Language of New Media* (Cambridge, MA: MIT Press, 2001), 163–64.

33. Laura He, "Tencent is First Asian Company to Top US$500 Billion in Value, Joining Apple

and Facebook," *South China Morning Post*, November 20, 2017, https://www.scmp.com/business/companies/article/2120712/tencent-breaches-us500b-valuation-shares-rally-above-hk41460.

34. Guobin Yang, "(Un) Civil Society in Digital China| Demobilizing the Emotions of Online Activism in China: A Civilizing Process," *International Journal of Communication* 12, (2018): 21.

35. Eric Harwit, "WeChat: Social and Political Development of China's Dominant Messaging App," *Chinese Journal of Communication* 10, no. 3 (2017): 312–27.

36. Larissa Hjorth, Natalie King, and Mami Kataoka, *Art in the Asia-Pacific: Intimate Publics* (London: Routledge, 2014), 3.

37. Hjorth, King, and Kataoka, *Art in the Asia-Pacific*, 2.

38. Qiaochu Li, Jiani Song, and Shuchi Zhang, "17 may Beijing Evictions, a Winter's Tale," *Made in China* 3, no. 1 (January–March 2018), http://www.chinoiresie.info/beijing-evictions-a-winters-tale/.

39. More information of the project can be found at: http://t.cn/RcgMQ9k.

40. A Chinese internet slang term referring to the next door neighbor who may be having an affair with your partner and who may also be used as a joke protagonist.

41. Weiwei Liu, "Australia| Liu Weiwei Project Launch," trans. Zimu Zhang, November 29, 2018, https://mp.weixin.qq.com/s/PQH-NbvKpqMa7uTPHRSulg.

42. Weiwei Liu, "Reply to Statement of Fate Decision Office," trans. Zimu Zhang, November 30, 2018, https://mp.weixin.qq.com/s/OSDzarHqY8-n-K9Jd_u-PA.

43. Weiwei Liu, "Rigging Votes, Worker and Event Art," trans. Zimu Zhang, accessed December 5, 2018, https://mp.weixin.qq.com/s/6RKkRloruH42R9OGUEVUqA.

44. Luigi Gamberti and Yongfeng Ma, "The 6th Ring Project," *Transnational Dialogues*, November 2, 2018, https://transnationaldialogues.eu/the-6th-ring-project/.

45. He Pan, "Local Variants," trans. Daniel Nieh, Ran Dian, June 14, 2018, http://www.randian-online.com/np_feature/local-variants/.

46. Pan, "Local Variants."

47. Gabriele de Seta, "Biaoqing: The Circulation of Emoticons, Emoji, Stickers, and Custom Images on Chinese Digital Media Platforms," *First Monday* 23, no. 9 (2018).

48. Limor Shifman, *Memes in Digital Culture* (Cambridge, MA: MIT Press, 2014), 8.

49. Jia Li, "Earth and Image (Direct Proximate Translation from Chinese Title as 土土土图图图)," trans. Zimu Zhang, January 8, 2017, https://mp.weixin.qq.com/s/lSmNNhXBdGrIOZ4V_I7yUA.

50. 44 Vlog, "Failed Flirting," trans. Zimu Zhang, September 30, 2018, https://mp.weixin.qq.com/s/zc2pqvUK4aDnH9bMFVzgGw.

51. Theatre 44, "We are Only Left with Future (Review & Foreshow)," trans. Zimu Zhang, September 21, 2017, https://mp.weixin.qq.com/s/LW9a6m_U73ZQWe7LZn5oag.

52. Marshall McLuhan, *Understanding Media: The Extensions of Man* (Cambridge, MA: MIT press, 1994).

53. Peter Linebaugh, *The Magna Carta Manifesto: Liberties and Commons for All* (Berkeley, CA: University of California Press, 2008).

54. Brad Troemel, "Art after Social Media," *You Are Here: Art after the Internet* (2014): 36–43.

The Lure of Connectivity

Exploring US and Chinese Scientists' Use of Social Media to Address the Public

Hepeng Jia, Xiaoya Jiang, Dapeng Wang, and Weishan Miao

Near the end of 2019, word began trickling out of Wuhan about patients showing up in hospitals with acute flu-like symptoms; when some of those patients started to die unexpectedly, the medical community began to wonder if it was witnessing the evolution of some new and deadly virus. By early 2020, hospitals were swamped with patients, yet the official channels of Party-run media were slow to respond. Worse yet, Party-run institutions and government agencies repressed discussion about the crisis, fearing the negative publicity that might follow if China was once again seen as the origin of a novel virus. But while the official media and government institutions sat on the news, concerned doctors took to social media, using Weibo, WeChat, and other Chinese social media to spread the word about the disease. The world was only alerted to COVID-19, then, because the scientific community used social media to work around the usual forms of communication control in China. We will not dive into the details of the COVID-19 crisis in this chapter but have opened with these comments to demonstrate that the future of public communication about science is going to take place on social media. Moreover, international tensions rise around such issues. So it is safe to say that the future of US–China relations will be influenced, at least in part, by how scientists in both countries use social media to educate their publics, to work with each other, and occasionally to rebuke their governments.

The story of Chinese doctors using social media to share news about COVID-19 comes as no surprise, for in the past decade, social media have significantly shaped how science is communicated.[1] Scientists have been making use of social media both in their internal, scholarly exchanges and in their public science communication efforts.[2] While studies have examined how scientists adopt social media platforms to disseminate scientific information and to engage the public,[3] few comparative studies across countries have been made.[4] This chapter tries to fill this gap by focusing on how US and Chinese scientists use social media to communicate science to the public.

The United States and China are the world's top two research powerhouses, and they host the most popular social media platforms such as Facebook, Twitter, WeChat, and Weibo. Therefore, for students of science communication and social media studies, it is more than necessary to learn incentives and barriers for scientists in the two countries to use social media for public science communication. Meanwhile, the two countries have different political systems, cultural preferences, research organizations, and science communication regimes. So, comparing US and Chinese scientists' social media use in their efforts to disseminate science will illustrate how varying political, societal, and institutional factors shape social media use among members in specific societies. As the COVID-19 crisis is raising antagonism between the two countries, the collaboration between scientists in the United States and China becomes more crucial today than at any other time. Without the partnership, the struggle to find a solution against the novel coronavirus will be much harder, if not impossible. Comparing social media use by scientists in the two countries, therefore, is more appealing than ever. This chapter offers an opening step toward fulfilling these objectives.

We analyze blogs, microblog sites (Twitter and Weibo), and social networking sites (Facebook and WeChat). Other popular social media tools frequently used by scientists—such as Mendeley, a desktop program for managing and sharing research papers, discovering research data, and collaborating online,[5] and Academia.edu and ResearchGate[6]—are internal to the scholarly community, meaning they are not used to communicate with broader publics, and hence were excluded from our investigation.

In this chapter, data used to probe the US scientists' social media behaviors are based on published scholarly studies; for Chinese scientists, we primarily use empirical data, including an online survey of Chinese researchers' communication activities, in-depth qualitative interviews with thirty online celebrity scientists, and participatory observation. We conducted the interviews from late 2016 to early 2019, and some of these interviews were implemented for a previous project.[7] Still, the data used here are customized for the specific purpose of this chapter. To explain this data to readers, we first delineate the status of social media use by US and Chinese scientists. Then we investigate their motivations and strategies for utilizing different social media. After that, we sketch the impact of social media use on public engagement in the two countries.

The Status of US and Chinese Scientists' Social Media Use

By the late 2000s, communication-savvy scientists and science writers were widely using blogs.[8] In the United States, science blogs are diverse in type. There are specialized science blog sites, such as scienceblog.com, realclimate.org, and LabSpaces; science-focused blogs on public blog sites like wordpress.com (e.g., The Research Whisperer at theresearchwhisperer.wordpress.com); blog sections of institutional websites such as the Institute of Physics blog (iopblog.org); and blogs operated by publications (such as SciLogs operated by Nature Publishing Group). In short, science blogs in the United States indicate a range of platforms with different institutional affiliations, different user communities, and different discourse styles. As in American democracy broadly, the relationships between science and social media are disjointed, user-driven, and so diverse as to border on chaos.

Science bloggers in the United States also have diverse identities and affiliations. Research indicates that many of them have a high level of education. A survey of over 600 science bloggers found 48 percent of the bloggers had doctorate degrees, and up to 47 percent (N = 288) respondents self-identified as academic researchers.[9] In a Pew survey of 3,748 US-based members of the American Association for the Advancement of Science (AAAS), 24 percent reported having blogged about science and their research in the past.[10] Another study found 23 of the 303 surveyed US scientists blogged.[11] The difference could be attributed to sampling characteristics. One central mission of AAAS is to promote public understanding of science, and its members often have a higher percentage than average in utilizing various communication tools.[12] Despite the relatively small number of blogging scientists, 92 percent of scientists reported that they read science blogs, according to a separate survey.[13] While more research is needed before reaching any firm conclusion, this body of data suggests that blogs have become a regular, if unevenly used, feature in US-based scientific communication.

There are few studies on the status of social media use by Chinese scientists. Based on existing literature, it seems that more US scientists use blogs than Chinese scientists. This situation implies that Chinese scientists may generally be more passive in public science communication.[14] Several factors drive this situation. First, the number of platforms where Chinese scientists can blog is much lower than those in the United States. Second, few Chinese research institutions have offered weblog services on their institutional websites. Third, perhaps because of a combination of points one and two, few scientists blog on public blog sites such as Sina Blog (http://blog.sina.com.cn), the country's largest blog site operated by Sina Corporation. Chinese scientists, therefore, face a shortage of attractive platforms and a lack of institutional support, hence driving their low usage of public blogs. Within this context in China, the primary science blog portals are ScienceNet.cn, founded under the Chinese Academy of Sciences (CAS) in 2006, and Songshuhui. net, which gathers several hundred science writers in an emerging community of online and public-facing science bloggers.

Though fewer Chinese scientists use science blogs, scientists who do blog tend to be active users. By April 2, 2014, up to 69,559 have registered as ScienceNet. cn's bloggers, among whom, 68,924 self-identify as researchers. Most of them are in natural science fields. Between March 31, 2013, and March 30, 2014, bloggers published 105,842 blog posts on ScienceNet.cn, resulting in 91 million visits.[15] The limited number of science blog portals in China makes it easier to estimate the percentage of blogging scientists, which is approximately 2 percent of the country's total research workforce.[16] These numbers suggest that science blogging in China is remarkably limited, amounting to emerging communication practices.

Of those Chinese scientists who use social media, their blogs provide scientific knowledge that might not be available on other media platforms. For example, active bloggers on ScienceNet.cn often posted articles on the newest scientific progress and scientists' views neglected by conventional media.[17] Science writers on Songshuhui.net and the commercial website Guokr.com, a leading popular science site in China derived from Songshuhui.net, also blogged about trendy science stories. In both the United States and China, the blog has opened science beyond the ivory tower and encouraged open dialogue between scientists and non-scientists.[18] It also provides alternative routes for scientists to acquire academic information, enhance scholarly exchanges, and reach other professional audiences. One possible conclusion, then, is that social media platforms have played encouraging roles for both Chinese and American scientists, facilitating the exchange of ideas, data, and labor. An alternative reading, of course, is that skirting formal peer-review to discuss science can lead to sloppy work—as seen during the COVID-19 crisis; social media may not be the ideal vehicle for life and death information about complicated scientific questions.

While the blogs mentioned above were early entrants in the world of science blogging, Twitter soon penetrated the science community. The survey mentioned above among AAAS members found 47 percent of them used social media to talk about science or read about scientific developments at least some of the time.[19] Similarly, Yeo et al. found 40 percent of the tenure-track scientists at a Midwestern research university used Twitter.[20] On Twitter, the US scientists, like their colleagues elsewhere, regularly share academic information, post links to references, and brief their research progress.[21] Twitter is also widely used at conferences to "broadcast" keynote points of speakers.[22] In the United States, institutional use of Twitter to communicate science to the general public and invite public feedback is common.[23] As a whole, studies reveal a positive association between Twitter mentioning of research and its citations.[24] Scientists whose research was mentioned on Twitter also had significantly higher h-indices, the metrics to examine the overall impact of a scientist's research.[25] Nevertheless, scientists are not necessarily active science communicators on Twitter. An analysis of Twitter users of the top 100 tweets for the release of the *Fifth Assessment Report of Intergovernmental Panel on Climate Change* (IPCC) found that the category "scientist" had the lowest level of prevalence among actors such as government, non-elite and journalist, though the most retweeted user in the sample was a climate scientist with more than 17,000 followers.[26]

Weibo, the equivalent of Twitter (which is blocked in China), has two different features from Twitter. First, before increasing their maximum length for a single post, the information contained in Weibo's 140-character-limit is much more luxurious than a Twitter microblog, since a single character in Chinese can represent an entire English word. The difference may have been intensified, as Weibo users now can post many more characters in a single tweet. Second, on Weibo, discussion threads can be attached to individual posts, so that it is easier to get involved in public dialogue around specific themes. These two typical Weibo characteristics make Weibo function more like an open forum than a social networking tool.[27]

Weibo, together with blogs, WeChat's public accounts (to be discussed below), and the Toutiao account, which is an algorithm-based site both for microblogging and blogging, are broadly called We Media in China. Weibo's monthly active users reached 446 million in the third quarter of 2018.[28]

Even while We Media use has exploded across China (as seen in the previous chapters in this book), Chinese scientists seem somewhat uninterested in using We Media for the purposes of public science education. Our survey of 522 scientists in 2016 indicated that only 27 percent (n=142) of the respondents owned a We Media account (including Weibo, WeChat public account, and Toutiao). Chinese scientists' actual percentage of owning such an account should be much lower, however, as our survey, implemented by popular science site Guokr.com, was administered in a sample of its scientist readers, who are presumably much more active in science communication than average Chinese scientists. We, therefore, sought to supplement this survey data with in-depth qualitative interviews with Chinese scientists who are leading internet-based science communicators. This work revealed that even among these online celebrities, the majority did not use Weibo. Among the thirty interviewees, only six actively used Weibo for science communication, with a small number of other interviewed scientists reporting their use of Weibo just for private purposes. Our combined survey and interview data suggest, then, that while Chinese scientists use We Media for personal communication, they tend not to use these platforms to engage in public science education. Later in this chapter, we will analyze in detail the factors leading to the low We Media use among Chinese scientists. Their reluctance to have a direct dialogue with the public, lack of time, low peer recognition, and the worry about unfriendly social media environment inhibit them from choosing these media.

In line with blogs and microblogging, scientists also utilize social networking platforms such as Facebook and WeChat for science communication. Facebook is the world's largest social networking site in terms of users. As of January 2019, it had more than 2.27 billion active monthly users.[29] Despite the public popularity of Facebook, individual scientists do not frequently use it for professional purposes.[30] American scientists have a higher personal, but lower professional use of Facebook.[31] Another survey of scientists' Facebook use showed that each of its 203 respondents reported 519 friends, and 27.5 percent among them were scientists. The number of scientist friends rose together with academic seniority.[32] The phenomenon shows that while scientists tend to use Facebook for private purposes, the social media platform still plays a role in professional social networking.

On Facebook, scientists often share science, but with close friends and family members.[33] Nevertheless, these findings do not necessarily indicate that Facebook is not an ideal platform to disseminate science. A Pew study identified the thirty most impactful science-related Facebook pages, which produced 130,932 posts in 2017 and were followed by 44 million users by the end of that year (with each page having at least 3 million followers).[34]

In terms of media function, China does not have a media platform equivalent to Facebook (which was also blocked in China). However, in terms of the number of users, WeChat is a comparable social networking platform, which we can investigate for scientists' social media behavior. In 2018, WeChat hosted 1.08 billion active monthly users who sent 45 billion messages and made 410 million audio/ video calls.[35] By the end of 2018, China had 829 million internet users, including 817 million who used a smartphone to surf the internet. The report indicated that most phone users used the WeChat application.[36]

Different from Twitter or Weibo, WeChat is a more closed social media platform. WeChat had the Moments (in Chinese known as "Friends' circle") function to allow its users to share pictures, statuses, and website links. But the Moments posts are available only to friends. Joining one's friends' circle on WeChat and hence reading Moments feeds from that person requires permission.[37] Despite its "closed platform" feature, WeChat has two functions for "publicness." One is its public account, which can be subscribed to by any user, and more importantly, can be published by any individual or organization without a license (whereas licensing is a must for traditional media in China). These features make WeChat public accounts typical examples of We Media. The second publicness function is WeChat's group chat. Each group allows up to 500 members. Information from a WeChat public account can be quickly transmitted first by being posted into a chat group and then transferred to other chat groups by overlapping group members.[38]

Like ordinary citizens, all Chinese scientists we interviewed have their personal WeChat accounts. All of them join multiple professional chat groups featuring their areas of expertise, their research institutions and teams, and public affairs in the science community. Science popularization is one of common themes across scientists' chat groups. A small number of online celebrities have their public accounts, but most others are writers for popular WeChat public accounts. Nearly all of them read popular science articles published by WeChat public accounts.

WeChat group chat is also a channel for Chinese scientists to interact with journalists and professional science communicators. Although Chinese scientists seldom raise new issues in group chats or reach out to journalists on WeChat, the WeChat friends of most of our interviewees include journalists, who can, therefore, read the scientists' posts in their friends' circles. One environmental scientist even set up an environmental journalism group inviting dozens of science and environment journalists to join. He is often an issue initiator and actively guides journalists' reporting in the group. Our participant observations also reveal that, for their public communication of science, Chinese scientists actively seek knowledge they are not familiar with from peer scientists in WeChat groups exclusive to scientists and science communicators.

Motivations and Strategies to Utilize Different Social Media

Using a variety of social media platforms, scientists have shared their views on scientific progress, questioned dubious breakthroughs,[39] communicated hot scientific topics such as climate events on Twitter, and explored multimedia formats of science communication.[40] There are a couple of standard dimensions for the US and Chinese scientists' social media use, ranging from empowering them to bypass legacy media to networking with both science community peers and other likeminded friends.

Given social media's functions to demythologize science and allow scientists to contribute contents directly, early studies found that American scientists hailed it as an alternative to conventional science journalism so that they could bypass journalism, which they had long held in doubt.[41] Similarly, in China, the majority of our interviewees said that new social media have empowered them with the capacity to express their opinions and avoid inaccurate media representations. Chinese scientists also expressed their strong disbelief in the media's capacity to report science.[42]

However, several other studies find that scientists have no motivation to use science blogs (let alone microblogs) to replace science journalism. Instead, American scientists continue to rely more on legacy journalistic media than social media to promote the public impact of their research.[43] Blogging scientists consider themselves as explainers of science and public intellectuals instead of reporters of science.[44] Chinese scientists share this belief. According to our interviews, scientists do not think blogs or WeChat public accounts would replace legacy media. Instead, some said their relationship with legacy media had become better with the help of social media, as journalists can read their articles or comments in their blogs to understand their points better. They prefer to be commentators of hot scientific events or interpretative storytellers of what they consider to be essential discoveries and significant scientific progress. The findings and progress identified by Chinese scientists often do not overlap with media interests.

Meanwhile, in our interviews, Chinese scientists stressed social media's vast and measurable impact, unparalleled by conventional media. For example, science videos on space immigration co-produced by a planetary scientist and a leading internet streaming service won 15 million visits. A high-energy physicist who provided articles to a WeChat public account said WeChat's functions of forwarding and sharing articles make the items reach a much broader and more relevant audience than traditional mass media and their websites. Another motivation for social media use pertains to science education. Both US and Chinese scientists have expressed concerns about the fragmentation of science information and the flood of false science news on social media. This perception has motivated scientists in both countries to fulfill their public intellectual roles with the opportunities provided by social media.[45]

In addition to their role as an alternative to conventional media, social media platforms also offer channels for peer networking. Studies seem to reveal that the average scientist's use of social media is primarily for peer communication rather than science dissemination. In her research of scientists in America, Germany, and Taiwan, Lo found that scientists' use of social media is passive, mainly "to keep informed" or "stay in touch with my friends" rather than to "communicate."[46] Other studies also revealed that sharing information related to professional practice and teaching, requesting assistance from and offering suggestions to others, networking, and engaging in social commentary are the primary motivations for US and other Western scientists to use social media.[47]

At first glance, in these activities, scholarly networking overweighs public communication of science. However, since most social media platforms are open environments, the boundaries among academic, public, and personal connections are often blurred.[48] To the lay public, this means the chance to access not only more science-related—often relatively more precise—information but also scientists' views and comments and their internal communication, though this does not necessarily enhance public engagement with science.

Similarly, in China, the scientists we interviewed applauded social media for helping them access updated information more efficiently and reach both broader and specific audiences, and for bringing them more interdisciplinary collaborations, external funding support, academic–industry partnerships, and in rare cases (such as fossil collection), more research materials. The aforementioned high-energy physicist told us that the public and peer scientists outside one's immediate research circles are not mutually excluded, and algorithm-based audience location or peer recommendation (through WeChat groups) help identify more potential collaborators and increase academic recognition while expanding likeminded readership. As in America, the boundaries among scholarly communication, public science communication, and the science-industry are repeatedly crossed on Chinese social media. Most interviewed scientists report a similar blurring of boundaries among different types of communication tasks.

Besides facing different audiences, scientists who use social media also need to deal with different platforms. Our study examines American and Chinese scientists' cross-platform use of social media. Scholars have found that people adopt different social media platforms to expand their online influence,[49] and both keep boundaries between platforms and allow content and audience to permeate across these boundaries.[50] Yet, few studies have examined scientists' usage of a whole range of social media in their work and public outreach efforts. In this section, we explore US and Chinese scientists' strategic use of multiple social media platforms from the perspectives of affordability, technology transformation, and the pursuit of controllability.

Technology affordability, which refers to how a new technology meets users' demands so that they can afford to direct their time, money, energies, and other resources toward it, is widely used to predict people's media choice. Few studies systematically probe US scientists' alternative social media use. Some briefly touch on their media choices based on a specific platform's affordability. For example, American scientists favor Twitter over Facebook in science communication. Still, they regularly use Facebook for personal communication because of the perceived publicness of Twitter and the privacy features of Facebook.[51] Scientists use different online media for various purposes, with personal websites used primarily for internal scientific communication, social networks dominated by private use, and blogs primarily serving as an information source related to science.[52]

Some studies traced American scientists' reactions to a controversial "arsenic life" study that "found" arsenic can replace the fundamental-for-life element phosphorus in a bacterium isolated in a Californian lake.[53] They revealed that blogs, science journalism, and tweets were strategically combined to whisper scientists' suspicions, enlist peer support, and eventually form public pressure to question the "arsenic life" study's credibility.[54] While maintaining that social media users perceive features of different sites "affording" different types of activities, these studies went beyond affordability and placed scientists' cross-platform media use "within the context of their overall assessment of all available platforms."[55]

Technology transformation is another aspect that is found to link to people's media choices. In addition to social media's affordability, technology developments also shape Chinese scientists' cross-platform social media use. Unfortunately, we cannot identify literature tracing how technology transformation shapes American scientists' social media use. Most of our interviewees in China have or had a blog account on ScienceNet.cn. Their choice of blog aims to reach a public sphere on a relatively controllable platform. But due to technological developments, many of them have stopped updating their blogs.

According to an editor at ScienceNet.cn, WeChat public accounts are increasingly replacing blogs on ScienceNet.cn because they can better meet users' needs. A scientist can lie in bed to read and update public account articles. Interviewed scientists also report that regular blogging requires so much time but offers so little return, both in money and influence. Some scientists also believed that WeChat and other social media platforms such as a Toutiao account and Zhihu (the Chinese equivalent of question-and-answer site Quora) could help locate readers more accurately than blogs. Despite the findings above, technological developments alone cannot explain changes in media use. The Chinese scientists who continue to blog think that ScienceNet.cn has created a sense of community. "When I publish a blog, old friends (blog readers) will greet me with, 'Great to see you again.'"

In our studies, we also have found scientists have a strong desire to pursue controllability in their social media use. The use (or non-use) of Weibo and its underlying pursuit of controllability distinguish American and Chinese scientists' social media use. American and Western scientists use Twitter as a public information hub, where they post short comments, links to journal papers, and blogs and recommend and receive academic resources.[56] Their Twitter use results in citations and easier access to journalists.[57] Although the primary goal of most American and Western scientists' Twitter use is networking with peers, the blurring boundaries have facilitated the public communication of science.

Surprisingly, the blurring boundary between scholarly and public communication seems to be something Chinese scientists want to avoid, even among those who are already online celebrities. More than half of our interviewed scientists have never had a microblogging account. For those who own Weibo accounts, except for the aforementioned six active users, they primarily use the accounts for private purposes. Two obstacles for Weibo use emerged during our interviews. For scientists, dealing with readers' feedback is too time-consuming, and they might receive some rude or emotional comments.[58] But underlying the reluctance is the consideration of controllability. This consideration has driven Chinese scientists to WeChat, where most functions are under their control. For one's friends' circle, one can decide who to befriend; for public accounts, owners (or editors) can choose which reader feedback to display and whether to address the feedback; for chat groups, one can select the group with likeminded friends to join and exit any time if the chat becomes unacceptable.

Nevertheless, not every Chinese scientist is concerned with Weibo. In our interviews, the six scientists who maintain Weibo as their primary social media platform for public communication said they gained a lot from microblogging. One of them obtained external funding by making friends and winning recognition on Weibo. Another active Weibo user, a paleontologist, benefitted from his followers' fossil contribution, which has produced one-fourth of his lab's scientific findings. A third active Weibo user popularized food nutrition knowledge, and according to her, the mass readership of Weibo allows her reach a wider audience than other platforms. However, her graduate students have to be involved in her Weibo account management to deal with its significant time demand. The other three active Weibo users all enjoyed the pride of being public-opinion leaders on science topics.

In summary, this section finds that the intention to circumvent rather than replace legacy media, the lure of connectivity first with peers but also with external audiences, the affordability of technologies and technological development, the social context, and the desire for controllability have motivated scientists to use social media and choose alternative platforms. But American and Chinese scientists use these platforms differently. American scientists enjoy easier access to the public while many Chinese scientists avoid the openness of Weibo and instead choose WeChat for its limited publicness and higher controllability. Although our sample for Chinese scientists mainly includes online celebrities, our conclusion likely holds for ordinary Chinese scientists. They likely have a greater desire to control their public presentation due to their lack of experience in civic engagement.[59]

Social Media Use and Public Engagement with Science

So far, we have examined the US and Chinese scientists' social media use for public science communication and the motivations and constraints underlying it. It is also important to examine the implications of scientists' social media use to engage the public, the ultimate goal of science communication. In their conventional science communication process, scientists had favored the deficit model, which attributes public skepticism or hostility to science to a lack of understanding, resulting from a lack of information. Following this model, scientists widely believe the goal of communicating science is to improve scientific knowledge among the general public.[60] By contrast, scholars have hailed social media as powerful dialogic platforms for promoting public engagement with science in different disciplines.[61] For example, over 72 percent of US synthetic biologists regard social media as crucial civic engagement platforms.[62]

Despite the potential, many scientists do not think the public should play an essential role in conversations about science. Smith found scientists' attitudes to public engagement through social media were imbued with beliefs or narratives linked to the deficit model, such as "educating the public" or "improving their scientific literacy."[63] Although Smith's sample mainly consists of UK scientists, her conclusion might apply to the American scientists too, as UK and US scientists have shared "educating the public" as their primary goal for science communication.[64] Several studies showed that most scientists view their social media use primarily to serve their professional work. For example, most biology articles are shared within professional communities with limited diffusion to the public.[65] Others reported the followers of faculty members in ecology and evolutionary biology are predominantly (~55 percent) peer scientists.[66]

Major US federal agencies, universities, and academic societies set up their profiles, news release channels, and feedback gateways on different social media platforms.[67] However, agencies' social media communication is often in one-way mode, receiving few responses from the audience and responding to even fewer.[68] Scientists' and agencies' emphasis on scientific certainty of topics communicated in their social media accounts can make them vulnerable to charges of unpreparedness or obfuscation because social media can suddenly amplify uncertain aspects of these topics.[69] The situation implies that besides technology accessibility and affordability, digital public engagement also requires the determination of scientists, agencies, and stakeholders to participate in dialogues positively.[70]

China has a similar situation both in terms of the deficit model implied in scientists' claimed intention to educate the public and in their effort to avoid direct dialogues with the public. During our interviews, several scientists emphasized the irrational and scientifically illiterate audiences, and most interviewees were reluctant to talk with non-scientist audiences on social media. Chinese scientists generally prevent their social media chats from being involved in public controversies such as the debate on genetically modified (GM) food or the therapeutic effect of traditional Chinese medicine. There are also widespread complaints among Chinese scientists on the poor environment for online public opinion, effectively inhibiting their intention to dialogue. A study on Weibo-based reaction to a scandalous experience of unethically feeding children to test the nutrition of already controversial GM food shows that Chinese scientists were reluctant to join online debates on GM food in the polarized public environment.[71]

The subsection above indicates that both American and Chinese scientists generally evade direct online dialogue with the public. However, this should not be interpreted as a failure of social media–based science communication. In her interview with Twitter-using scientists, Smith found while the logic of deficit model dominated their spontaneous actions, they were highly flexible and happy to explore chances for online dialogue.[72] In the aforementioned study on scientists' followers, peer scientists accounted for the majority; however, when the number of followers surpassed a threshold of 1,000, the types of followers became more diverse. They included research and educational organizations, media, members of the public, and a small number of decision-makers.[73] The study indicates that although scientists' regular communication on social media primarily targets peers, those who are active online have a broader body of audience/followers. The interactive platform provides the opportunity to create a discussion that engages the public.

The research on the arsenic life controversy reveals a similar pattern.[74] Although opposing scientists' initial intention in their blogs and Twitter responses to the disputed study was to enlist peer comments and supports, they did not exclude the involvement of the mass media and even the general public. In another case study, Simis-Wilkinson et al. examined tweets with the hashtag #overlyhonestmethods that revealed some behind-the-scene details of scientific research.[75] They found that by placing insiders' conversation in a public space, often in humorous styles and with 75 percent of the language accessible, lay audiences are likely privy to scientists' inner world. Social media platforms thus provide chances for public engagement with internal science, potentially helping the public to dialogue with scientists.

Chinese scientists also show some flexibility in welcoming meaningful public engagement, though sometimes in patterns different from US scientists. One trend is to encourage objectivity in assessing scientific advances amid the official media's regular efforts to propagandize scientific progress.[76] Although our sample features communication-savvy scientists, most of them are reluctant to appear in the media to avoid being hyped. A recent example was in February 2019, Chinese media widely applauded a study by a Guangzhou-based CAS team to use malaria infection to treat cancer (initially promoted by a CAS social media platform). In WeChat groups focused on science communication, some young life scientists cautiously questioned the unclear mechanism underlying the treatment and pointed out the announced therapeutic effect was not based on the team's published papers. These comments led an independent media outlet (*The Intellectuals*, operated in the form of a WeChat public account) to launch impactful investigative reporting into the hyped treatment.[77]

A more influential case is the effort of young Chinese scientists, organized through WeChat, to question a 2016 study published in *Nature Biotechnology* by a Chinese lab on a new (and potentially revolutionary) method of genomic editing hailed by the Chinese media as a Nobel Prize–level study.[78] After over one hundred labs worldwide failed to replicate the study, young Chinese scientists published several rounds of open letters urging the lab to publish raw data and publicize its experimental details.[79] These efforts, followed by the media's investigations, pushed *Nature Biotechnology* to launch an investigation and asked the lab to retract its paper when the data was found to lend no support to their study conclusion.[80] Our interviews have covered several participating scientists who signed the open letters. One of them, who authored one open letter, confirmed the role of social media in helping coordinate peers and transform the growing scientific consensus to intense social pressure. Interestingly, while this scientist would not talk with journalists for his studies, he was active in receiving media interviews about the open letter because he wanted the scientific consensus questioning the published genomic editing method widely disseminated.

When discussing the idea of "public engagement with science," Lewenstein clarifies that two interpretations of public engagement are most common: "engagement" as an aspect of learning and "engagement" as part of participatory democracy.[81] In terms of the participatory democracy of science governance, Chinese scientists' social media use seems not to have provided a significant breakthrough. Still, in terms of "engagement" as an aspect of interactive learning, social media platforms have made significant impacts. The aforementioned fossil collection by paleontological lovers guided by the celebrity paleontologist through Weibo is one example, which can be called a Chinese version of citizen science. Other public engagements include the timely provision of popular science contents by Chinese scientists to meet the public demands identified by trending online opinions in fields like food nutrition and atmospheric pollution. Social media–based streaming services also enable scientists to visualize their lab activities and field studies (in ecology and zoology disciplines and the space exploration mentioned previously) and to receive more audience feedback.

In the sense of "engagement" as learning, American scientists and institutions also have developed a variety of practices to engage the public and promote their participation in research, often involving the use of social media.[82] For example, scientists at Boston-based Northeastern University and partners developed a video game to help citizen science participants manipulate and compare 3D protein structures to finish scientific tasks.[83] In these cases, learners can learn science by doing, and social media platforms offered the channel to engage scientists into this process. The interactions are hardly possible in pre–social media era.

In summary, although US and Chinese scientists have not widely adopted the dialogic mode of science communication through social media, the interactivity and boundary blurring created by these media still facilitate public engagement. For example, with social media, science journalists can more conveniently produce investigative reporting thanks to their access to scientists' internal disputes. When we consider the learning aspect of public engagement, we can find that social media plays a more significant role. While both US and Chinese scientists can now utilize video, audio, vivid narrative, and audience location to create a more participatory science learning environment, there are differences between their endeavors. American scientists develop social media platform-based citizen science projects, whereas in China, social media help scientists partially overcome the propaganda role of official media to promote science. Social media platforms also enable the direct provision of popular science information to meet perceived public demands.

Conclusion

In this chapter, we examined the status of US and Chinese scientists' use of social media for public science communication, as well as their motivations and strategies to use various social media platforms. Our review, survey, interviews, and observation show that social media assist scientists in bypassing the limitation of legacy media to reach wider audiences, as well as harvest more interdisciplinary collaborations and realize multiple returns. In the process, these scientists strategically choose different social media platforms for their specific affordability. Yet, contextual elements also shape their multi-platform social media use, particularly in controversial settings. Compared with their US counterparts (at least based on what existing literature has revealed), Chinese scientists are more active to minimize uncontrollability.

However, as discussed, social media has yet to become a ready tool for public engagement with science. Scientists prioritize their internal networking demands on social media over civic engagement with science; research institutions and government agencies utilize social media to make their information reach a broader audience without fully considering and responding to public feedback. Nevertheless, the boundary obscuring of social media and scientists' effort to enlist social supports through these media platforms offer more chances for the public to be engaged. Social media also better serve the educational aspect of public engagement with science than the element of participatory democracy.

Therefore, a more meaningful civic engagement with science on social media calls for constructive inputs by scientists, research institutions, government agencies, and the public itself. Further studies are needed to explore more social media–based options for science communication; measure the effect of the media's blurring of boundaries on public involvement; and examine the consequences of scientists' effort to balance scholarly networking, controllability, and public outreach on various social media platforms.

NOTES

1. Dominique Brossard and Dietram A. Scheufele, "Science, New Media, and the Public," *Science* 339, no. 6115 (2013): 40–41.
2. Cassidy R. Sugimoto, Sam Work, Vincent Larivière, and Stefanie Haustein, "Scholarly Use of Social Media and Altmetrics: A Review of the Literature," *Journal of the Association for*

Information Science, Technology and Culture 68, no. 9 (2017): 2037–62. Hans Peter Peters, Sharon Dunwoody, Joachim Allgaier, Yin-Yueh Lo, and Dominique Brossard, "Public Communication of Science 2.0: Is the Communication of Science via the 'New Media' Online a Genuine Transformation or Old Wine in New Bottles?," *EMBO Reports* 15, no. 7 (2014): 749–53.

3. Holly M. Bik and Miriam C. Goldstein, "An Introduction to Social Media for Scientists," *PLoS Biology* 11, no. 4 (2013): e1001535; see Stuart Allan and Vinciane Colson, "Science Blogs as Competing Channels for the Dissemination of Science News," *Journalism* 12, no. 7 (2011): 889–902; also see Paige Brown Jarreau, "Science Bloggers' Self-Perceived Communication Roles," *Journal of Science Communication* 14, no. 4 (2015): A02. Alison Smith, "'Wow, I Didn't Know That Before; Thank You': How Scientists Use Twitter for Public Engagement," *Journal of Promotional Communications* 3, no. 3 (2016): 320–39.

4. Yin-Yueh Lo, "Online Communication beyond the Scientific Community: Scientists' Use of New Media in Germany, Taiwan, and the United States to Address the Public" (PhD dissertation, Freie Universität Berlin, 2016).

5. Stefanie Haustein, Vincent Larivière, Mike Thelwall, Didier Amyot, and Isabella Peters, "Tweets Vs. Mendeley Readers: How Do These Two Social Media Metrics Differ?," *Information Technology* 56, no. 5 (2014): 207–15.

6. Steven Ovadia, "ResearchGate and Academia.Edu: Academic Social Networks," *Behavioral & Social Sciences Librarian* 33, no. 3 (2014): 165–69.

7. Hepeng Jia, Dapeng Wang, Weishan Miao, and Hongjun Zhu, "Encountered but Not Engaged: Examining the Use of Social Media for Science Communication by Chinese Scientists," *Science Communication* 39, no. 5 (2017): 646–72.

8. Geoff Brumfiel, "Supplanting the Old Media?," *Nature* 458, no. 7236 (2009): 274–77.

9. Paige Brown Jarreau, "All the Science That Is Fit to Blog: An Analysis of Science Blogging Practices" (PhD dissertation, Louisiana State University, 2015).

10. Lee Rainie, Cary Funk, and Monica Anderson, *How Scientists Engage the Public* (Washington, DC: Pew Research Center, 2015).

11. Lo, "Online Communication beyond the Scientific Community."

12. Bruce V. Lewenstein, "'Public Understanding of Science' in America, 1945–1965" (PhD dissertation, University of Pennsylvania, 1987).

13. Kimberley Collins, David Shiffman, and Jenny Rock, "How Are Scientists Using Social Media in the Workplace?," *PLoS One* 11, no. 10 (2016): e0162680.

14. Hepeng Jia, Lin Shi, and Dapeng Wang, "Passive Communicators: Investigating the Interaction of Chinese Scientists with the Media," *Science Bulletin* 63, no. 7 (March 2018): 402–4.

15. Liang He, "The Research of the Science Blog (in Chinese)" (MA thesis, Hunan University, 2014).

16. Chinese Ministry of Science and Technology, *2016 S&T Human Resources Status in China* (Beijing: China S&T Statistics Service, 2018).

17. Xiaohui Huang and Yan Zhan, "Scientific Content Analysis of Scientific Researchers' Blog: Blogs in ScienceNet.Cn as Examples" (Chinese), *Studies on Science Popularization* 5, no. 2 (2010): 24–29.

18. Jarreau, "All the Science That Is Fit to Blog"; and see Huang and Zhan, "Scientific Content Analysis of Scientific Researchers' Blog."

19. Bernard J. Jansen, Mimi Zhang, Kate Sobel, and Abdur Chowdury, "Twitter Power: Tweets as Electronic Word of Mouth," *Journal of the American Society for Information Science Technology and Culture* 60, no. 11 (2009): 2169–88.

20. Sara K. Yeo, Michael A. Cacciatore, Dominique Brossard, Dietram A Scheufele, and M. Xenos, "Twitter as the Social Media of Choice for Sharing Science" (paper presented at the 13th International Public Communication of Science and Technology Conference, Salvador, Brazil, May 5–8, 2014).

21. Kim Holmberg, Timothy D. Bowman, Stefanie Haustein, and Isabella Peters, "Astrophysicists' Conversational Connections on Twitter," *PLoS One* 9, no. 8 (2014): e106086; and see Collins et al., "How Are Scientists Using Social Media in the Workplace?"

22. Sara P. Bombaci, Cooper M. Farr, H. Travis Gallo, Anna M. Mangan, Lani T. Stinson, Monica Kaushik, and Liba Pejchar, "Using Twitter to Communicate Conservation Science from a Professional Conference," *Conservation Biology* 30, no. 1 (2016): 216–25.

23. S. Bhattacharya, P. Srinivasan, and P. Polgreen, "Engagement with Health Agencies on Twitter," *PLoS One* 9, no. 11 (2014): e112235; Nicole M. Lee and Matthew S. Vandyke, "Set It and Forget It: The One-Way Use of Social Media by Government Agencies Communicating Science," *Science Communication* 37, no. 4 (2015): 533–41; and see Nicole M. Lee, Matthew S. VanDyke, and R. Glenn Cummins, "A Missed Opportunity?: NOAA's Use of Social Media to Communicate Climate Science," *Environmental Communication* 12, no. 2 (2018): 274–83.

24. Stefanie Haustein, Isabella Peters, Cassidy R. Sugimoto, Mike Thelwall, and Vincent Larivière, "Tweeting Biomedicine: An Analysis of Tweets and Citations in the Biomedical Literature," *Journal of the Association for Information Science, Technology and Culture* 65, no. 4 (2014): 656–69.

25. Xuan Liang, Leona Yi-Fan Su, Sara K. Yeo, Dietram A. Scheufele, Dominique Brossard, Michael Xenos, Paul Nealey, and Elizabeth A Corley, "Building Buzz (Scientists)

Communicating Science in New Media Environments," *Journalism & Mass Communication Quarterly* 91, no. 4 (2014): 772–91.

26. Todd P. Newman, "Tracking the Release of IPCC Ar5 on Twitter: Users, Comments, and Sources Following the Release of the Working Group I Summary for Policymakers," *Public Understanding of Science* 26, no. 7 (2017): 815–25.

27. Adrian Rauchfleisch and Mike S. Schäfer, "Multiple Public Spheres of Weibo: A Typology of Forms and Potentials of Online Public Spheres in China," *Information, Communication & Society* 18, no. 2 (2015): 139–55.

28. China Internet Watch, "Weibo Mau Increased to 446m in Q3 2018, 93% Mobile," China Internet Watch, December 4, 2018, https://www.chinainternetwatch.com/27603/weibo-q3-2019/.

29. Statista, "Most Popular Social Networks Worldwide as of January 2019, Ranked by Number of Active Users (in Millions)," *Statista: The Statistics Portal*, January 2019, https://www.statista.com/statistics/272014/global-social-networks-ranked-by-number-of-users/.

30. Michael Nentwich and René König, "Academia Goes Facebook? The Potential of Social Network Sites in the Scholarly Realm," in *Opening Science: The Evolving Guide on How the Internet Is Changing Research, Collaboration and Scholarly Publishing*, ed. Sönke Bartling and Sascha Friesike (Cham, Switzerland: Springer International Publishing, 2014), 107–24.

31. Stacy Loeb, Christopher E. Bayne, Christine Frey, Benjamin J. Davies, Timothy D. Averch, Henry H. Woo, Brian Stork, Matthew R. Cooperberg, Scott E. Eggener, "Use of Social Media in Urology: Data from the American Urological Association," *Bju International* 113, no. 6 (Jun 2014): 993–98; and see Yeo et al., "Twitter as the Social Media of Choice for Sharing Science."

32. Craig R. McClain, "Practices and Promises of Facebook for Science Outreach: Becoming a 'Nerd of Trust.'" *PLOS Biology* 15, no. 6 (2017): e2002020.

33. Yeo et al., "Twitter as the Social Media of Choice for Sharing Science."

34. "The Science People See on Social Media," Pew Research Center, March 2018.

35. China Internet Watch, "WeChat Year in Review 2018," China Internet Watch, January 14, 2019, https://www.chinainternetwatch.com/28056/wechat-2018/.

36. China Internet Network Information Center (CNNIC), "The 43rd Statistical Report on Internet Development in China," CNNIC, 2019.

37. Eric Harwit, "WeChat: Social and Political Development of China's Dominant Messaging App," *Chinese Journal of Communication* 10, no. 3 (2016): 312–27.

38. Xiaobo Wang and Baotong Gu, "The Communication Design of WeChat: Ideological as Well as Technical Aspects of Social Media," *Communication Design Quarterly Review* 4, no.

1 (2016): 23–35.

39. Sara K. Yeo, Xuan Liang, Dominique Brossard, Kathleen M. Rose, Kaine Korzekwa, Dietram A. Scheufele, and Michael A. Xenos, "The Case of #Arseniclife: Blogs and Twitter in Informal Peer Review," *Public Understanding of Science* 26, no. 8 (May 26, 2016): 937–52.

40. Dustin J. Welbourne and Will J. Grant, "Science Communication on YouTube: Factors That Affect Channel and Video Popularity," *Public Understanding of Science* 25, no. 6 (February 19, 2015): 706–18.

41. John S. Wilkins, "The Roles, Reasons, and Restrictions of Science Blogs," *Trends in Ecology & Evolution* 23, no. 8 (2008): 411–13; and see Vinciane Colson, "Science Blogs as Competing Channels for the Dissemination of Science News," *Journalism* 12, no. 7 (2011): 889–902; also see Brumfiel, "Supplanting the Old Media?"

42. Jia et al., "Encountered but Not Engaged."

43. Joachim Allgaier, Sharon Dunwoody, Dominique Brossard, Yin-Yueh Lo, and Hans Peter Peters, "Journalism and Social Media as Means of Observing the Contexts of Science," *BioScience* 63, no. 4 (2013): 284–87.

44. Jarreau, "Science Bloggers' Self-Perceived Communication Roles."

45. Hauke Riesch and Jonathan Mendel, "Science Blogging: Networks, Boundaries, and Limitations," *Science as Culture* 23, no. 1 (2014): 51–72; and see Jarreau, "Science Bloggers' Self-Perceived Communication Roles."

46. Lo, "Scientists' Use of New Media in Germany, Taiwan, and the United States."

47. George Veletsianos, "Higher Education Scholars' Participation and Practices on Twitter," *Journal of Computer Assisted Learning* 28, no. 4 (Aug 2012): 336–49.

48. Timothy David Bowman, "Investigating the Use of Affordances and Framing Techniques by Scholars to Manage Personal and Professional Impressions on Twitter" (PhD dissertation, Indiana University, 2015).

49. Harsh Taneja, James G. Webster, Edward C. Malthouse, and Thomas B. Ksiazek, "Media Consumption across Platforms: Identifying User-Defined Repertoires," *New Media & Society* 14, no. 6 (2012): 951–68.

50. Xuan Zhao, Cliff Lampe, and Nicole B. Ellison, "The Social Media Ecology: User Perceptions, Strategies, and Challenges" (paper presented at the 2016 Conference on Human Factors in Computing Systems, Santa Clara, CA, May 7–12, 2016), 89–100.

51. Yeo et al., "Twitter as the Social Media of Choice for Sharing Science."

52. Lo, "Scientists' Use of New Media in Germany, Taiwan, and the United."

53. Felisa Wolfe-Simon, Jodi Switzer Blum, Thomas R. Kulp, Gwyneth W. Gordon, Shelley E. Hoeft, Jennifer Pett-Ridge, John F. Stolz, Samuel M. Webb, Peter K. Weber, Paul C.

W. Davies, Ariel D. Anbar, Ronald S. Oremland, "A Bacterium That Can Grow by Using Arsenic Instead of Phosphorus," *Science* 332, no. 6034 (2011): 1163.

54. Gunver Lystbaek Vestergaard, "The Science Grapevine: Influence of Blog Information on the Online Media Coverage of the 2010 Arsenic-Based Life Study," *Journalism* 18, no. 5 (2017): 626–44; and see Yeo et al., "The Case of #Arseniclife: Blogs and Twitter."

55. Zhao et al., "The Social Media Ecology."

56. George Veletsianos and Royce Kimmons, "Scholars and Faculty Members' Lived Experiences in Online Social Networks," *Internet and Higher Education* 16 (January 2013): 43–50; and see Veletsianos, "Higher Education Scholars on Twitter."

57. Haustein et al., "Tweeting Biomedicine"; also see Liang et al., "Communicating Science in New Media Environments."

58. Jia et al., "Encountered but Not Engaged."

59. Hepeng Jia, Lin Shi, and Dapeng Wang, "Examining Chinese Scientists' Media Behaviors: Institutional Support and Media Experience Predict Involvement" (paper presented at the 2018 Annual Conference of Association for Education in Journalism and Mass Communication (AEJMC), Washington DC. August 6–9, 2018).

60. John C. Besley and Matthew C. Nisbet, "How Scientists View the Public, the Media, and the Political Process," *Public Understanding of Science* 22, no. 6 (2013): 644–59; also see Molly J. Simis, Haley Madden, Michael A. Cacciatore, and Sara K. Yeo, "The Lure of Rationality: Why Does the Deficit Model Persist in Science Communication?," *Public Understanding of Science* 25, no. 4 (2016): 400–14.

61. María José Luzón, "Public Communication of Science in Blogs: Recontextualizing Scientific Discourse for a Diversified Audience," *Written Communication* 30, no. 4 (2013): 428–57; and see Miguel Valdez Soto, Joyce E. Balls-Berry, Shawn G. Bishop, Lee A. Aase, Farris K. Timimi, Victor M. Montori, and Christi A. Patten, "Use of Web 2.0 Social Media Platforms to Promote Community-Engaged Research Dialogs: A Preliminary Program Evaluation," *JMIR Research Protocols* 5, no. 3 (2016): e183; also see G. Fauville, S. Dupont, S. von Thun, and J. Lundin, "Can Facebook Be Used to Increase Scientific Literacy? A Case Study of the Monterey Bay Aquarium Research Institute Facebook Page and Ocean Literacy," *Computers & Education* 82 (March 2015): 60–73; and Moritz Büchi, "Microblogging as an Extension of Science Reporting," *Public Understanding of Science* 26, no. 8 (2017): 953–68.

62. Dominique Brossard, "Science and Social Media" (presentation at the National Academy of Sciences and National Academy of Medicine: Committee Science of Science Communication; A Research Agenda, Washington DC, February 25, 2016), https://sites. nationalacademies.org/cs/groups/dbassesite/documents/webpage/dbasse_171456.pdf.

63. Smith, "'Wow, I Didn't Know That Before.'"

64. Besley and Nisbet, "How Scientists View the Public, the Media, and the Political Process."

65. Juan Pablo Alperin, Charles J. Gomez, and Stefanie Haustein, "Identifying Diffusion Patterns of Research Articles on Twitter: A Case Study of Online Engagement with Open Access Articles," *Public Understanding of Science* 28, no. 1 (2018): 2–18.

66. Isabelle M. Côté and Emily S Darling, "Scientists on Twitter: Preaching to the Choir or Singing from the Rooftops?," *Facets* 3, no. 1 (2018): 682–94.

67. Laura Van Eperen and Francesco M. Marincola, "How Scientists Use Social Media to Communicate Their Research," *Journal of Translational Medicine* 9 (November 15, 2011). Sanmitra Bhattacharya, Padmini Srinivasan, and Phil Polgreen, "Engagement with Health Agencies on Twitter," *PLoS One* (November 7, 2014), https://doi.org/10.1371/journal.pone.0112235; and see Lee et al., "Set It and Forget It."

68. Lee and VanDyke, "One-Way Use of Social Media by Government Agencies"; and see Lee et al., "NOAA's Use of Social Media to Communicate Climate Science."

69. Kajsa E. Dalrymple, Rachel Young, and Melissa Tully, "'Facts, Not Fear': Negotiating Uncertainty on Social Media During the 2014 Ebola Crisis," *Science Communication* 38, no. 4 (June 22, 2016): 442–67.

70. Ann Grand, Gareth Davies, Richard Holliman, and Anne Adams, "Mapping Public Engagement with Research in a UK University," *PLoS One* 10, no. 4 (April 2015): e0121874.

71. On the study on Weibo, see Jingqun Fan, Hepeng Jia, Guangmang Peng, and Feng Zhang, "A Study on Scientific Controversies on Social Media: Genetically Modified Golden Rice Communication in Chinese Weibo" (Chinese), *Journalism & Communication*, no. 11 (2013): 106–16. The controversial nutrition study was published as Guangwen Tang, Yuming Hu, Shi-an Yin, Yin Wang, Gerard E. Dallal, Michael A. Grusak, and Robert M. Russell, "B-Carotene in Golden Rice Is as Good as B-Carotene in Oil at Providing Vitamin a to Children," *American Journal of Clinical Nutrition* 96, no. 3 (2012): 658–64.

72. Smith, "'Wow, I Didn't Know That Before.'"

73. Côté and Darling, "Scientists on Twitter."

74. Vestergaard, "The Science Grapevine"; and see Yeo et al., "The Case of #Arseniclife."

75. Molly Simis-Wilkinson, Haley Madden, David Lassen, Leona Yi-Fan Su, Dominique Brossard, Dietram A. Scheufele, and Michael A. Xenos, "Scientists Joking on Social Media: An Empirical Analysis of #Overlyhonestmethods," *Science Communication* 40, no. 3 (2018): 314–39.

76. Hepeng Jia and Zhenhua Liu, "The Separation of Propaganda about Science Research and Mass Media: Quantitative and Qualitative Analysis of Science Institutions in China" (Chinese), *Studies on Science Popularization* 4, no. 1 (2009): 17–23.

77. Shuisong Ye, "Infecting Malaria to Treat Cancer? Let's Start from Dead Patient's Feedback" (Chinese), *The Intellectual* (March 5, 2019), http://www.sohu.com/a/299127482_120026231?sec=wd.

78. Feng Gao, Xiao Z. Shen, Feng Jiang, Yongqiang Wu, and Chunyu Han, "DNA-Guided Genome Editing Using the Natronobacterium Gregoryi Argonaute," *Nature Biotechnology* 34, no. 5 (2016): 768–73 (retracted).

79. David Cyranoski, "Replications, Ridicule and a Recluse: The Controversy over Ngago Gene-Editing Intensifies," *Nature* 536 (August 11, 2016): 136–37.

80. David Cyranoski, "Authors Retract Controversial Ngago Gene-Editing Study," *Nature* (August 3, 2017), https://www.nature.com/news/authors-retract-controversial-ngago-gene-editing-study-1.22412.

81. Bruce V. Lewenstein, "Public Engagement," *Informal Science* (January 2016), http://www.informalscience.org/news-views/public-engagement.

82. David Shiffman, "Twitter as a Tool for Conservation Education and Outreach: What Scientific Conferences Can Do to Promote Live-Tweeting," *Journal of Environmental Studies and Sciences* 2, no. 3 (2012): 257–62; and see Samantha Z. Yammine, Christine Liu, Paige B. Jarreau, and Imogen R. Coe, "Social Media for Social Change in Science," *Science* 360, no. 6385 (2018): 162; also see Shupei Yuan, Anthony Dudo, and John C. Besley, "Scientific Societies' Support for Public Engagement: An Interview Study," *International Journal of Science Education, Part B* (2019), doi:10.1080/21548455.2019.1576240.

83. Thomas Muender, Sadaab Ali Gulani, Lauren Westendorf, Clarissa Verish, Rainer Malaka, Orit Shaer, and Seth Cooper, "Comparison of Mouse and Multi-Touch for Protein Structure Manipulation in a Citizen Science Game Interface," *Journal of Science Communication* 18, no. 1 (2019): A05.

All in One Place?

Reluctance in Everyday Mobile Communication in China

Lei Vincent Huang

Mobile communication technologies offer users opportunities to connect and communicate with others anytime and anywhere. In China, the past decade has witnessed the rapid growth of the number of mobile phone users and high penetration of mobile technologies in people's lives. As of the end of 2018, the number of mobile phone users had reached 820 million.[1] Recent developments in mobile technologies and the wide adoption of smartphones have brought opportunities to use such technologies in not only one-to-one, text-only communication but also in multi-sided, multimedia communication. In addition, mobile communication technologies such as mobile instant messengers (MIMs) on smartphones are incorporating features that increase their utility, such as social network service (SNS), blogging, and mobile payment. WeChat, as one of the leading examples of such integrative design, is the most popular mobile instant messenger in China and has been leading the innovation of mobile communication technologies globally. These mobile communication technologies offer high integration of various functions and bring a person's various social contacts into one place. For example, a typical Chinese user will use her phone to make traditional phone calls to family, to use WeChat instant messaging with friends, to send and receive email and other communication from work, to pay online bills, to swipe her phone in the subway station instead of using a card or coins, to play games while on the subway, and then to pay for groceries on the way home—the mobile phone has thus become an "all in one place" life tool. But as our mobile technology has become integrated into virtually every aspect of our daily lives, concerns have arisen that this integration may cause numerous problems, including information and communication overload,[2] context collapse,[3] and tensions in identity presentations.[4] In short, infinite connectivity and non-stop communication may be producing some unwelcome conflicts.

The aforementioned problems have resulted in disconnection practices, where users choose to go offline or withdraw from using a smartphone application.[5] Studying non-use or disconnection practices can help us understand concerns and problems in using communication technologies. However, disconnecting from online communication is not always the best way to avoid the problem. More importantly, the high integration of communication functions may make it impossible to completely leave a mobile technology or a smartphone application. In other words, people may wish to turn off only certain functions and at the same time stay connected or show their presence to others. In addition to the impact of technological integration, users may also find it difficult to withdraw from using the mobile technologies because they experience social pressure to use them from their peers or employers.[6] User experience of mobile communication is therefore shaped by technological as well as social factors. While studying non-use will not capture the full complexity of communication technology uses, exploring people's struggles, contradictions, and hesitancies in their everyday use of communication technologies will point to reluctance in use and how such emotions are shaped by cultural, social, and technological factors.[7] In short, if most of our emerging literature on mobile communication technology has focused up to now on how users adopt new platforms, building ever more complicated and integrated communication networks, I am asking the opposite question: how do users opt out of these technologies?

As a first step toward answering this question, I focus in this chapter on reluctance in using WeChat, the most popular MIM and social media platform in China. Reporting data collected from interviews with WeChat users, I show how the integrative design of WeChat, the open network people have to maintain using WeChat, and overly positive self-presentation norms on WeChat Moments contribute to reluctance in user experience. This study contributes to our understanding of contradictions in mobile communication that is no longer dyadic and text-based but is multi-sided, multi-modal, and multi-functional. It also contributes to understandings of mobile communication in China in the smartphone era and extends previous research on mobile phone use to investigate how smartphone and MIM design and social and cultural understanding of the technologies interact to shape user experience. In what follows, I first briefly review research on reluctance in user experience and introduce mobile communication in China and WeChat. Then I present an interview study that illustrate three points of reluctance in WeChat use. Finally, I discuss the implications of this study in terms of mobile communication, MIM research and design, and future directions. I conclude that reluctance is a powerful and likely increasing response to communication integration, perhaps suggesting that even in our networked and postmodern world, users still want to cling to the boundaries separating family, friends, and work. While my data focuses on users in China, it would make sense to speculate that reluctance is likely on the rise in the United States as well, suggesting that future research could offer comparative insights into reluctance both in and between American and Chinese mobile communication users.

Reluctance and the Complex Uses of Social Media

As people embrace the always-on mode of smartphone use, communication scholarship has evolved from a duality view—that people either connect or disconnect from mobile communication technologies—to a view suggesting that people regulate their connectivity, adjust their volumes of communication based on different circumstances, and constantly manage the direction of communication as time and space changes.[8] Although people regulate their connectivity, they do not always prefer to do so; recent research on social media suggests that even though they use them constantly, people feel reluctant to engage in some elements of social media.[9] For instance, Cassidy found that users of Gaydar, a gay dating app, had to determine how to use the app after it was deemed to be a site for seeking casual sex.[10] Likewise, in America, users who thought they were communicating in closed threads on Facebook have been shocked to learn that their every personal bit of information is being mined by data-trackers and surveillance programs. In both cases, users have had to adjust expectations and habits pending new information, in both cases leading to less trust in the app. As these two examples indicate, as users regulate their connectivity via mobile communication, they often experience reluctance.

To complicate matters, recent developments in mobile technologies and the expansion of integrative design logics are likely to increase reluctance in user experience. In Chinese society, mobile communication is no longer enabled by limited types of modality, such as texting and calling; rather, mobile communication is now multi-modal, as indicated in the examples listed above.[11] Such developments introduce conveniences as well as new issues into people's everyday lives, as people enjoy but occasionally are bothered by the high connectivity afforded by the technologies. Furthermore, norms of mobile technology use that are not necessarily favored by the users have developed. For instance, employees could perform commitment to their jobs by showing constant connection and making themselves available at and after work using mobile technologies, a practice that may not always be productive as constant connection may be disruptive to work and bring problems to work/life balance.[12] Thus, problems in mobile technology use are not determined by advances in the technology alone, but are shaped by the entanglement of material features (e.g., technological features and application design) and human factors (e.g., social norms and individual identities). While our technologies have been evolving rapidly, our human understanding of them is lagging behind—so we have more technology than we know how to manage, leaving users with a sense of being overwhelmed.

To flesh out these claims, this study explores reluctance in the use of the most popular mobile communication technologies in China. Specifically, this study examines the use of WeChat, a smartphone-based social networking application that enables various functions for communication and social interaction. WeChat is famous for its "all in one place" design. While it started as an instant messenger, WeChat now provides functions of multimedia instant messaging, by which users can send text/voice messages, pictures, videos, and files to another user or a group of users. It also provides a social networking service (SNS) called Moments. Through Moments users can post original content (e.g., texts, photos, and video clips) as well as content shared from other websites. In addition to supporting social interactions, WeChat also provides a platform for organizations and individuals to manage mini-websites called "official accounts," where users can subscribe to these accounts and receive updates or interact with chosen organizations and their individuals. Lastly, WeChat incorporates utility functions such as bill payment, booking services, and more.[13]

The integrative design facilitates connectivity among users while also leading to unexpected outcomes, such as fear of surveillance. For example, Yu and his colleagues found that parents constantly checked their children's life statuses through sending private messages and reading their posts.[14] To resist such surveillance, children regulated their behaviors by posting only positive content on Moments. In addition, WeChat users usually connect with people from various aspects of their life. Therefore, people face a *collapsed context* on WeChat, where assumptions and norms of different social contexts are blended in one place.[15] Research suggests that diversity and specificity of user groups results in difficulty of managing various expectations for responsiveness and accessibility across different user groups from different life contexts.[16] That is to say, when an MIM user connects to diverse user groups, they may feel pressure when managing communication through the application because they sense boundary concerns: users might not want their work and family lives to intermingle quite so much. As for specificity, research suggests that when users connect to communities (e.g., chat groups of teams, departments, and organizations) rather than specific users (e.g., peers, managers, and clients), they feel more stressed to manage expectations because they become harder to predict. Similarly, on WeChat, I would expect that users may need to manage expectations of responsiveness and accessibility and encounter difficulties when they wish to connect to a group of users while disconnecting from another group. Across all these instances, we see mobile communication technologies leaving users feeling caught between different discourse groups, hence collapsing the previously discrete contexts of daily life. This can, on the one hand, lead to a thrilling sense of connectivity and convergence, but on the other hand, it can lead to serious confusions, embarrassments, or awkward moments—these latter experiences are what lead to a spike in user reluctance.

Also, as previous research suggests, Chinese users, in contrast to their Western counterparts, manage an open network of contacts and develop distinctive interaction rituals that feature contextualized mobility.[17] High-context interaction patterns and relationships in China are reflected in the use of mobile technologies. That is to say, although being offered spatial and temporal flexibility in connection, Chinese users consider social hierarchies and the need of maintaining harmony in using mobile phones. Those who are in a relatively less powerful position are expected to be more careful in observing the etiquette of using mobile phones, whereas those who are powerful are more intrusive in mobile communication. Chinese users are also subtle in mobile communication. For instance, not answering phone calls may be used as a signal of refusal or as a way to maintain some social distance with acquaintances. With the enhanced connection provided by WeChat, the power-oriented interaction patterns and the needs of maintaining harmonious relationships may become sources of reluctance, because there are more constraints to contextualized mobility and maintaining different patterns of interactions in one place. In this instance, user reluctance regarding mobile communication technologies overlaps with the need for more analysis of organizational norms in China, where workplace hierarchies are still very powerful.

Methods: Interviews with Knowledge Workers

This study draws on qualitative data collected for a larger research project that explores WeChat use in work and social contexts. The participants were recruited using snowball sampling. Starting from my social and professional networks, I first identified WeChat users who frequently used various functions of the platform (e.g., WeChat Moments, file exchange, mobile payment, and reading and following official accounts) and used the platform in professional contexts. These users provided more comprehensive insights into user experience than those who only used limited functions of the platform. One of the benefits of recruiting participants from the researcher's social network is that, in Chinese contexts, without trusted relationships with respondents, researchers may have limited access to data, as Chinese respondents are likely to withhold important information from unfamiliar individuals.[18] Due to this limitation, researchers may fail to gain deep insights into the phenomenon under investigation because of the low-quality data. Therefore, snowball sampling starting from the researcher's social networks (i.e., *guanxi* network) is an effective participant recruitment method for research in the Chinese context.[19] One of the limitations of this *guanxi*-based snowball sampling is that the researchers may have homogenous social networks, which limit the diversity of study samples. To avoid this limitation, I purposefully selected contacts from different occupations and in different locations.

In total, I recruited thirty participants, including twenty-five from mainland China and five from Hong Kong. There were ten male and twenty female participants. The average age of the participants was twenty-two years old (SD = 0.81). It should be noted that all the participants are working and living in what are considered first-tier cities in China (Beijing, Shanghai, Shenzhen, and Qingdao). They are all knowledge workers (e.g., teachers, government officials, public relations executives, and marketing professionals), and WeChat is frequently used in their work. Semi-structured interviews were conducted with the participants. The interview protocol covered grand-tour questions exploring the participants' general experience of using WeChat in social, instrumental, and professional contexts. It also included questions asking the participants to share their experiences and thoughts on specific functions (one-to-one and group chat, WeChat Moments, subscribing official accounts, and utility functions). Lastly, the protocol probed norms perceived by the participants and their concerns in using WeChat. Since the protocol aimed at setting the stage for the participants to share their experience, during the interviews, I just relied on it to ensure consistency of topics and allowed the emergence of unanticipated topics.[20] All the interviews were conducted in Mandarin and were recorded with the participants' permission. All the interviews were transcribed and imported to NVivo 12, a qualitative data analysis software. Open coding, axial coding, and selective coding procedures were adopted in data analysis.[21] During open coding stage, I created codes from reading transcripts of the interviews. Next, in axial coding, I established high-order codes to organize the codes generated in opening coding. Through identifying connections among codes, I combined open codes into axial codes. Finally, in selective coding, I organized the codes around three broader themes corresponding to points of reluctance identified from the data and factors that contributed to them.

Findings: Reluctance in Social Media Use

The data suggest that the participants use WeChat in social and work life. Not only a tool for mobile communication, WeChat is referred to as an indispensable part of everyday life. Sally, an English teacher, said, "WeChat is the most frequently used smartphone app in my life. You cannot leave it. It's more than a communication tool." Although the participants appreciated the high integration of functions afforded by WeChat, they also perceived reluctance in their everyday WeChat use. In the following, I describe three points of reluctance identified in the data. These points of reluctance are associated with the integrative design of WeChat, the open networks people have to maintain when using WeChat, and evolving norms of self-presentation on WeChat Moments.

Reluctance 1: "WeChat Can Do Anything"

The first point of reluctance involves WeChat's all-in-one-place design. To the participants, WeChat is not only a communication tool but also a platform offering multiple utilities, such as paying bills, engaging in social networking, and reading news. Such high integration of multiple functions brings convenience. For example, Felicia, a marketing executive in a media organization in Beijing, stated that WeChat's integrative design makes it easy to manage everyday logistics: "WeChat is probably the most-used application in my everyday life. I interact with my friends on Moments. I scan QR codes to make payment. I read articles from the subscribed public WeChat accounts." For Felicia, then, WeChat integrates a wide array of both communication and everyday functions, proving the utility of the "all-in-one-place" design.

My interview participants all mentioned the various communication contexts in which WeChat was used. For instance, on WeChat, people can join chat groups based on interests, work, and life events. They can also interact with their contacts on Moments, which is a collapsed context in which their contacts from various aspects of life are brought together and their posts are aggregated in a timeline. Further exploring this multiplicity of communication contexts suggests that not only integrative design but also social norms could contribute to the use of WeChat for communication with a user's different kinds of contacts, such as coworkers, clients, friends, and relatives. When I asked the participants why they chose to add their coworkers on WeChat, many of them expressed their reluctance in doing so; however, they said that they had to because it was required by their companies or managers. Kevin, a lawyer in Qingdao, said, "On the first day of my work, I added the law firm partners' WeChat and I was added to WeChat work groups. Then my colleagues added my WeChat. It's just natural." The same multi-tasking efficiency that Felicia praised was, then, for Kevin, the source of some reluctance, as he felt pressured by his workplace to melt the boundaries between work and daily life.

Indeed, the most common point of reluctance identified in my interview data is related to the integrative design of WeChat. The participants enjoyed such design but at the same time they sometimes needed context separation because the high integration of functions brought high integration of different communication contexts. This reluctance is especially evident in users who adopt WeChat for work-related interactions, as they experience difficulties in separating work and personal life. "I feel that I never will be off work," said Bailey, an English teacher in

Qingdao. She described how she was in many work groups, such as class groups, where she could find parents of her students; internal work groups, where she could find her chairman and other colleagues; and task-related groups, where she discussed work-related tasks with her colleagues. For Bailey, the integration of these different discourse communities into one app created challenges:

> Because we have different work schedules. For instance, on Monday, I have a day off but most of my colleagues are working. In this case, I will still receive lots of messages from these groups. Do I need to reply? Well, I am having a day off. I should relax and do whatever I want. But if I do not reply, I will have to deal with it later, when I go back to work. It's hard to not to check about these messages.

Bailey's words suggest a sense of reluctance: she is bothered by the emergence of work-related communication on her day off.

In another example, the reluctance points in a different direction, as Lily, a product assistant in Shenzhen, was sometimes bothered by lots of messages and information from her friends during working hours. She explained:

> It's just few clicks and you can see your friends' posts and sometimes they share something very emotional and I will be affected at work. They also know that I use WeChat for work, so I must check out new messages frequently at work, so they message me and would assume that I can reply immediately. This is impossible. I have lots of work-related messages to reply to. How can I manage communication with my friends in that situation? It's even bothering if my manager goes to my desk and talks to me and she sometimes could see incoming messages from my WeChat on my PC.

Lily's example suggests that not only can the high integration of functions—and thus, integration of interaction contexts—bring concerns to users, but also that people's expectations and assumptions of an always-on mode results in a sense of reluctance around using WeChat. For Bailey, the reluctance was triggered by too-much-work intruding on the assumed quiet of a day off; for Lily, the opposite was true, as friends and family expected her to engage in communication with them while she was at work—in both cases, the reluctance follows from a lack of boundaries between daily life and work.

Reluctance 2: "I Have Everyone on WeChat"

The second point of reluctance reflects concerns over the fact that on WeChat users have to maintain an open network. When mobile phones provided only telephony and short text messages, Chinese users, different from their western counterparts, maintained an open network of their social contacts, which means that Chinese mobile users tended to maintain a contact list that was comprised of not only close friends but also acquaintances and professional contacts.[22] In other words, for Chinese users, mobile phones serve as "less an extension of private self than a mobile interface to their social universe."[23] Now, mobile phones support multiple functions, affordances, and modalities, and more importantly, telephony and short text messages are conducted and exchanged using smartphone applications. This is partly due to the rapid development of and easy, low-cost access to high-speed cellular networks in China. For example, Miranda, a user interface designer in Beijing, explained some of the changes brought by the wide adoption of smartphones and WeChat in recent years:

> Years ago, when we did not have WeChat, we usually sent messages and made phone calls using the functions provided by the mobile phones. Now, it seems that everyone is using WeChat and it is unnecessary to know each other's cell phone numbers. We just need to know each other's WeChat account number. (We did this) because the cost is very low. Now we have WiFi everywhere, at home, at office, at shopping malls.

Other participants' reflections on the changes brought by mobile phone use resonated with Miranda's comments. It is becoming common nowadays that people do not ask for each other's mobile phone numbers, instead using their WeChat account numbers when they know each other and wish to maintain connections. In addition to the wide adoption of WeChat and smartphones, people now tend to believe that everyone is on WeChat and is always online, which makes connecting and communicating using WeChat a taken-for-granted setting in everyday life in China. In this context, maintaining this large and open network can be tricky. Previously, people maintained an open and large network of contacts using contact lists, wherein users could have a high level of control of their presence (e.g., when to make phone calls and send text messages). Now, since WeChat and the like have provided an integrative design, users can have multiple opportunities to signal their presence. For instance, a user could signal his/her presence on WeChat Moments by sending a post. Another user who sees the post would believe that the user is available and may send a private message to him/her or make an audio call using WeChat. That signaling presence, to help users to learn if others are available for interaction, was impossible in the early age of mobile communication. Now, this integrative design enabling users to easily gain knowledge of others' availability has become a source of reluctance to some participants—for signaling your presence to friends and family now means your coworkers can see it as well, meaning there is virtually no privacy, no sense of personal space and time disconnected from access by others. For example, Donald, a sales executive, shared his experiences in this regard:

> Sometimes my client would follow my WeChat Moments, and I guess they would sometimes see if I posted something to learn whether I was available. It is good of course that I always have a presence to them because I want to leave an impression, but that's it. That's the only purpose. I don't want them to use this to learn whether I am available and use it against me when I don't reply to their messages. Sometimes, I just need more time to craft my replies because it is an important inquiry. . . . That's why I would always prefer emails when it comes to inquiries or professional communication, because I would always have time to think how to reply.

Reflecting this reluctance, some participants mentioned in the interviews that they would prefer asking for mobile phone numbers when they first meet someone and wish to keep in touch. However, what complicates matters is how power positions in a relationship influence what is asked for and how WeChat is used. Those who use WeChat for work-related purposes frequently mentioned the influence of power relations. Power structures in organizations seemed to be reproduced in the use of WeChat and those in the lower power positions seemed to have little flexibility in how WeChat should be used for work. Renee, an internal communication executive, shared that when she just started working for her employer, she was added to the company's WeChat groups and felt that she had no choice, although she would describe herself as a private person who wished to set a boundary between work and life by not dealing with work-related matters on WeChat. And yet, she felt that she could not resist the connections required to fuel work-related communication. "Because it would be impolite," Renee explained, "and more importantly, I am just a newcomer. I don't want to upset my boss and have a bad review in my probation period." In this case, Renee's reluctance at collapsing daily life and work functions was overridden by her boss's expectations: Of course she would join the WeChat group, for that demonstrated her team spirit.

This sense of workplace hierarchies determining a user's experiences with online communication apps was shared in an example from Eric, a university professor:

> Last year, I met some senior administrative member of the university, and I felt that I had to wait until he said, "Let's add each other's WeChat account." I could not say it because I did not know if he was willing to.

In Eric's case, he felt reluctance at making a WeChat request, for he did not know if asking a superior was acceptable. On the other hand, some participants who are veteran employees seemed to show more control over what to use for communication and were less likely to feel reluctant to connect with everyone they knew on WeChat. Miranda explained that she did not like using WeChat for work because there was too much personal stuff on Moments. "So, I just did not reply to messages on WeChat but on QQ, and gradually my colleagues knew that they could find me on QQ," Miranda said. Since her company also frequently uses QQ, another instant messenger, for work-related communication, Miranda could successfully separate her work-related and personal communication. The question, however, which my data set does not answer, is how much influence Miranda's sense of job security had on her communication practices? Eric, who was unsure of workplace protocols, responded one way, whereas Miranda responded another way—their communication preferences and practices probably reflect different levels of power at work.

Summarizing the above findings about the technological affordances of WeChat for an integrative user experience, I conclude that Chinese mobile phone culture, in which users tend to maintain open and large networks, and the social norms in Chinese society, wherein workplace hierarchies as still powerful, contribute to an emerging sense of reluctance to connect to all the people a person knows on WeChat. This is because of the integrative design of WeChat and having an open network can facilitate context collapse, wherein different discourse communities can intermingle, sometimes in embarrassing or awkward ways. Especially when different understandings about the appropriate enactments of some affordances abound, people have to deal with unwanted interactions, which affect their work-life balance. Similarly, when the social norm is to add coworkers' WeChat accounts but not mobile phone numbers for the sake of connections and interactions, and when those in high power positions decide such matters, people become reluctant to connect via these apps.

Reluctance 3: "Seeking for Presence (*Cun Zai Gan*)"

The third point of reluctance is the need to construct identities for certain types of audiences on Moments, which results from the perceived need of having a presence to people on WeChat. The identity work is described by some of the participants as a "job" or a "task," because usually they feel this reluctance when they connect with their coworkers, superiors, and clients on WeChat. Creating some face time on WeChat to work-related contacts is considered as something necessary and helpful for workplace and client relationship development. In this case, WeChat Moments use becomes instrumental. What is posted might not represent people's true selves but carefully crafted content for certain audiences.

Although not willing to use WeChat Moments, some participants feel the pressure of using it and showing something to their contacts. Iris, a university teaching assistant, felt that she had to post something on WeChat Moments once in a while.

> It's been a while that I post something to WeChat Moments. My friends one day told me that she felt that I disappeared in Moments. I was thinking, what does she mean? Does it mean that some people expect to see me on Moments?

Showing presence on Moments becomes a norm. According to some participants, they have to put "I turn off Moments," or "No posts in my Moments" in profiles to declare that they do not use Moments. "I do not want to offend anyone, so I have to say it in my profile," a participant explained why he had to put a similar line in his profile. The very act of putting a declaration of not using Moments just shows how people feel that everyone is using Moments and "disappearing" from the space by not posting anything might lead to social exclusion.

In addition to adding explanations to avoid misinterpretation, one participant mentioned that he found "a middle ground that could make everyone happy." On Moments, users can control how much content could be accessed. Moments offers three options: to show posts within three days, to show posts within half a year, and to show all the posts. Some participants choose the first option and never post anything on Moments.

> It means that I do not block you, but you actually can see nothing. I feel that it helps me to say that I do post things on Moments, but I would rather only show what is posted within three days. It will not offend people if a person may feel upset if he/she only sees a flat line.

Frank, a marketing executive, provided this explanation. A flat line could be interpreted as being blocked from a person's WeChat Moments. Frank's strategy is to not violate the social norm that everyone is using Moments. Instead, he appears to follow the social norm but sets a boundary that is acceptable both socially and technologically.

Offline contexts also play an important role in affecting users' perception of reluctance and possibility of disengagement. Some participants feel that they have to return to Moments not because WeChat does not provide an effective feature to turn off the function but due to users' offline experience: many of their friends, coworkers, and family members talk about content from Moments. The feeling of missing possibly useful information leads these users to turn on WeChat Moments again. However, they choose to not to let Moments display new post notifications.

In sum, the reluctance of seeking for presence on WeChat (Moments) is related to an emerging social norm of self-presentation cultivated by the wide adoption of WeChat. Since WeChat is the most frequently used application now, it is hard to escape from the expectation of using Moments. In the participants' words, being absent from WeChat Moments is considered "weird," "questionable," and even "not acceptable." The very act of claiming not to use WeChat Moments indicates that it is becoming a norm to use the function and to have some presence. It is with this norm that the participants perceive a point of reluctance to demonstrate a presence on the app.

Concluding Discussion

This chapter explores how users of MIM and integrative social media perceive reluctance in their user experience. The three points of reluctance described above are related to the integrative design of WeChat, open networks people have to maintain using WeChat, and norms of presence on WeChat Moments. Behind these points of reluctance are contradictions between technological features of WeChat and human factors such as Chinese mobile communication culture and power-oriented interaction rituals. Since WeChat is now being used in many different contexts (e.g., work, personal life, and dating), users have to deal with multiple cultures (e.g., organizational culture and local culture) when they use WeChat. Without being provided with opportunities for technological separation in order to deal with the multiple cultures, users are likely to be reluctant to use WeChat. Findings also suggest that Chinese organizational, relationship, and mobile communication culture is reproduced through the use of WeChat. Although WeChat's design, like many other social technologies, offers flexibility and openness of communication, user factors such as organizational culture that prescribes engagement in WeChat group communication shapes the process of WeChat use.

This study extends research on reluctance in social media use by examining how reluctance is shaped by the contradiction between an integrative design logic of social media technologies and users' need of contextual separation, the differences in perception of technological affordances, and relation-oriented cultural norms. This study extends research on reluctance in social media use to a new context: mobile social media use in everyday life.[24] Moving beyond prior research, this study also explores how social media users respond to reluctance. Similar to investigating reluctance as negotiations between individual preferences and social norms as well as contradictions between users' motivations and technological affordances, exploring responses and choices made by users would shed light on how social media use is a tension-filled experience rather than simply a matter of use or non-use. Furthermore, this study shows that exploring reluctance in social media could help us understand how individual technological frames as well as group and social norms and technological features interact to shape user experience. That reluctance is shaped by both human and technological factors suggests that the reluctance perspective on social media use takes a sociotechnical stance, similar to perspectives of paradoxes and adaptive structuration in studying technology use.[25]

Through investigating the use of WeChat, the most popular mobile social networking smartphone app in China, this study also contributes to the understanding of mobile communication in Chinese society. It extends previous work that mainly focuses on earlier generations of mobile technologies that offer limited functions such as text messaging and phone calling.[26] Chinese mobile phone users still maintain large and open networks even as their mobile communication has been migrating to smartphone applications. However, such large and open networks may become a source of tension when the network is maintained in a context offering high integration of functions. It is not the integrative design but what such design has provided—such as multiple social presence opportunities and availability signaling occasions—that make users feel reluctant to use WeChat to maintain the large and open networks. In addition, Chinese culture norms and values, such as power relations determining communication patterns and harmony, still play an important role in the next generation of mobile communication that features uses of highly integrative smartphone applications.[27] Moreover, such cultural factors also influence how people respond to reluctance in their user experience. For instance, as suggested in the findings, one participant chose not to show that he blocked another user but instead used a technological feature as an excuse to protect his and the user's personal feelings. Future research could further explore how technological features could help users to deal with their reluctance, taking into consideration cultural influences in mobile communication.

Several limitations of this study should be noted. First, this study draws on data collected from people in their twenties and thirties who use WeChat for work. Identity work and work socialization are key concerns among users in this demographic. Future research can explore whether reluctance exists in other demographics, such as senior users, how this reluctance differs, and what factors play key roles shaping the reluctance. Second, this study draws on data from a small sample, which may limit generalization of the findings. However, findings from this study resonate with many reports from the trade literature and public press. Since resonance with people in a similar context is regarded as an important criterion when evaluating a qualitative study's generalizability,[28] it could be argued that this study provides generalizable findings. Lastly, this study focuses only on WeChat as an initial exploration for reluctance in social media use. Future studies could draw on this theoretical perspective to further explore how other social media are used and how reluctance is perceived. For instance, scholars can investigate reluctance in using interest-based social media, such as Douban.com, and explore what technological affordances and human factors shape reluctance in user experience.

Notes

1. CNNIC, "The 43rd China Statistical Report on Internet Development," February 2019, http://cnnic.cn/gywm/xwzx/rdxw/20172017_7056/201902/W020190228474508417254.pdf.

2. Pamela Karr-Wisniewski and Ying Lu, "When More Is Too Much: Operationalizing Technology Overload and Exploring Its Impact on Knowledge Worker Productivity," *Computers in Human Behavior* 26, no. 5 (2010): 1061–72, https://doi.org/10.1016/j.chb.2010.03.008; Keri Stephens, Dron M. Mandhana, JiHye J. Kim, Xiaoqian Li, Elizabeth M. Glowacki, and Ignacio Cruz, "Reconceptualizing Communication Overload and Building a Theoretical Foundation," *Communication Theory* 27, no. 3 (2017): 269–89, https://doi.org/10.1111/comt.12116.

3. Alice Marwick and danah boyd, "I Tweet Honestly, I Tweet Passionately: Twitter Users, Context Collapse, and the Imagined Audience," *New Media & Society* 13, no. 1 (2011): 114–33, https://doi.org/10.1177/1461444810365313.

4. Katie Davis, "Tensions of Identity in a Networked Era: Young People's Perspectives on the Risks and Rewards of Online Self-Expression," *New Media & Society* 14, no. 4 (2012): 634–51, https://doi.org/10.1177/1461444811422430.

5. Elija Cassidy, "Social Networking Sites and Participatory Reluctance: A Case Study of Gaydar, User Resistance and Interface Rejection," *New Media & Society* 18, no. 11 (2016): 2613–28; Cliff Lampe, Jessica Vitak, and Nicole Ellison, "Users and Nonusers: Interactions Between Levels of Facebook Adoption and Social Capital," in *CSCW '13: Proceedings of the 2013 Conference on Computer Supported Cooperative Work Companion* (2013): 809–19; Eric Baumer and Phil Adams, "Limiting, Leaving, and (Re) Lapsing: An Exploration of Facebook Non-Use Practices and Experiences," in *CHI 2013*, (AMC, 2013): 3257–66.

6. Rich Ling and Chih-Hui Lai, "Microcoordination 2.0: Social Coordination in the Age of Smartphones and Messaging Apps," *Journal of Communication* 66, no. 5 (2016): 834–56; Avery E. Holton and Logan Molyneux, "Identity Lost? The Personal Impact of Brand Journalism," *Journalism* 18, no. 2 (2017): 195–210.

7. Cassidy, "Social Networking Sites and Participatory Reluctance," 2613–28; Ben Light, *Disconnecting with Social Networking Sites* (London: Palgrave Macmillan, 2014).

8. Kristine Dery, Darl Kolb, and Judith MacCormick, "Working with Connective Flow: How Smartphone Use Is Evolving in Practice," *European Journal of Information Systems* 23, no. 5 (2014): 558–70, https://doi.org/10.1057/ejis.2014.13.

9. Light, *Disconnecting with Social Networking Sites*; Cassidy, "Social Networking Sites and Participatory Reluctance."

10. Cassidy, "Social Networking Sites and Participatory Reluctance," 2613–28.

11. Di Cui, "Beyond 'Connected Presence': Multimedia Mobile Instant Messaging in Close Relationship Management," *Mobile Media & Communication* 4, no. 1 (2016): 19–36, https://doi.org/10.1177/2050157915583925; Ling and Lai, "Microcoordination 2.0."; Qian Yu, Peiying Huang, and Liming Liu, "From 'Connected Presence' to 'Panoptic Presence': Reframing the Parent–Child Relationship on Mobile Instant Messaging Uses in the Chinese Translocal Context," *Mobile Media & Communication* 5, no. 2 (2017): 123–38, https://doi.org/10.1177/2050157916688348.

12. Dery, Kolb, and Maccormick, "Working with Connective Flow," 558–70; Gillian Symon and Katrina Pritchard, "Performing the Responsive and Committed Employee through the Sociomaterial Mangle of Connection," *Organization Studies* 36, no. 2 (2015): 241–63, https://doi.org/10.1177/0170840614556914.

13. Eveline Chao, "How WeChat Became China's App for Everything," *Fast Company*, January 2, 2017, https://www.fastcompany.com/3065255/china-wechat-tencent-red-envelopes-and-social-money.

14. Yu, Huang, and Liu, "From 'Connected Presence' to 'Panoptic Presence.'"

15. Marwick and boyd, "I Tweet Honestly, I Tweet Passionately."

16. Sharon F. Matusik and Amy E. Mickel, "Embracing or Embattled by Converged Mobile Devices? Users' Experiences with a Contemporary Connectivity Technology," *Human Relations* 64, no. 8 (2011): 1001–30, https://doi.org/10.1177/0018726711405552.

17. Elaine J. Yuan, "From 'Perpetual Contact' to Contextualized Mobility: Mobile Phones for Social Relations in Chinese Society," *Journal of International and Intercultural Communication* 5, no. 3 (2012): 208–25, https://doi.org/10.1080/17513057.2012.670714.

18. Anton Kriz, Evert Gummesson, and Ali Quazi, "Methodology Meets Culture: Relational and Guanxi-Oriented Research in China," *International Journal of Cross Cultural Management* 14, no. 1 (2013): 27–46, https://doi.org/10.1177/1470595813493265.

19. Kriz, Gummesson, Quazi, "Methodology Meets Culture."

20. Thomas Lindlof and Bryan Taylor, *Qualitative Communication Research Methods*, 3rd ed. (Thousand Oaks, CA: Sage, 2011).

21. Juliet Corbin and Anselm Strauss, *Basic of Qualitative Research* (Los Angeles, Sage, 2015).

22. Yuan, "From 'Perpetual Contact' to Contextualized Mobility."

23. Yuan, "From 'Perpetual Contact' to Contextualized Mobility," 222.

24. Cassidy, "Social Networking Sites and Participatory Reluctance."

25. Heewon Kim and Jessa Lingel, "Working through Paradoxes: Transnational Migrants Urban Learning Tactics Using Locative Technology," *Mobile Media & Communication* 4, no. 2 (2015): 221–36, https://doi.org/10.1177/2050157915619650; Melissa Mazmanian,

Wanda J. Orlikowski, and Joanne Yates, "The Autonomy Paradox: The Implications of Mobile Email Devices for Knowledge Professionals," *Organization Science* 24, no. 5 (2013): 1337–57, https://doi.org/10.1287/orsc.1120.0806. Jeremy Birnholtz, Graham Dixon, and Jeffrey Hancock, "Distance, Ambiguity and Appropriation: Structures Affording Impression Management in a Collocated Organization," *Computers in Human Behavior* 28, no. 3 (2012): 1028–35, https://doi.org/10.1016/j.chb.2012.01.005; Gerardine DeSanctis and Marshall Poole, "Capturing the Complexity in Advanced Technology Use: Adaptive Structuration Theory," *Organization Science* 5, no. 2 (1994): 121–47, https://doi.org/doi:10.2307/2635011.

26. Yuan, "From 'Perpetual Contact' to Contextualized Mobility."

27. Yuan, "From 'Perpetual Contact' to Contextualized Mobility."

28. Sarah J. Tracy, "Eight 'Big-Tent' Criteria for Excellent Qualitative Research," *Qualitative Inquiry* 16, no. 10 (2010): 837–51, https://doi.org/10.1177/1077800410383121.

Contributors

David Craig is a clinical associate professor at USC Annenberg where he teaches graduate courses in media industries. He is a Peabody fellow and associate professor at Shanghai Jiao Tong University in the Institute of Cultural and Creative Industries. His current research includes multiple books mapping the global social media entertainment and Chinese wanghong industries. Craig is also an Emmy-nominated Hollywood producer and former television executive.

Lei Vincent Huang is a lecturer in communication at Hong Kong Baptist University. His research examines how information and communication technologies structure, alter, and extend organizational and interpersonal communication. He is particularly interested in social media affordances and employee behaviors. In addition, he studies digitally mediated interpersonal communication, especially in the context of online dating.

Hepeng Jia obtained his PhD in science communication at Cornell University. He is a professor in the School of Communication of Soochow University. Dr. Jia was the former editor-in-chief of *Science News Magazine* of the Chinese Academy of

Sciences. His research interests include science and risk communication, science controversies, and science journalism.

Xiaoya Jiang is a PhD student in the School of Journalism and Mass Communication at University of Wisconsin–Madison. Her publications mainly focus on message effects.

Xiao Li is a graduate student at the Television School of the Communication University of China; her focus is broadcasting television journalism. She did her undergraduate study at Beijing University of Posts and Telecommunications, where she majored in information engineering. Her current research direction is the transformation and convergence of news media in China.

Junyi Lv is a PhD student at the Annenberg School for Communication and Journalism, University of Southern California. She holds a master of communication management also from USC Annenberg, and a bachelor of arts in broadcasting journalism from Hunan Normal University in China. Her research interests lie in the intersection of rhetoric and argumentation, object-oriented ontology, anthropology, and communication. Specifically, she studies the entanglement of humans and nonhumans; climate change and Anthropocene rhetoric; and public spheres and social media entertainment. Her works have been published in the *International Journal of Communication* and *International Journal of Cultural Studies*.

Weishan Miao is an associate professor at the Institute of Journalism and Communication Studies, Chinese Academy of Social Sciences. His research focuses on the interaction between new media, politics, and social change in China. He has a PhD from the School of Journalism and Communication of Tsinghua University in Beijing.

Jeremy Wade Morris is an associate professor in the Department of Communication Arts at the University of Wisconsin–Madison. He is the author of *Selling Digital Music, Formatting Culture* (2015) and a co-editor of the recent collection, *Appified: Culture in the Age of Apps* (with Sarah Murray, 2018). He has published widely on new media, software, music technologies, and podcasting in journals such as *New Media and Society, Popular Communication, Critical Studies in Media Communication, Popular Music & Society*, and more. He is also the founder of PodcastRE.org, a large database that tracks, indexes, and preserves podcasts, allowing researchers to analyze sonic culture. His current projects involve a co-edited collection (with Eric Hoyt) on podcasting, and a manuscript on the history of apps, tentatively titled *App Culture: A History of Mundane Software.*

Dapeng Wang is an associate professor at the China Research Institute for Science Popularization's Popular Science Writing Research Department. His research focuses on the interaction between scientists, media, and journalists. He is particularly interested in examining communication behaviors of celebrity scientists in China. He has published dozens of science communication papers and several translated books in the field.

Wei Wang is a lecturer at USC-SJTU Institute of Cultural and Creative Industry, Shanghai Jiao Tong University. She received her PhD from the Annenberg School for Communication and Journalism at the University of Southern California. She is interested in China's economic restructuring, rural–urban links, digital activism, and new economic forms. Her dissertation, "Agricultural Informatization and Agrarian Power Dynamics in Rural China," examines different modes of applying ICTs and the changing power structures in a glocalized and commercialized agriculture sector.

Yizhou (Joe) Xu is a PhD student in media and cultural studies at the University of Wisconsin–Madison's Department of Communication Arts. His research interest deals with the software development industry in China, particularly dealing with the roles of state policy, digital labor, and platforms. Prior to attending UW–Madison, Joe was a documentarian and broadcast journalist based in Beijing, working for new agencies including CBS News, NPR, and Swiss TV.

Qingjiang (Q. J.) Yao is an associate professor in the Department of Communication and Media at Lamar University, Beaumont, Texas. He obtained his master's degree in philosophy from Beijing Normal University and PhD in mass communication from the University of South Carolina, and worked at an educational newspaper in Beijing for six years before pursuing his doctorate. His research interest lies in examining the persuasive effects of the mass and social media and pop culture in the digital era and particularly on environmental, science, and health issues. He has published in such journals as *American Journal of Media Psychology, Asian Journal of Communication, Chinese Media Research, Journal of International Crisis and Risk*

Communication Research, Journal of Internet Law, Journal of Media and Religion, Public Relations Review, Science Communication, Telematics and Informatics, and other venues and presented for more than thirty studies to annual conferences of the International Communication Association, Association for Education in Journalism and Mass Communication, National Communication Association, and other conferences.

Fengjiao Yang is a professor at Television School of the Communication University of China. Her primary research interests include the structural change of China's TV news industry and media convergence. Her papers have appeared in a variety of journals such as *Modern Communication, China Journalism and Communication Journal*, and *China Radio & TV Academic Journal*. She is also a research fellow for the China Online Video Case Study Report 2017, 2018, and 2019.

Guobin Yang is the Grace Lee Boggs Professor of Communication and Sociology at the Annenberg School for Communication and Department of Sociology at the University of Pennsylvania, where he directs the Center on Digital Culture and Society and serves as deputy director of the Center for the Study of Contemporary China. He is the author of *The Red Guard Generation and Political Activism in China* (2016) and the award-winning *The Power of the Internet in China: Citizen Activism Online* (2009). He is also the editor or co-editor of four books, including *Media Activism in the Digital Age* (2017) and *China's Contested Internet* (2015).

Michelle Murray Yang is an assistant professor in the Department of Communication at the University of Maryland, College Park. Her book, *American Political Discourse on China*, was published in 2017.

Lin Zhang is an assistant professor of communication and media studies at the University of New Hampshire. Her research revolves around the cultural economy of information capitalism as it intersects with issues of class, gender, nation, and race in an age of globalization. She has published interdisciplinary articles in journals such as the *Journal of Consumer Culture, New Media and Society, International Journal of Cultural Studies, International Journal of Communication, Feminist Media Studies, Inter-Asia Cultural Studies*, and *China Information*. She's currently working on a book manuscript about digital entrepreneurial labor in China and the remaking of selves in post-2008 China.

Zimu Zhang is a moving image practitioner and researcher. She is currently conducting her PhD research at City University of Hong Kong. Her research interests include visual culture and art practices focused on ecology and the society of control. She holds a BA degree from Communication University of China, a joint master's degree in documentary filmmaking from the Docnomads Erasmus Mundus program. Her audiovisual works have been exhibited in international film and art festivals, such as the European Media Art Festival, Doclisboa, and the China Independent Film Festival, among others. She is also active in film curating, alternative space building, and socially engaged art practices.

Index